Insights on Teaching Speaking in TESOL

Edited by Tim Stewart

Maria Dantas-Whitney, Sarah Rilling, and Lilia Savova, Series Editors

TESOL Classroom Practice Series

 Teachers of English to Speakers of Other Languages, Inc.

Typeset in ITC Galliard and Vag Rounded
by Capitol Communication Systems, Inc., Crofton, Maryland USA
Printed by United Graphics, Inc., Mattoon, Illinois USA
Indexed by Pueblo Indexing and Publishing Services, Pueblo West, Colorado USA

Teachers of English to Speakers of Other Languages, Inc.
700 South Washington Street, Suite 200
Alexandria, Virginia 22314 USA
Tel 703-836-0774 • Fax 703-836-6447 • E-mail tesol@tesol.org •
http://www.tesol.org/

Publishing Manager: Carol Edwards
Copy Editor: Jean House
Additional Reader: Vanessa Caceres
Cover Design: Capitol Communication Systems, Inc.

ISBN 9781931185578
Library of Congress Control No. 2009902341

Table of Contents

Focus on Public Speaking

Focus on Feedback & Assessment

Dedication

I dedicate this book to the memory of my two big brothers.

Jack Stewart, 1947–2008

Dave Stewart, 1949–1977

Series Editors' Preface

The TESOL Classroom Practice Series showcases state-of-the-art curricula, materials, tasks, and activities reflecting emerging trends in language education and in the roles of teachers, learners, and the English language itself. The series seeks to build localized theories of language learning and teaching based on students' and teachers' unique experiences in and out of the classroom.

This series captures the dynamics of 21st-century ESOL classrooms. It reflects major shifts in authority from teacher-centered practices to collaborative learner- and learning-centered environments. The series acknowledges the growing numbers of English speakers globally, celebrates locally relevant curricula and materials, and emphasizes the importance of multilingual and multicultural competencies—a primary goal in teaching English as an international language. Furthermore, the series takes into account contemporary technological developments that provide new opportunities for information exchange and social and transactional communications.

Each volume in the series focuses on a particular communicative skill, learning environment, or instructional goal. Chapters within each volume represent practices in English for general, academic, vocational, and specific purposes. Readers will find examples of carefully researched and tested practices designed for different student populations (from young learners to adults, from beginning to advanced) in diverse settings (from pre-K–12 to college and postgraduate, from local to global, from formal to informal). A variety of methodological choices are also represented, including individual and collaborative tasks and curricular as well as extracurricular projects. Most important, these volumes invite readers into the conversation that considers and so constructs ESOL classroom practices as complex entities. We are indebted to the authors, their colleagues, and their students for being a part of this conversation.

Insights on Teaching Speaking in TESOL presents practical applications for implementing new ways of teaching speaking that are informed by an understanding of current theoretical knowledge. The volume reflects teaching approaches that include both an open engagement with meaningful tasks and consciousness-raising elements of a focus on form. It considers current developments in TESOL pedagogy that reflect the incorporation of sociopragmatic skills into the curriculum. Finally, the volume integrates technological advances that have allowed scholars to create large corpora of spoken language and opened up the way to reconsider written textbook language forms and traditional ideas of "correct" usage in conversation.

The chapters in this volume have been arranged in three main sections. The first and largest section focuses on the development of teaching materials and their implementation in lessons. The second section is devoted to illustrations of current practice in the teaching of public speaking. The book ends with a section dedicated to contemporary ideas on how to assess speaking tasks.

Maria Dantas-Whitney, Western Oregon University
Sarah Rilling, Kent State University
Lilia Savova, Indiana University of Pennsylvania

CHAPTER 1

Introduction: The Practice of Teaching Speaking in the 21st Century

Tim Stewart

This new Classroom Practice series of books, published by the association for Teachers of English to Speakers of Other Languages (TESOL), humbly aims to illustrate the state of the art in classroom teaching in the first decade of the 21st century. The series is focused on learning about what English for speakers of other languages (ESOL) teachers are doing in their classrooms and recording their reflections on why their practice has developed in certain ways; that is, theorizing about practice. Therefore, I open this volume with a brief description of its theoretical rationale.

REFLECTIVE PRACTICE

The thinking of teachers influences what they do in the classroom in fundamental ways. This thinking has been labeled *teacher cognition* (Woods, 1996). As a result of teacher educators' recognition of the influence that teacher cognition has on practice, ESOL practitioners today are encouraged to engage in reflective teaching (e.g., Richards & Lockhart, 1996; Zeichner & Liston, 1996). Yet, for second-language teachers, serious challenges to reflective practice remain because

> most L2 teachers continue to work in institutions in which they, their students, and their instructional practices are constructed by the positivistic paradigm that defines good teaching in terms of student performance on standardized tests and conceptualizes learning as internal to the learner. (Johnson, 2006, pp. 247–248)

For this reason, Johnson believes that teachers in all contexts need, "now more than ever," to neutralize their professional disempowerment in the counterproductive "educational climate of standardization and accountability" (p. 248) by reclaiming professional development in order to construct their own theories of practice. This ownership of professional development entails the responsibility of teachers to go beyond experience and create abstract knowledge by engaging in reflective practices that are transformative for themselves, their students, and their educational environment. Of course, this process would require ESOL teachers to make greater contributions to the professional discourse. Widdowson (2003, p. 2) lays down the challenge with typical clarity: "Teachers who insist that they are simply practitioners, workers at the chalkboard, not interested in theory, in effect conspire against their own authority, and against their own profession."

The question becomes: Are teachers exerting themselves in response to challenges such as those put forth by Widdowson and Johnson? The "artificial dichotomy between theory and practice" (Kumaravadivelu, 2006b, p. 166) remains a persistent theme in the contemporary literature (Allwright, 2005; Bailey & Nunan, 1996; Johnson, 2006; Stewart, 2006). This discussion is certainly impacting the field. Teaching ESOL, as a profession, is now experiencing a greater valuing of experiential practitioner knowledge. Thus, research in the field has broadened to permit teacher–researchers to investigate their own practice through, for example, narrative studies, exploratory inquiry, and action research (see Allwright, 2005; Bailey & Nunan, 1996; Edge, 2001; Farrell, 2007; Holliday, 2004; Johnson & Golombek, 2002; Richards & Lockhart, 1996; Shohamy, 2004). For reflective practice to have transformative impacts, practitioners must take the shared knowledge base of teaching ESOL into the classroom practice that they create, with the intention of reorganizing their practical understandings. This commitment to renew professional development is the pedagogical philosophy underpinning the contributions in this book.

The Teaching of Speaking in ESOL

Contributors to this volume are teacher–researchers who have chosen to explore puzzling aspects of their own classroom practice. This process involved them in reinterpreting practical knowledge through a dialogic interchange with their theoretical literature, experiential knowledge, and classroom research activities. Therefore, this book highlights dynamic interactions between teachers, students, texts, and contexts that shed light on current ESOL practice in teaching speaking.

"Knowing" a language most often means being able to converse in that language. It seems safe to presume that for most language learners today speaking is the most highly valued skill, but teaching a conversation class is not a simple undertaking. Brown (2001, pp. 267–268) notes that, "The goals and the techniques for teaching conversation are extremely diverse, depending on the student, teacher, and overall context of the class." Learning to speak another language is a very complex task that requires simultaneous attention to a range of subskills.

The fluency-versus-accuracy debate continues, but longitudinal studies of immersion students have convinced many practitioners of the need for a greater focus on form (e.g., Swain, 1985). This focus has led to a redirecting of the practice of teaching speaking from an open engagement with meaningful tasks (indirect approach), to a direct approach that "explicitly calls students' attention to conversational rules, conventions, and strategies" (Brown, 2001, p. 276). As examples of this trend, task-based and content-based approaches to language teaching both seek to include consciousness-raising elements of a focus on form (e.g., Fotos, 2002; Spada & Lightbrown, 2008).

Since the publication of Bernard Mohan's seminal work *Language and Content* (1986), content-based language instruction (CBLI) has taken hold in North American schools. It is commonly employed now to support ESOL students at all levels intent on entering mainstream classrooms. The implications of CBLI for the teaching of speaking are: first, the shift of focus from language form to acquiring information; second, a concern with using "authentic" materials and tasks; and third, the integration of skills. The task-based language teaching (TBLT) approach shares many commonalities with CBLI, and the two approaches are often used in combination (van Lier, 1996, p. 205).

Kumaravadivelu (2006a) describes the significance in the research literature of the shift from communicative language teaching to TBLT. Serious criticisms of task-based and content-based approaches have been made, however (Richards & Rodgers, 2001; Swan, 2005). Despite theorists' critiques, classroom teachers' enthusiasm for using these approaches has not appeared to dampen. In recognition of this fact, Richards and Rodgers predict: "we can expect to see CBI continue as one of the leading curricular approaches in language teaching" (p. 220). Moreover, rather than rejecting the teaching of grammar, as Swan claims, many ESOL practitioners who use CBLI and TBLT have integrated a focus on form that is informed by the content material: *The content drives the language* (see Doughty & Varela, 1998; Long, 1991). This approach to grammar instruction depends largely on the judgment of the classroom teacher. The teacher's analysis of texts and knowledge of his students ultimately determine what grammar needs to be taught. Whether form-focused instruction is integrated into the communicative lesson or taught at a separate time in isolation depends on a number of factors (see Spada & Lightbrown, 2008).

Likewise, the practice of teaching speaking has been impacted by incorporating sociopragmatic skills into ESOL pedagogy. Hinkel (2006, p. 116) cites Kasper's (2001) findings from an extensive review of the literature on teaching pragmatics, stating: ". . . explicit teaching and direct explanations of the L2 form-function connections represent a highly productive means of helping learners improve their L2 sociopragmatic skills."

Recent developments in the teaching of speaking in ESOL may be marked pre- and post-Internet. From computer-assisted language learning (commonly known as CALL) to corpus, the waves of technological advancement are influencing practice in varied ways. Digital cameras seem to be everywhere and are capable of recording extremely high-quality images and sound that can be sent around the world and posted very easily on the World Wide Web. But some things never change. No matter what tool is being used, practice remains the pivotal element:

"[I]t is not the technology per se that is effective or ineffective but the particular ways in which the technology is used" (Kern, 2006, pp. 188–189).

Technological advances have allowed scholars to create huge corpora of spoken language (O'Keefe, McCarthy, & Carter, 2007) that have opened up reconsideration of written textbook language forms and traditional ideas of "correct" usage in conversation. In light of this recent development, Hinkel posits: ". . . curricula that attend to the distinctions between conversational and formal oral production can prepare learners for real-life communication in EFL and ESL environments alike" (2006, p. 117). This observation takes us back to the key issue of tasks and materials. Being able to design or select engaging materials and coordinate a series of high-quality tasks is probably the most important classroom management skill needed by teachers of speaking (see Folse, 2006).

IN THIS VOLUME

The 16 remaining chapters in this book have been arranged in three main sections. Perhaps not surprising for a volume on current practice in teaching speaking in ESOL, the largest section focuses on the development of teaching materials and their implementation in lessons. More and more speaking courses seem to include public speaking tasks, so teachers should be pleased to find a section devoted to illustrations of current practice in teaching public speaking. The book ends with five chapters dedicated to contemporary ideas on the nagging problem of how to assess speaking tasks. All of the chapters detail practical applications for implementing new ways of teaching speaking that are informed by an understanding of current theoretical knowledge. This volume features the findings of teachers' research and provides a forum for teachers who have made inquiries into their own practice to share what they have learned. The 16 classroom narratives presented here represent the learning of practitioners who struggle every day with how to intervene in their classrooms so that they might improve their practice. By sharing their insights into the practice of teaching speaking in thoughtful narratives, these teachers are promoting their practical knowledge to the level of theory.

Section 1: Focus on Materials Development & Implementation

In "Exploring Values in English Through a Dilemma-Based Story," William Perry shares insights based on his lengthy experience using moral values topics in ESOL and cross-cultural training courses. He believes that the benefits of using values topics far outweigh the possible risks. His chapter explores the potential of a simple dilemma-based story for ESOL speaking classes. He outlines his adaptation of the story in detail and includes many examples of student work to illustrate an interactive teaching and learning process.

The new Test of English as a Foreign Language Internet-based test (TOEFL iBT) presents challenges and opportunities to ESOL practitioners. Dana Saito-

Stehberger and Jee-Eun Oh believe that the new test questions better represent authentic language tasks required in academic communities. Their chapter, "Authentic iBT Speaking Practice Using Open-Source Voice-Recording Software," describes techniques for teaching speaking that parallel the six speaking tasks on the iBT. Saito-Stehberger and Oh provide detailed advice for teachers on how to enhance speaking classes using materials that simulate the iBT.

How do teachers help students build speaking fluency in a grammar-based curriculum? Kevin McCaughey describes two speaking activities he has developed to achieve that goal with focused practice on syntactic and lexical items. He outlines six points for developing and implementing successful fluency tasks that focus on forms in his chapter, "Reinforcing Grammar and Vocabulary Learning With High-Volume Speaking Activities."

Bärbel Diehr introduces an action research project in her chapter, "Young Learners' Use of English: Imitation or Production?" The project investigated methods for getting young children learning English in Germany to move from imitation to production of the language. She describes "meaningful, communicative, and enjoyable tasks" that she and her colleagues developed to help elementary school teachers devise lessons that would allow their pupils to progress beyond repetition to produce coherent, communicative speech.

Healthcare professionals in Japan need to learn English today more than ever before, according to Yoshihito Sugita's chapter "Reframing and Reconstructing Situational Dialogues: Scaffolding Speaking Tasks for English for Occupational Purposes." After introducing situational dialogues and activities that are fairly standard textbook exercises, Sugita expands and scaffolds teaching tasks to match the communicative needs of his nursing students. With a focus on fluency and meaning, the students in his course follow a set five-stage sequence from listening to and recasting dialogues, to planning through writing of a final oral presentation.

Frustrated with the standard exercises in her course book, Hoa Thi Mai Nguyen introduced problem-posing tasks into her conversation course. By doing so, she challenged her own authority in the classroom, as well as the expectations of her students. Her conclusion, based on the reactions of her students—that this Western approach to developing critical thinking should be adopted in Vietnam—also challenges the presumptions of some ESOL scholars. "An Experimental Application of the Problem-Posing Approach for English Language Teaching in Vietnam" outlines her methods and students' responses.

In his chapter, "From Podcasting to YouTube: How to Make Use of Internet 2.0 for Speaking Practice," Robert Chartrand provides a glimpse into the vast applications related to the teaching of speaking currently available to teachers via the Internet. The practical nature of his descriptions should be comforting to teachers who lack enthusiasm for technology in teaching. His chapter shows teachers how to create podcasts for listening and speaking practice, as well as pedagogical uses of popular Internet social networking Web sites.

I explain in "(Re)Cycling Speaking Tasks on the Road to Pedagogical Renewal: Drama in the ESOL Classroom" how adapting to new teaching circumstances can be beneficial for professional development and describe a theme-based curriculum that I created after moving to a new university. The curriculum recycles language and skills through several learning tasks, such as poster presentations and drama activities, which are linked by a central theme engaging students in talk about controversial topics.

Section 2: Focus on Public Speaking

Jessie Carduner and Sarah Rilling outline a calorie-rich method of preparing graduate students for high-stakes presentations. In their chapter, "Data and Donuts: Preparing Graduate Students in Language Education to Speak at Conferences," Carduner and Rilling describe how they integrate simulated conference presentations in two graduate courses. They take a genre-based approach for training their students to present academic papers and posters of research projects. This approach is a significant innovation in their program with potentially broad application as it prepares young scholars to effectively share their knowledge in professional forums.

The difference between taking a mentoring and a coaching approach to prepare students for public speaking events is explored by Amanda Bradley in "A Holistic, Humanistic Approach to Developing Public Speaking Skills Through Speech Mentoring." Her chapter describes the processes she and her colleagues have used to ready students for speech contests, as she explains the concept of *deep approaches* to learning that underlies her practice.

In her investigation into English for academic purposes (EAP) students' use of presentation aids, Caroline Brandt discovered a mismatch between subject faculty expectations and EAP tutors' practice. In particular, she cites the overuse of PowerPoint as having possible negative effects on presentation content, style, and comprehensibility. "PowerPoint or Posters for EAP Students' Presentation Skills Development?" shows how poster presentations might be a better presentation aid to promote the type of critical interaction and oral communication skills that faculty members regard as vital to academic success.

Section 3: Focus on Feedback & Assessment

In his chapter, "The Speaking Log: A Tool for Posttask Feedback," Tony Lynch introduces the speaking log, which he describes as a tool students can use for self- and peer-assessment and feedback on speaking tasks. Recording speaking assignments is central to this review process as it "creates an opportunity for learners to capture, analyze, and reflect on their own speech, which under normal circumstances is fleeting and hard to recall."

With the goal of overcoming students' fear of public speaking by demystifying the process of assessing oral presentations, Jeff Popko guided his graduate students as they created a grading rubric used for self-, peer-, and teacher-assessments. "Demystifying Presentation Grading Through Student-Created Scoring Rubrics" details the steps his students used to prepare, practice, present, and assess their class presentations. The course aims are to help students understand a range of attributes beyond content that make oral presentations successful.

Aiden Yeh encourages ESOL educators to experiment with Web 2.0 tools in their classes. In her chapter, "Practical Strategies for Assessing Students' Oral Speeches Through Vlogs," she describes her course, Professional Public Speaking, through a five-stage process she calls the *learning cycle*. This process includes different steps for evaluation and revision that incorporate peer-, teacher-, and self-feedback. Yeh claims that ESOL students and teachers can benefit significantly from the enhanced audio and video features of Web 2.0 technology.

Stephen Soresi's chapter, "Promoting Oral Proficiency Through In-Class Speaking Tests," shows teachers how they can promote, as well as monitor, speaking fluency through in-class speaking tests. He presents his quick (low-stakes) and milestone (higher-stakes) tests as being very practical to implement and score. Besides the simplicity of the test prompts, key features of these speaking tests are the use of a response time limit and a target speech rate range. He provides teachers with ample advice on how they can implement these speaking tests in courses.

Joann Chernen laments the fact that teachers of speaking and pronunciation tend to avoid oral journals. In her chapter, "Taking Pronunciation Further With Oral Journals," she seeks to debunk some common misconceptions about oral journals. She presents the results of her research and makes a strong case for the effectiveness of oral journals in the teaching of pronunciation and oral skills.

What Is the Direction for the Teaching of Speaking?

ESOL practitioners should find the descriptions of teaching practice in this book useful for their own professional development. Indeed, the ideas contained in each of the chapters indicate the currents in the field and show us some of the directions in which we might expect to see the teaching of speaking move. For a snapshot of the major areas addressed in this volume, consider Table 1.

Learning technologies are certainly having a significant impact on the practice of teaching spoken English. Representative samples of practice in this book range from materials developed based on the new TOEFL iBT speaking section (chapter 3), to teacher podcasts (chapter 8), to student self-recording (chapters 5, 8, 13, 15, and 17). While a direct focus on form is evident in fewer than half of the chapters, feedback–assessment is referred to in 13 chapters. This would seem to indicate that teachers of speaking continue to struggle to balance fluency and accuracy objectives. The majority of the descriptions of current practice in the field in this volume are linked to task-based, content-based, or English for specific purposes curricula. This trend is unlikely to change in the near term. Another picture of ESOL speaking curricula that emerges is the growing prevalence of speeches, formal oral presentations, and other public speaking events (chapters

Table 1. Selection of Topics Covered in this Book by Chapter

Chapter	CBLI/ TBLI	English for specific purposes	Grammar/ Focus on form	Learner groupings	Autonomous learning	Professional development	Critical thinking	Presentation aids	Assessment/ Feedback	Learning technologies
2. Perry	✓			✓	✓	✓	✓	✓	✓	
3. Saito-Stehberger & Oh	✓			✓	✓		✓		✓	✓
4. McCaughey			✓	✓		✓		✓		
5. Diehr	✓		✓	✓	✓	✓			✓	✓
6. Sugita		✓	✓	✓					✓	
7. Nguyen	✓		✓	✓	✓	✓	✓			
8. Chartrand	✓	✓			✓	✓	✓	✓	✓	✓
9. Stewart	✓			✓		✓	✓	✓		
10. Carduner & Rilling	✓	✓		✓	✓	✓	✓	✓	✓	✓
11. Bradley	✓			✓	✓	✓	✓	✓	✓	
12. Brandt		✓					✓	✓	✓	
13. Lynch		✓	✓	✓	✓				✓	✓
14. Popko		✓		✓	✓		✓	✓	✓	✓
15. Yeh			✓		✓		✓	✓	✓	✓
16. Soresi	✓		✓	✓	✓	✓			✓	
17. Chernen					✓	✓			✓	✓

2, 3, 6, 8–12, 14, and 15). Since presentation, discussion, and debate seem to be required in many mainstream courses (e.g., Ferris, 1998), ESOL professionals are seeking effective techniques for teaching students the skills of public speaking. Ideas for incorporating critical thinking, something of a controversial concept in the field, into ESOL speaking courses are described in many of the chapters (chapters 2, 3, 7–12, 14, and 15). In addition, teachers of speaking courses generally are very concerned with the issues of teacher talk and student time on task. As a result, many of the chapters in this book highlight the practical matters of grouping students in lessons and encouraging out-of-class practice. Finally, concerns with the professional development of teachers and the emphasis on autonomous learning found in the volume point to the reciprocal link between teachers and the students in their classrooms, that is, the interdependence between teacher and learner autonomy. Many of the teacher–researchers in this volume commented on what they have learned from their students and how important that learning was in their self-development.

A number of the contributors to this book are nonnative writers, while many others teach in contexts where English is not the vernacular. This professional mix reflects changes in the global political and economic environment. Globalization and digital communications have fused to accelerate the spread and power of English so that it is now the language of global communication. Many of the authors in this volume refer either directly or indirectly to the impact these trends have had on their practice.

Critical discourse in ESOL spotlights cornerstone issues in the field, such as: *correctness* and the teaching of strategies rather than rules of usage; standard–nonstandard English and the question of *competence*; the multiplicity of *speech communities*; and the *language identity* of learners (Canagarajah, 2006). It seems clear that the growth of World Englishes will continue to influence ESOL teaching practice (Kirkpatrick, 2007). While the direction of change is unknown, "there is a growing notion that we should be teaching English *as* an international language, rather than as a language attached to a specific culture from the English-speaking West" (Holliday, 2005, p. 8). A good example related to teaching speaking in ESOL is the shift away from "native speaker" models of pronunciation (Jenkins, 2000), although this trend is not without controversy (Holliday, 2005, pp. 8–9).

The authority of ESOL classroom teachers worldwide should continue to grow in the new century because, "We need to learn from diverse traditions of professionalization in different communities to develop a richer TESOL discourse," what Canagarajah calls "plural professional knowledge" (2006, p. 27). Obviously, practitioners are the bedrock of the ESOL community. Therefore, the place of teachers in developing the knowledge base of the field must be recognized and embraced (Farrell, 2007; Johnson, 2006; Stewart, 2006). This volume is a small contribution to that end.

Tim Stewart enjoys working with ESOL practitioners to help them shape their descriptions of classroom practice for publication. He hopes to continue doing that, while spending a bit more of his time on writing fiction, ice skating, snorkeling, and avoiding consumerism.

Focus on Materials Development & Implementation

CHAPTER 2

Exploring Values in English Through a Dilemma-Based Story

William Perry

INTRODUCTION

Finding materials for speaking activities that are consistently successful and that work with a wide range of learners is a challenge for most practitioners who teach English for speakers of other languages (ESOL). In this chapter, I would like to share the work I have done with a simple story, "Alligator River," originally designed for moral development and values clarification (Simon, Howe, & Kirschenbaum, 1972). My first contact with the story was in the early 1990s as a trainer for the Peace Corps in a program designed for U.S. volunteers living and working in new cultures. I have since used it in numerous educational contexts for developing both cross-cultural awareness and English-language skills. In the following sections, I present the origins of the dilemma-based story as well as my most recent adaptation and use of it with Japanese university students in English as a foreign language (EFL) speaking courses.

The origins of "Alligator River" can be traced to a book entitled *Values Clarification* (Simon, Howe, & Kirschenbaum, 1972). Subsequently, Holmes and Guild (1979) adapted the story for use in cross-cultural training, calling it "The Parable." Levine and Adelman (1992) further adapted the story but retained its original name, "Alligator River," in their cross-cultural communication textbook *Beyond Language*.

The story involves five characters: a young woman (Rosemary) engaged to a man on the other side of Alligator River (Geoffrey); a close friend of Rosemary's on her side of the river (Frederick); the owner of the only boat on her side of the river (Sinbad); and another friend of Rosemary's on Geoffrey's side of the river (Dennis). Rosemary needs to cross the alligator-filled river to reach her fiancé, Geoffrey, but in order to do so she must negotiate with Sinbad, the owner of the only boat in town. In the version of the story that I used, Sinbad tells Rosemary that he will take her across the alligator-filled river on the condition that she spend a week with him before they cross. She is disturbed by his request and seeks counsel from her close friend Frederick. Unfortunately, Frederick finds the problem very difficult and is unable to offer Rosemary any advice. She decides to spend the week with Sinbad and then crosses the river in his boat to meet Geoffrey. The two are happy to see each other, but when Rosemary tells Geoffrey how she was able to cross the river, he rejects her out of hand and says that he would not marry her if she were the last woman on earth. Rosemary then goes to her friend on Geoffrey's side of the river, Dennis, for advice. Dennis feels compassion for her and says that while he does not love her, he will marry her (see the full text of the story in Appendix A).

The story ends at this point and, depending on the aims of the class or workshop, follow-up activities begin. In ethics courses, students rank the characters, and a detailed discussion of the rankings typically ensues. Through group discussion, students not only become aware of their own values but also gain an understanding of the values of others. In a cross-cultural training setting, participants read or listen to the story, rank the characters, and then discuss the rankings in relation to cultural and personal values. Goals of this cross-cultural training are to help the participants gain a greater awareness of their own values, to see the extent to which these values are shared by others from the same culture, and to appreciate the inevitable conflicts in values that take place in a new cultural setting.

In this chapter, it is my intention to demonstrate how to use "Alligator River" effectively to help university-level students at varying proficiencies develop English-speaking skills. As the students' motivation and desire to communicate increase, so do opportunities for language practice based on their own ideas and values. The activity outlined below reflects my use of the story with more than 200 Japanese university students in 10 classes over a 2-year period.

CONTEXT

The idea of adapting values clarification activities for English-language learning is not a new one. Numerous English as a second language (ESL) textbooks and other teacher resource books cite the power of affective activities to motivate learners, build their self-esteem, and increase an understanding of their own values (Arnold, 1999; Brown, 1987; Moskowitz, 1978). Too often, English ESOL teachers shy away from opportunities for language learners to make decisions and expose their values to others. Moskowitz suggests a concrete approach to gradually integrating what she refers to as "humanistic" activities, a category that includes self-esteem and values clarification activities, into the language classroom. She argues that these activities can help a learner develop greater self-awareness, which, in turn, can lead to an acceptance of one's self and a broader acceptance of others. Moskowitz further suggests that humanistic strategies can give more meaning to school learning and help students deal more effectively with the real world.

In her classic book on communicative competence, Savignon (1983) discusses personalized language use with a specific focus on activities that encourage self-expression and that may stimulate controversy. She cites values clarification exercises as a good means of helping students get to know themselves and others through the medium of the second language. Savignon reminds us that the primary aim of using these exercises is for language development and self-expression, and not for advocating a particular set of values. The goal should be to develop an awareness of one's own values and to learn to respect the values of others.

Reid (1999) points out some potential difficulties in what she terms "the implementation of affect in the language classroom" (p. 298). The research in this area is limited, and as teachers, we may make unwarranted assumptions concerning learning styles and strategies, particularly in a cross-cultural setting. Reid cautions teachers to be aware of the tendency to stereotype groups, such as Japanese EFL students, because there are as many individual differences as commonalities within a given cultural group. She does concede, however, that Japanese students, because of their formal education, may be more "focused on consensual decision-making, reserved, formal and cautious" (p. 303).

Having a fairly clear sense of the risks and benefits of introducing affective activities in a foreign language classroom, I chose to use "Alligator River" as a values clarification activity with 10 different classes of 1st-year Japanese university students. There were approximately 25 students in each class. The goal of all of these general English classes was to help the students, most of them advanced beginners, develop their communication skills in English. In most classes, the activity was completed during one 90-minute class period.

CURRICULUM, TASKS, MATERIALS

The first steps in my formulation of the "Alligator River" activity were similar to those presented in *Beyond Language* (Levine & Adelman, 1992). Their adaptation appears in a chapter entitled "Cross-Cultural Contact with Americans" and is designed to help students learn to discuss differing perceptions and values. In their book, Levine and Adelman warn teachers that some students may have difficulty expressing themselves because of the personal nature of the content of "Alligator River."

In a typical lesson sequence, first students read the story and rank the five characters in their own order of approval. Next, they write reasons for their first and last rankings. After that, students sitting in groups of five explain their individual rankings of the "best" (number-one ranking) and "worst" (number-five ranking) character. Group discussion focuses on the source of the values (personal and/or cultural) that led to the rankings. The Levine and Adelman (1992) exercise concludes with interpretive comments on how people have differing values, but if they share a common culture, there are likely more similarities than differences in the values systems.

In my adaptation of this activity for 1st-year Japanese university students, it was necessary to consider some specific classroom challenges. My students had focused primarily on grammar and translation in their study of English and generally found the communicative use of English difficult. In addition, Japanese students typically are reluctant to share their personal values openly with others in a classroom setting. These considerations underlie the procedures in my adaptation of the following activity.

Reading the Story and Ranking the Characters

First, I passed out the text of "Alligator River" and asked the students to read it. After approximately 10 minutes, I directed them to rank the characters using a simple form (Appendix B). After the students had completed their individual rankings, they put them aside and moved to randomly assigned groups. A group size of five students worked best, ensuring that each student would eventually work with only one of the characters in the story. Throughout the activity, students could use either English or Japanese, but all of my interaction with them was in English as were the students' concluding presentations to the class. The requirements of retelling the story to the teacher and subsequently presenting the rankings to the entire class in English helped to motivate most groups to use English throughout the activity.

Checking for Comprehension

Next, I asked each group to go back to the text of "Alligator River" and sketch their understanding of the story on the large sheets of paper that I had distributed. I instructed each group to draw one picture together representing their comprehension of the text. This part of the activity took approximately 20 minutes, including the time needed to have groups retell the story to me based on their picture. During this process, I addressed misunderstandings of the basic story and modeled language as necessary. Figures 1 and 2 illustrate two different group approaches to this task. The students who produced Figure 1 chose to show a summary picture of the story, while the group that drew Figure 2 presented the story sequentially. In both cases, they were able to retell the story in English easily with reference to their drawings.

I discovered that having students work together in groups to draw pictures of the story rejuvenated their motivation just at the point when the individual rankings had been completed. At this point, some students may have felt that they were done, having completed the group-ranking task. Bringing them back to the story for a comprehension check through drawing rekindled their interest in the details.

Figure 1. A Summary Picture of the Story

Group Ranking

I had each group do a group ranking that included clear reasons for each of the rankings. To do this, students went back to their individual ranking sheets and engaged in animated discussions. Because they had retold the story as part of the previous step, discussions were mostly conducted in English. Typically, students were able to reach a consensus after about 5 minutes, but in some cases there was extended debate about the ranking order because of contrasting values. Sample group ranking sheets are shown in Figures 3 and 4.

These group ranking sheets clearly show differences in values between the two sample groups. The group in Figure 3 respected Geoffrey's "purity" and Frederick's willingness to listen to Rosemary, while the group in Figure 4 valued Dennis' gesture to marry Rosemary and Rosemary's commitment to action.

The task of arriving at a group consensus on ranking the five characters brought a different set of skills into play. The students had to listen, discuss, and compromise, as necessary. I recall that one group found the process so challenging that members finally agreed to rank all of the characters at "3." When all of the groups reached agreement on one ranking, many of the students again seemed to feel that the activity was over; they had done individual rankings and also had shared their values with the other group members in the process of arriving at a group ranking. But there was still more to the lesson.

Figure 2. A Sequential Picture of the Story

Drawing the Characters' Faces

After the students had agreed on a common group ranking, I asked them to try to visualize the five characters, thinking about the characteristics they had attributed to each in their discussions and rankings. Following this visualization process, I asked them to draw the faces of each character on large pieces of paper: one face on each piece of paper along with the ranking and the key reasons for the ranking. The students' initial reaction was typically one of surprise, but they quickly shifted their attention to the drawing task. During the drawing activity, I walked around the classroom and reminded the students to do their best to show the characteristics they had cited in their rankings when drawing the characters' faces. The pictures in Figure 5 illustrate student work in one group on this part of the exercise.

Although many students were surprised that they had to draw the characters, this task boosted their motivation again. Because of their formal training in school, most Japanese students can express themselves well through drawing, and some take great pleasure in doing so. This part of the exercise gave students an opportunity to illustrate the reasoning they used in the ranking process and group discussion. Critical thinking, drawing, and practice using English in speaking and writing were integrated in this task.

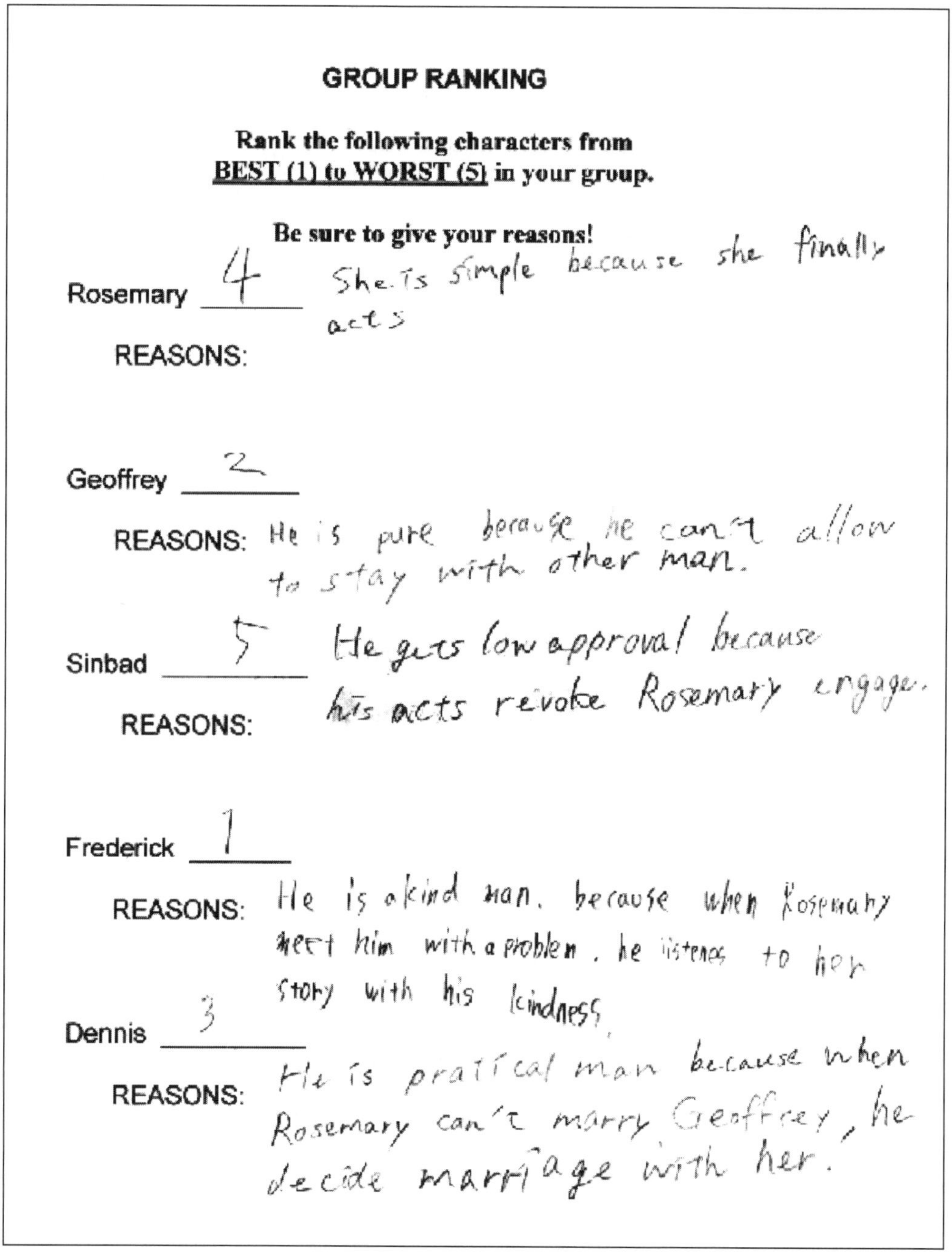

GROUP RANKING

**Rank the following characters from
BEST (1) to WORST (5) in your group.**

Be sure to give your reasons!

Rosemary _4_   She is simple because she finally acts

REASONS:

Geoffrey _2_

REASONS: He is pure because he can't allow to stay with other man.

Sinbad _5_   He gets low approval because his acts revoke Rosemary engage.

REASONS:

Frederick _1_

REASONS: He is a kind man. because when Rosemary meet him with a problem. he listens to her story with his kindness.

Dennis _3_

REASONS: He is pratical man because when Rosemary can't marry Geoffrey, he decide marriage with her.

Figure 3. Sample Group Ranking Sheet

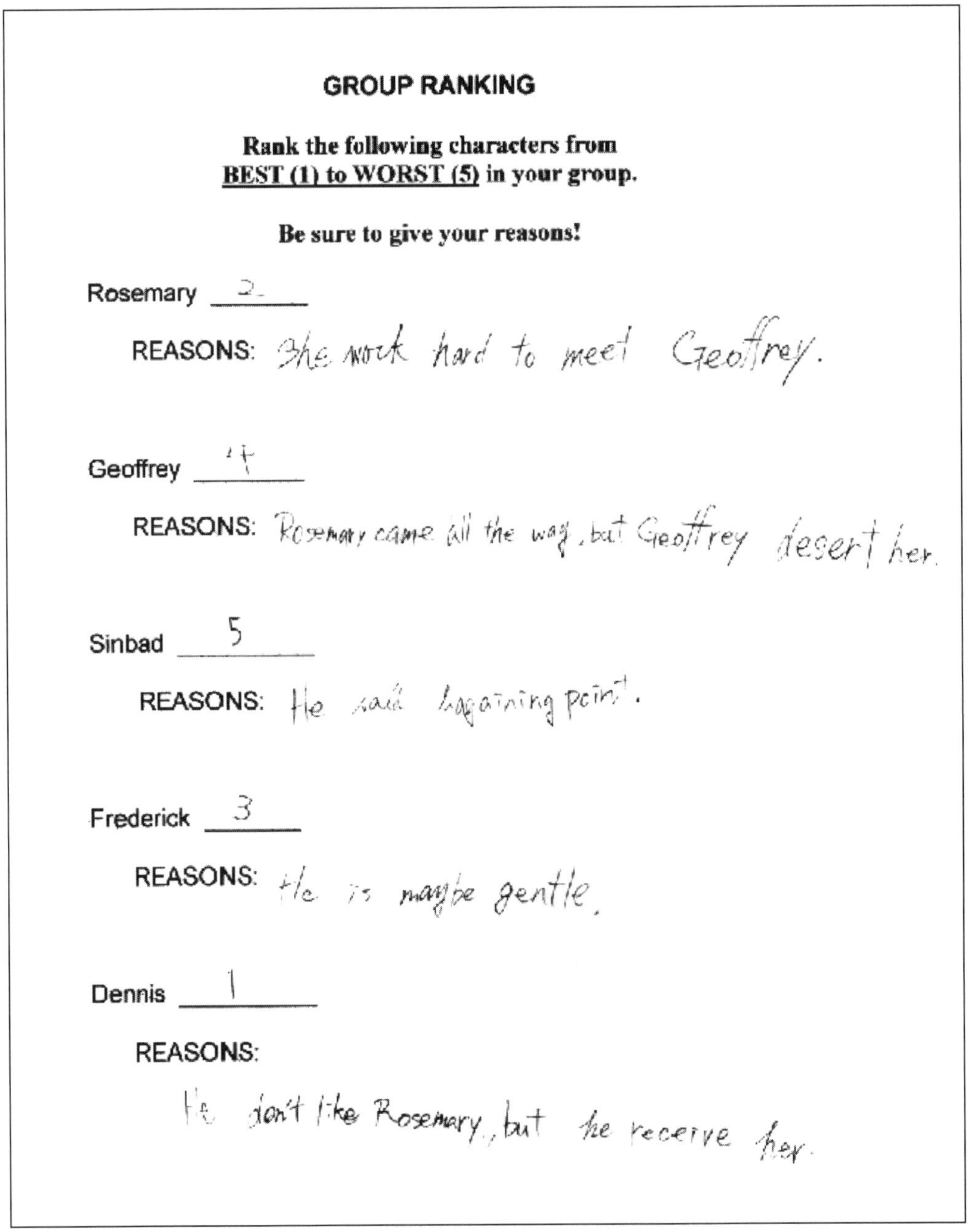

GROUP RANKING

**Rank the following characters from
BEST (1) to WORST (5) in your group.**

Be sure to give your reasons!

Rosemary ___2___

    REASONS: She work hard to meet Geoffrey.

Geoffrey ___4___

    REASONS: Rosemary came all the way, but Geoffrey desert her.

Sinbad ___5___

    REASONS: He said bargaining point.

Frederick ___3___

    REASONS: He is maybe gentle.

Dennis ___1___

    REASONS:

        He don't like Rosemary, but he receive her.

Figure 4. Sample Group Ranking Sheet

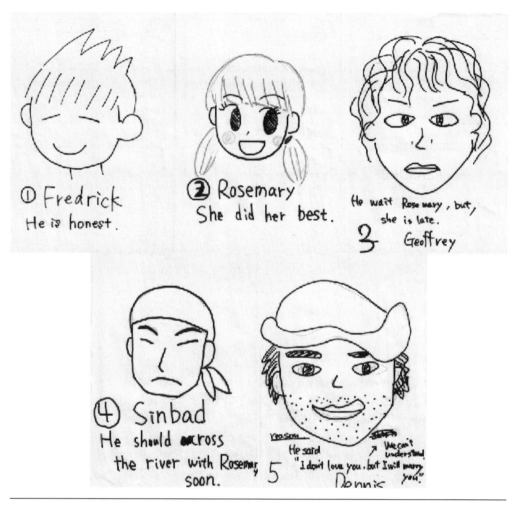

Figure 5. Pictures of the Characters' Faces

Presenting Pictures and Rankings in English

When the groups had finished drawing their pictures, they prepared short oral presentations. The objective of the class presentations was to present and justify rankings while talking about and showing the group pictures to the class. While they made their presentations, I tabulated the results as shown in the sample data from one class in Table 1.

After the presentations were finished, I drew the students' attention to the ranking data that I had tabulated on the board. I asked them to think about generalizations they could make concerning all of the rankings and to write their generalizations on a piece of paper. This kind of thinking was quite difficult for the 1st-year Japanese university students, but after I modeled a few possible generalizations, they began to come up with more on their own. These included

Table 1. Comparative Group Rankings in One Class

	Group 1	Group 2	Group 3	Group 4	Group 5
1st	F	D	F	G	R
2nd	D	F	D	R	F
3rd	R	R	R	F	D
4th	G	G	S	G	S
5th	S	S	G	S	G

Note. 1 is the highest approval. R =Rosemary; F = Frederick; D = Dennis; S = Sinbad; G = Geoffrey.

general statements such as, "In our class, all of the groups ranked Geoffrey and Sinbad either fourth or last," or "All of the groups except one ranked Frederick either first or second," or "None of the groups in our class ranked Rosemary and Frederick fourth or last."

Closing the Activity

To bring the activity to a close, I asked students to think about the generalizations they had generated and write down their ideas about why some of these general tendencies surfaced in the data. I asked them about cultural and personal values regarding judgments of what is "good" and what is "bad," and gave them an opportunity to express themselves on this topic in writing. There was always at least one student in each of the 10 classes who asked what the "right" answer was. In response, I would redirect the question to the entire class and was never disappointed with their answers. Most of the students seemed to understand that there was no right answer: They had found their own answers based on a combination of personal and cultural values.

REFLECTIONS

Discovering classroom activities that work time after time is vital to foreign- and second-language teachers' enthusiasm for the profession and also allows insights into the mysteries surrounding the process of second-language learning. The "Alligator River" exercise is one that I have found consistently works well with students at a wide range of proficiency levels. Although the content of the story may not be suitable for some students, activities of this type that involve making decisions, expressing ideas through multiple channels such as drawing, and generalizing about data clearly can help university students develop both their language and thinking skills. In addition, through this activity, learners can gain a greater awareness of their own values as well as those of their classmates.

Why Did the Activity Work So Well With All of the Groups?

The fact that students in all 10 of the classes were able to remain on task for an entire 90-minute lesson indicates that there was something about the activity that naturally motivated them. The story is simple and accessible even to students at lower proficiency levels. Humans enjoy stories and try to identify with characters to whom they are attracted, while separating themselves from those they find less attractive. Given the important role that stories play in most aspects of human life, it is hardly surprising that a story like "Alligator River" would immediately catch students' attention.

I believe that adding a decision-making dimension to the exercise further motivated learners. Through this process, I felt that my students were empowered as they evaluated the behavior of the characters in the story. This empowerment increased motivation and, in turn, kept them on task.

As the activity moved through the next stages, drawing a picture of the story and reaching a group consensus, student motivation remained at a high level, and they became more interested in what the other groups were thinking. When I next asked all of the groups to draw the individual characters' faces, their motivation surged again because of the investment they had made in the story and because of the decisions they had made, both individually and collectively, about the characters.

Although some of the classes showed less enthusiasm for the oral presentations that followed and far less for processing the results of the rankings, it was important for all of the groups to have an opportunity to show their drawings and report on their work. The final step, having students make generalizations based on class results, was at times tedious. Since some of the generalizations were crucial to understanding value systems, both personal and cultural, and since some learners needed to see the bigger picture, it is a step in the exercise that should not be omitted. To sustain motivation during this part of the activity, I think it is helpful to have the students fill in their own group's data as in Table 1 and to have each of them write down three or four generalizations before the full-class discussion begins. Asking the students to share their ideas with others in small groups prior to opening a full-class discussion can also make this concluding part of the activity run more smoothly.

What Are Some Other Ways to Use the Same Story?

When a teacher finds an activity that works in one particular learning context, it is only natural to think about using it in others. I have had the opportunity to work with some of the same groups of students in different classes over a 2-year period, and tried to use the same story in different ways with them. These students first became acquainted with "Alligator River" in the activity described previously and subsequently were able to work with the same story in a writing class as well as in a class that featured debates. In the writing class, I directed the students to summarize the story in their own words and rank the characters with appropriate written justifications for the rankings. Recycling the story for another purpose not only gave the students a chance to write with confidence about something they knew but also helped them to refine their reasons for the rankings. Similarly, when I used the story in an introductory debate class, the students knew the characters well and felt confident in presenting arguments for one character or another (for another view on recycling tasks, see the Stewart chapter in this volume).

To further test the versatility of the story, I decided to use it with a 1st-year English oral communication class as a final oral examination. The students in this class worked with the story as described here, but instead of doing oral presentations in front of the entire class, they presented their group rankings and pictures as their final oral examination for the course. They were highly motivated and well prepared for the exam, and I had the opportunity to follow up with questions for individual students regarding either the rankings or the drawings. I was also able to draw their attention to some general differences in ranking tendencies between Japanese students and U.S. Peace Corps volunteers. Typically, students were eager to try to explain the cross-cultural differences. They clearly enjoyed this kind of oral exam, and as a teacher I was able to evaluate students based on more English communication data than is usually available in an examination context (also see the Soresi chapter in this volume).

How Can Teachers Find Other Stories Like This One to Use in the Classroom?

Stories like "Alligator River" have grown out of the tradition of questioning one's values and of questioning what is "right" and what is "wrong." Similar dilemma-based stories can be found in the works of psychologists, theologians, and philosophers (among others) who specialize in ethics and moral development. Kohlberg's (1963) dilemma stories, developed for his research on the stages of human moral development, present situations in which people have to make decisions based on their values and beliefs. Stories such as Kohlberg's well-known "Heinz Dilemma" are widely available and can be easily adapted for use in the foreign or second-language classroom (see Appendix C for the original text of this story).

Another good source for dilemma-based stories requiring participants to make value-based decisions can be found on the Wilderdom Web site (2006). Initially designed for corporate team-building, these activities are divided into two basic types: (a) choose equipment scenarios and (b) choose people scenarios. The Moon Survival scenario is an example of the former. In this activity, participants learn about the situation and are then required to rank available equipment for survival on the moon. The Plane Crash Survival scenario involves making decisions about people: Nine people survive a plane crash, and there is only space for four people in the life raft. Participants have to make decisions about which people should survive and need to justify their decisions. Although the emphasis in these activities is typically on group process and team-building, they can also be used effectively to stimulate discussion based on student values. To increase the likelihood of success with ESOL students, however, it is important to carefully think through the learning tasks and include clear steps for ensuring comprehension of the stories. It is also essential to provide an opportunity to express personal values in a nonthreatening context through alternative means of expression, such as drawing.

Should "Alligator River" be Adapted for Particular Learning Contexts?

In the 10 years that I have used "Alligator River" in my teaching, I have found that it is a robust, self-motivating activity that is likely to be effective regardless of the educational context; however, I continue to refine and adapt the story and the related tasks as I use it. Most recently, I found it necessary to change the names of two of the characters: Rosemary and Sinbad. Based on discussions with colleagues and on the results of student rankings and justifications, I realized that many felt that Rosemary's name in itself made her appear "good" (*rose* plus *marry*) and that Sinbad (*sin* plus *bad*) because of his name alone was often destined to receive the lowest ranking. I changed the names to Roxana and Sidney, respectively, and have found that this small change requires deeper thinking on the part of the students as they make their value judgments.

Teachers who use this activity should consider the unique characteristics of their own teaching contexts and adapt it to meet the needs of their students. Each time that I have adapted the text or modified my classroom approach in some way for a particular group, the effectiveness of the activity has increased. I encourage teachers to adapt the basic story as necessary and to share their new ideas.

In closing, I return to the question of whether the benefits of values clarification activities in a classroom learning situation outweigh the risks. Based on my experience of the past 30 years in both ESOL education and Peace Corps cross-cultural training, it has become abundantly clear to me that the risks are minimal compared with the opportunities that such activities offer students to explore their own values and express themselves. Certainly there are specific groups of students for whom "Alligator River" is not appropriate, but exploring values—whether with university students making moral choices about crossing an alligator-filled river or elementary school students thinking and talking about their dreams for the future—positions learners in the center of the learning process. I suggest that ESOL teachers at all levels could take this risk and reach out to connect with students at a deeper level to reap the benefits of increased motivation and language practice focused on the learners' own ideas and values.

William Perry has been involved in English language teaching for more than 25 years in countries throughout the world and currently teaches at Kobe University, in Japan. He has maintained a parallel career with the U.S. Peace Corps and is interested in the role of values and beliefs in language learning.

APPENDIX A

Alligator River

Rosemary is a woman of about 21 years of age. For several months she has been engaged to a young man named Geoffrey. The problem she faces is that between her and her fiancé there lies a river: no ordinary river, but a deep, wide river filled with hungry alligators.

Rosemary wonders how she can cross the river. She remembers Sinbad, who has the only boat in the area. She then approaches Sinbad, asking him to take her across. He replies, "Yes, I'll take you across if you'll stay with me for one week." Shocked at this offer, she turns to a close acquaintance, Frederick, and tells him her story. Frederick responds by saying, "Yes, Rosemary, I understand your problem, and I wish I could help you, but it is just too difficult for me." Rosemary decides to return to Sinbad, and stays with him for a week. Sinbad then takes her across the river.

Her meeting with Geoffrey is warm. On the evening before they are to be married, however, Rosemary feels she must tell Geoffrey how she succeeded in getting across the river. Geoffrey responds by saying, "I wouldn't marry you if you were the last woman on earth."

Finally, Rosemary turns to her friend Dennis. Dennis listens to her story and says, "Well, Rosemary, I don't love you—but I will marry you."

That is all we know of the story.

(adapted from Levine & Adelman, 1992, p. 32)

APPENDIX B

Your Ranking

Rank the following characters from *best* to *worst* in your opinion.

Rosemary _____
   reasons:

Geoffrey _____
   reasons:

Sinbad _____
   reasons:

Frederick _____
   reasons:

Dennis _____
   reasons:

1 = high approval
5 = low approval

APPENDIX C

Heinz Steals the Drug

In Europe, a woman was near death from a special kind of cancer. There was one drug that the doctors thought might save her. It was a form of radium that a druggist in the same town had recently discovered. The drug was expensive to make, but the druggist was charging 10 times what the drug cost him to make. He paid $200 for the radium and charged $2,000 for a small dose of the drug. The sick woman's husband, Heinz, went to everyone he knew to borrow the money, but he could only get together about $1,000, which is half of what it cost. He told the druggist that his wife was dying and asked him to sell it cheaper or let him pay later. But the druggist said: "No, I discovered the drug and I'm going to make money from it." So Heinz got desperate and broke into the man's store to steal the drug—for his wife. Should the husband have done that?

(Kohlberg, 1963, p. 19; see Galbraith & Jones,1976,
for additional ideas for using Kohlberg's dilemma stories.)

CHAPTER 3

Authentic iBT Speaking Practice Using Open-Source Voice-Recording Software

Dana Saito-Stehberger and Jee-Eun Oh

INTRODUCTION

In September 2005 the newest version of the Test of English as a Foreign Language (TOEFL), the TOEFL Internet-based test (iBT), debuted. Some of the most significant changes in this version are: (a) the elimination of the independent structure–grammar section; (b) the integrated speaking and writing tasks that require test-takers to comprehend spoken conversations, lectures, and written texts in order to respond sufficiently; and (c) the inclusion of a new speaking section. Because the TOEFL has been widely institutionalized to measure nonnative academic English-language proficiency since 1964, the iBT promises to become the new gatekeeper in many educational institutions where English is the primary language of instruction.

As English for speakers of other languages (ESOL) instructors, we celebrate the changes in the TOEFL: The iBT tasks are more authentic and reflect the kind of tasks that are likely to occur in academic settings. Moreover, the previously neglected skill of speaking is being tested directly. At the same time, we realize that as the TOEFL changes, English as a second language (ESL) or English as a foreign language (EFL) teachers of academically oriented students are burdened to alter their curricula accordingly. Among the most challenging tasks is to devise practical and effective ways to prepare students for the speaking tasks that have strict time limits as well as listening and speaking requirements initially unfamiliar to students. Our response to this demand was to create a curriculum that resembles the six iBT speaking prompts. Students digitally record their responses using the open-source (i.e., free for our teaching purposes) voice-recording software Audacity, and we guide them through a self-reflection process.

The aim of this chapter is to support teachers who are looking for more authentic and practical ways of teaching speaking skills. In this chapter, we will (a) provide specific information on the six speaking tasks that iBT test-takers are asked to perform; (b) explain our record, transcribe, evaluate, and correct (R-TEC) technique and the guidelines we created to design speaking prompts that resemble those in the iBT; and (c) share handouts, assessment techniques, and our reflections on how well this curriculum helps students develop their speaking skills. Schmidt (1990) claims that learners will be more inclined to correct their errors and therefore make progress toward more accurate and fluent speech by noticing the gap between the rules and structures they have studied compared with their own language production. We will show how we use free voice-recording software as well as the learning tasks and assessment techniques that are supported by Schmidt's hypothesis.

CONTEXT

Teaching Context

This curriculum has been taught in an intensive English program (IEP) on a university campus, where most students aspire to attend a university in an English-speaking country. It is integrated into our higher level listening and speaking classes, which meet between 5 and 8 hours a week for 10 weeks. The in-class activities account for approximately 10% of class time. Because the iBT speaking tasks require students to perform common, everyday functions using an *integration* of the language skills, the test has very *positive washback*; that is, it has positive effects on the students' language development as they prepare for the test, and the test provides "useful diagnoses of strengths and weaknesses" (Brown, 2004, p. 29). Whether students intend to study English in an academic setting or not, practicing iBT-like speaking tasks supports the development of skills that are essential for fluency in everyday conversation. For example, the test aims to assess the clear organization and presentation of ideas, the ability of the speaker to summarize written and aural passages and to logically support his personal opinion (Educational Testing Service, 2005). The learning activities created for our intensive English program could be easily adapted to many different classroom settings, from business English to EFL settings, and from K–12 settings to adult education settings. The adaptation of the tasks is discussed in the *Curriculum* section.

The Output Hypothesis, the Noticing Hypothesis, and Consciousness-Raising Activities

In the fifth edition of his classic *Principles of Language Learning and Teaching* textbook, H. D. Brown (2007) added a new section entitled "Hot Topics in SLA Research," and among the first topics presented is the role of awareness, or conscious learning, in the process of second-language acquisition. Research in the past 2 decades has led theorists away from Krashen's (1981) view that "acquisition," or unconscious learning, is primarily responsible for the fluency in second-language performance. Although no one argues that unconscious learning plays a part in second-language acquisition, many researchers now challenge the idea that it is the primary means (e.g., Ellis, 1997b; Schmidt, 1990). The general consensus is that Krashen's Input Hypothesis, which states that second-language acquisition is a result of input alone, does not sufficiently explain the complex process. Learners not only need to be exposed to input, but the input must also be internalized. This has come to be called "intake" (Corder, 1967; Gass & Selinker, 2001). Once the new information has been taken in, the next step is to use it in production. Swain (2000) has argued that the learner's use of the language actually facilitates the acquisition. Her Output Hypothesis explains two ways that learner production of the target language, or output, facilitates language acquisition; first, it challenges learners to process the target language more deeply, and, second, it gives learners a chance to notice their own mistakes.

Our curriculum is grounded in these three concepts: (a) conscious learning is significantly more important to second-language acquisition than previously believed, (b) information in the target language that a learner receives must be internalized, or noticed, by the learner in order for it to make a greater impact on language acquisition, and (c) the production of the target language facilitates language acquisition. Schmidt proposes that intake is necessary for second-language acquisition to occur, and that "intake" is what learners consciously notice. He goes on to state that the requirement to notice is "meant to apply equally to all aspects of language (lexicon, phonology, grammatical form, pragmatics)" (Schmidt, 1990, p. 149). Schmidt and Froda (1986, pp. 310–315) coined the phrase *noticing the gap,* which describes the necessary process of the learner noticing the gap between input and his current target language production. They suggest that learners must notice the gap in their own production before noticed input can become internalized.

In responding to the iBT practice tasks we have created, learners are given the opportunity to notice the gap between their verbal response and what they have learned in class, such as intonation, rhythm, stress, pauses, pronunciation of problematic phonemes, vocabulary, specific grammar points, topic sentences, supporting details, and signal words. We provide our students with instruction on the structure and the expectations of the iBT tasks, including how much time they have to prepare and then to speak. By staying within the time constraints during the practice tasks, our students can notice the gap between their response and the guidelines set by the Educational Testing Service (ETS), the organization that produces the iBT. In addition, we require students to reflect in writing on their observed gaps, which is a metacognitive learning strategy that has also been credited as facilitating the language learning process (Fotos, 1996; O'Malley & Pierce, 1996).

The Six iBT Speaking Tasks

Most students who take the iBT have a goal of attending an academic institution. The tasks that test-takers are asked to perform are related to situations that take place in university settings, such as lectures, study groups, and meetings with professors. The speaking section consists of six types of tasks, which are briefly explained in Table 1. The task names in our table (i.e., Announcement/Discussion Task and General/Specific Task) describe the type of skill being tested and were borrowed from Rogers (2007). The first two tasks are "independent tasks," which means that a student's response is based on his own previous knowledge or experience and that no other information source is necessary to answer the questions. Test-takers are asked a question, given 15 seconds to organize a response, and then given 45 seconds to speak. The next four tasks are integrated, which means that students must comprehend a reading or listening passage in order to respond to the prompt. Test-takers can take notes on the reading and listening passages. They are given 20 or 30 seconds to organize their thoughts and then have 60 seconds to state their response. Tasks 3 and 5 involve campus situations, such as a meeting with a professor or a discussion between two students, while tasks 4 and 6 relate to a professor's lecture. Although the tasks pertain to academic settings, they are meant to test general skills necessary to speak accurately and fluently in any setting. Some of those general skills include: expressing and defending a personal opinion; synthesizing two different sources of information, such as a movie review and information from friends talking about the movie; being faced with a problem and giving an opinion of the best solution; and summarizing what someone has said.

All six responses are scored against a rubric with three criteria: delivery, language use, and topic development. A high score in the delivery category means that the speech is well paced with relatively clear pronunciation and intonation. A high score in language use reflects an effective use of grammar, vocabulary, and sentence structures. Last, a high score in topic development means that the response was well developed and coherent, the relationships between the ideas are clear, and there is a logical progression of ideas. Important elements that contribute to a coherent response include a topic sentence, supporting details, and signal phrases, such as *first, second, in addition*, and *according to the reading passage/ lecture/conversation*. See Appendix B for directions on accessing the iBT speaking rubrics.

Audacity: Open-Source Voice-Recording Software

In the past, speaking skills were challenging to teach and assess because capturing students' responses was tedious and time-consuming. Traditionally, responses were recorded on analog tapes to make students aware of their progress and ensure that teachers were accountable for assessments. A new technology has made the process of recording students' oral responses affordable and time

Table 1. Descriptions of the Six iBT Speaking Tasks[1]

Task	Task name	Description	Prep. Time	Response Time
1	**Independent Free-Choice Task Personal Preference Task**	Students see a single question that asks them to express and defend a personal choice.	15 seconds	45 seconds
2	**Independent Paired-Choice Task**	Students see a single question that asks them to make and defend a personal choice between two contrasting behaviors or actions.	15 seconds	45 seconds
3	**Announcement/ Discussion Task Read/Listen/Speak: Campus**	Two sources of information: — a **reading passage** (75–100 words) on a campus-related issue (45 seconds to read) — a **listening passage** (60–80 sec.) comments on an issue in the reading Students see a question that asks them to pull together (synthesize or integrate) and express information from both sources.	30 seconds	60 seconds
4	**General/Specific Task Read/Listen/Speak: Academic**	Two sources of information: — a **reading passage** (75–100 words) with background information on an academic topic (45 seconds to read) — a **listening passage** (60–90 sec.) gives an excerpt from an academic lecture with a more specific aspect of the same topic Students see a question that asks them to combine and convey important information from both sources.	30 seconds	60 seconds
5	**Problem/Solution Task Listen/Speak: Campus**	One source of information: — a **listening passage** (60–90 sec.) of a conversation between a man and a woman about a student-related issue and two possible opinions or solutions Students see a question that asks them to demonstrate understanding of the problem and express an opinion about the best solution.	20 seconds	60 seconds
6	**Summary Task Listen/Speak: Academic**	One source of information: — a **listening passage** (90–120 sec.) that explains a term or concept and gives two examples to illustrate it Students see a question that asks them to summarize the lecture, demonstrating understanding of its structure and the relationship between the examples and the overall topic.	20 seconds	60 seconds

[1] TOEFL materials adapted from *Helping Your Students Communicate with Confidence*, 2005. Used by permission of ETS, the copyright owner; however, the test questions and any other testing information are provided in their entirety by Teachers of English to Speakers of Other Languages. No endorsement of this publication by ETS should be inferred.

efficient. Audacity is an open-source voice-recording software that can be downloaded from the Internet and installed on a computer in a matter of minutes (http://audacity.sourceforge.net). *Open-source* means that the source code for the program is available to the public; the software is free for educational uses. The Audacity interface is straightforward; as long as students know the record, stop, and play symbols on most music devices, they will be able to use this software. Voice recordings can be saved in a number of different audio formats, including MP3, which compresses the file, making it faster to e-mail. In most cases, these files can be stored in an audio CD format and played in a CD player. Audacity makes it possible for all of the students in a class to respond to the prompt at the same time and learn from their mistakes because they can easily review their own responses (for more on recordings and student error correction, see the Lynch and Chernen chapters in this volume).

CURRICULUM, TASKS, MATERIALS

In this section, we explain the different aspects of our curriculum. We will outline step-by-step guidelines on how to create authentic speaking prompts.

The Six Speaking Tasks

The types of speaking tasks we have created (see Table 2) closely resemble those on the iBT and stay within the parameters stated in Table 1. Although iBT test preparation books exist with good practice activities for the six tasks (e.g., Phillips, 2005; Rogers, 2007), not enough class time in our course is dedicated to the iBT to justify having students buy a large and costly book. To suit the purposes of the course, we have created three different prompts for each of the six types of tasks. We have either authored the reading and listening passages or have credited their source. We recorded the listening passages ourselves using the Audacity software and saved them in MP3 format. All of the prompts can be downloaded from our Web site (see Appendix B). We have chosen topics that are common at university campuses and of interest to the general student population. Examples of tasks 3 and 6 are in Appendix A.

Methodology

We begin the iBT speaking unit by clearly describing the six tasks listed on the task description sheet (Table 2). We focus on two tasks at a time. Students practice in class first, getting used to the time limits and the task requirements. Then we have the students record in the computer lab.

The first two tasks are free response prompts that do not require students to read or listen to anything besides the question. This is easy to practice in pairs in class because it takes less than 5 minutes: about 15 seconds to read the prompt on the board, 15 seconds to prepare to speak, and 45 seconds to respond. Next, the sequence is repeated as the partner responds to a different question prompt. This

Table 2. Sample Speaking Prompts and Topics

Task 1: Free-Choice Task (examples) Tell us about a person you admire. Use reasons and details to support your response. If you could take any course at a university for free, which one would you choose? Use reasons and details to support your response.
Task 2: Paired-Choice Task (examples) Do you think it is better to marry before or after the age of 30? Use details and examples to support your response. Would you rather do indoor or outdoor housework? Use details and examples to support your response.
Task 3: Read, Listen, Speak: Campus 1. Student schedule 2. Transportation (bus strike) 3. Plagiarism
Task 4: Read, Listen, Speak: Academic 1. Criminal court 2. Alternative fuel 3. Multiple intelligences
Task 5: Listen, Speak: Campus 1. Extension on exam, issue: priority of family versus school 2. Eating lunch, issue: bringing a lunch versus eating out 3. Sale at campus computer store, issue: buying a new model versus an inexpensive older model
Task 6: Listen, Speak: Academic 1. Racial profiling 2. Torts 3. Affirmative action

activity engages students at the beginning of class since it provides everyone with speaking practice. If there is extra time, the listeners give feedback to the speakers. They report the main idea of the response, the supporting details, and the signal words that the speakers used. This becomes good listening practice and reinforces the idea of structure in a response. Students also work in pairs on tasks 3–6. Two of the three prompts that we created are used for practice in class. The third prompt is played in the computer lab when they record their responses.

In the computer lab, the students begin the R-TEC process, described in detail below.

Record: Each student, with a headset on, sits in front of a computer. The Audacity program is already opened, ready for the students to record when they are prompted. The questions are displayed through the projector or on the individual computers. If there is no projector, the questions and the reading texts can be distributed on paper. For tasks 1 and 2 (see Table 2), students only need to read the questions before they give their response. In tasks 3 and 4, students need to read a passage and listen to a conversation. The teacher needs

Teacher Evaluation of the Student Transcript

Student: _____

	Yes	No
Did you complete the self-evaluation chart appropriately?	Yes No 4 3 2 1 0	
Did you accurately edit your transcription?	Yes No 4 3 2 1 0	
Did you state a topic sentence?	Yes No 4 3 2 1 0	
Did you state your main idea and two reasons or examples in your response?	Yes No 4 3 2 1 0	
Did you use signal words?	Yes No 4 3 2 1 0	
(For tasks 3–6) Did you summarize the situation or information accurately?	Yes No 4 3 2 1 0	
Did you use reported speech? *The reading passage was about…* *The conversation/lecture was about…*	Yes No 4 3 2 1 0	
Score: ____ / 28		

Figure 1. Teacher Evaluation Form

to pay close attention to the 45-second time limit for the reading. Tasks 5 and 6 involve only listening to a passage. For each task, a set amount of time is given for students to plan their response after the question is read. The response is then recorded. Students can keep track of how much time has elapsed with the Audacity software. The students save their recordings as MP3 files and e-mail them to themselves so that they can complete their transcriptions as homework. The teacher neither needs to listen to nor evaluate the spoken response. The focus of this practice is, first, for students to self-assess and, second, for the teacher to look at the language use and topic development of the response, which is done when students turn in their written transcripts. The teacher's evaluation of the transcript is recorded on the form in Figure 1. Feedback on pronunciation is not given in this assignment (see the Chernen chapter in this volume for feedback on pronunciation).

Transcribe: The next step in the process is for students to listen to their recording and transcribe it word for word, including any false starts, repetition, and mistakes. Students are encouraged to mark any hesitation or pause with a single backslash (/); a longer pause should be denoted with a double backslash (//). As a student records more slash marks, he becomes aware of problems with fluency. Transcripts should be double spaced and either typed or handwritten very clearly. See Figure 2 for a student sample of the R-TEC process.

Evaluate: As students listen to their responses and read through their transcript, they evaluate their own response with a checklist and two open-ended questions: "What did you do well?" and "What would you like to improve on?"

Name_____

iBT Task: #3Assignment

Notes on the reading passage: *KJ*

O.C.T. Authority went on Strike Satur buses x until further alternate means → student

(1) taxi (949) 469·8294

(2) Carpool

(3) friends → Activity office.

Notes on the listening passage:

email 1 hour

options (taxi — tight budget / family, friend, → aunt 15 years / criss → 3 student ride already

#3 Announcement/Discussion Task
Give each characteristic a score between 0 and 4, "4" being excellent.

Delivery Of Response	I spoke clearly and didn't mumble.	④ 3 2 1
	I spoke at an appropriate speech; not too slowly or too fast.	4 3 ② 1
	I spoke fluently. I didn't make long pauses.	4 ③ 2 1
	I used good intonation and clear pronunciation.	4 ③ 2 1
Use of Language	I used appropriate and proper grammar and vocabulary.	4 ③ 2 1
	I used vocabulary and grammar that I am familiar with.	④ 3 2 1
Development of Topic	I stated the topic of the memo/announcement in the first sentence of my response and then summarized it.	4 ③ 2 1
	I used my notes to organize my thoughts.	④ 3 2 1
	I summarized the student(s)'s opinion and explained why the student feels this way.	4 ③ 2 1
	I cited the source that I referred to (ex. *According to the announcement/newspaper article/memo . . .* and *"The man/woman says that . . ."*).	4 3 ② 1

1. What do you do well?

I didn't mumbled a lot.
My notes were well organized.

2. What specific things do you want to improve on?

I should speak more faster!
I should cite the source that I reffeted to.

Continued on p. 38

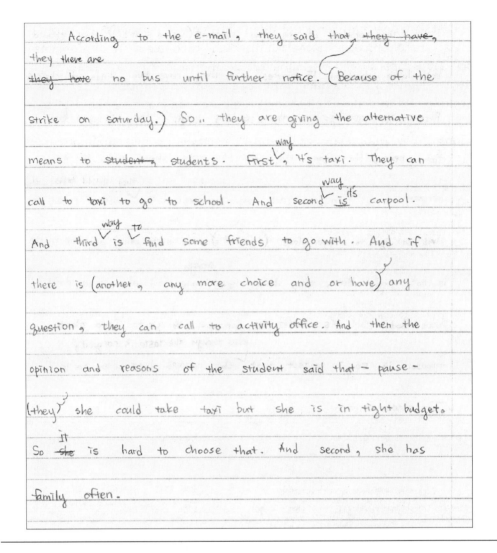

According to the e-mail, they said that, ~~they have~~, ~~they~~ there are ~~they have~~ no bus until further notice. (Because of the strike on saturday.) So.. they are giving the alternative means to ~~student~~, students. First, way it's taxi. They can call to taxi to go to school. And second way is it's carpool. And third way is to find some friends to go with. And if there is (another, any more choice and or have) any question, they can call to activity office. And then the opinion and reasons of the student said that — pause — (they) she could take taxi but she is in tight budget. So ~~she~~ it is hard to choose that. And second, she has ~~family~~ often.

Figure 2. Example of Student Work for Task 3

We found that students engage in significant reflection on the speaking tasks even when rating their performance on a simple scale of 1–4 with the checklist (also see the Popko and Yeh chapters in this volume).

Correct: The last step is for students to edit their transcripts for organizational, grammatical, and lexical errors. It is interesting for the teacher as well as the student to see the gap between a student's actual production and his explicit knowledge of English.

Assess: The way we assess this task provides helpful feedback for the student, yet it is not too time-consuming for teachers (for more on the time involved in assessing recorded speech, see the Chernen chapter in this volume). As stated previously, we don't actually listen to each recording. Rather, we look at the transcripts and evaluate the topic development (i.e., topic sentences, main points, supporting ideas, and the use of signal words) and give credit based on the quality of responses to the two open-ended self-reflection questions. Through this process, students develop the skills of self-reflection and noticing that will lead them to become independent learners. Teachers use the evaluation sheets to provide systematic feedback. A big advantage for teachers is that this feedback does not take a lot of time to produce (see Figure 1). Figure 2 is an example of a student's self-assessment and self-corrected transcript. This student sample is a response to the task 3 example prompt in Appendix A (i.e., giving a classmate advice on alternative forms of transportation to school during a bus strike).

Material Development: Tips in Creating Speaking Tasks

Developing prompts for the independent tasks 1 and 2 shown in Table 2 was a matter of creating discussion questions; however, creating appropriate prompts for tasks 3–6 required much more planning and organization. Next, we offer teachers some advice about creating iBT speaking practice prompts based on our experience.

1. **Brainstorm a theme or topics:** For academic tasks, start with an academic discipline. Then, narrow down to a specific concept or theory. For campus tasks, think about student issues (e.g., housing, cafeteria, classes, professors, exams, grades). Teachers who are not preparing students for the iBT have an even greater range of topics, such as travel advice, a business complaint, parents' day at school, a bus schedule, coupons, taxes, and library late fines.

2. **Research the topic:** Find or write a listening passage and, for tasks 3 and 4, a reading passage of 75–100 words. Based on what ETS has written about the integrated tasks and on practice iBT questions we have reviewed, we have drawn conclusions about some reoccurring characteristics of the integrated task passages.

   a. **Task 3: Reading passage (75–100 words)** on a campus issue. This passage is in the form of some kind of announcement, memo, newspaper article, or e-mail that informs the college campus community of a particular situation, such as a new policy.

   Listening passage (60–80 seconds) that comments on the issue in the reading. This listening passage is between a male and female student who are expressing their opinions about the situation described in the reading passage. Test-takers are to describe the situation, how the students feel about it, and the reasons they feel that way.

b. **Task 4: Reading passage (75–100 words)** on an academic topic.

   Listening passage (60–90 seconds) gives an excerpt from an academic lecture with a more specific aspect of the same topic, such as an example of something mentioned in the reading passage. Test-takers are instructed to summarize the two passages, making the relationship between the passages clear.

c. **Task 5: Listening passage (60–90 seconds)** of a conversation about a student issue and two possible solutions. Test-takers are asked to explain the problem and the two options discussed. Then they are told to give their opinion of the best solution and why they think it is best.

d. **Task 6: Listening passage (90–120 seconds)** that explains a term or concept and gives two examples to illustrate it. Test-takers must summarize the main ideas.

3. **Record:** The conversations or lectures should be recorded using a headset and the Audacity voice-recording software. The iBT conversations are always between a man and a woman to make it easier for the test-taker to cite the source of the information.

To write the questions, consider the skills listed below, and refer to our example prompts (see Appendix B).

Task 1: Express and defend a personal choice.

Task 2: Make and defend a personal choice between two contrasting behaviors or actions.

Task 3: Summarize information from two sources.

Task 4: Integrate the important information from two sources.

Task 5: Summarize the problem, and choose the best solution.

Task 6: Summarize the lecture, and comment on its structure and how the examples relate to the main idea.

REFLECTIONS

The initial aim of this curriculum was to prepare students for the speaking section of the iBT. As we became more familiar with the iBT, however, we realized that all of our students would benefit from practicing speaking tasks that resemble those on the iBT. As a result, the types of tasks we have outlined in this chapter are not just part of our iBT preparation course, but have been integrated into our general speaking classes as well. From our experience developing the curriculum, we end with four key observations that we believe will resonate with instructors who are using iBT tasks in classes that are not entirely focused on preparation for the iBT.

- To avoid student complaints of too much test preparation, we explicitly explain the skills that these tasks help develop, such as giving an organized response in a reasonable amount of time and being able to identify their own mistakes by correcting their transcripts.

- Expect students' confidence level in their speaking to drop initially because they are put under strict time pressure to respond. As their familiarity with the tasks and with hearing their own voices increases, so will their confidence.

- Although initially students find the timed impromptu responses unnatural and uncomfortable (15-second preparation, 45 seconds to speak), after routine practice they have commented on how it has helped them to organize their thoughts faster and give a more confident response.

- Last, when developing this curriculum, we found it faster and easier to write and record our own dialogues and lectures rather than search the Internet for prerecorded listening passages that fit the topics and word count we were looking for.

Dana Saito-Stehberger is an ESL and teaching English as a foreign language (TEFL) instructor at the University of California Irvine Extension, in the United States. She teaches in the teaching ESOL master's program at Alliant International University in San Diego, California. Her research interests include the instruction of pragmatic competence, online learning communities, and online instruction.

Jee-Eun Oh teaches in the Intensive English Program at the University of California Irvine Extension. She also teaches foundation courses in the teaching ESL and TEFL certificate programs. Her research interests include technology in language teaching and effective learning environments.

APPENDIX A: EXAMPLES OF TASKS 3 AND 5

Task 3

Reading Passage (e-mail)

Dear all:

As many of you may know, the Orange County Transportation Authority went on strike on Saturday. No public buses will run until further notice. Students who rely on the public buses to get to school every day will need to find an alternate means of transportation. The activities office suggests one of the following three options: (a) make arrangements with a taxi by calling (999) 469 8294; (b) carpool with classmates; or (c) notify a friend, relative, or host parent. If students need additional information, please direct them to the Activities office. Thank you.

Regards,

D. Santiago

Director of Student Activities

Listening Passage

Woman: Did you get the e-mail about the bus strike?

Man: Yeah. I can't believe that no buses will be running. That is so inconvenient!

Woman: Tell me about it. I practically live on the public buses. I live about an hour away from school. I have no idea how I am going to get to school every day.

Man: Well, the e-mail lists several options. Can you take the taxi?

Woman: Well . . . I'm on a very tight budget. I can't take the taxi every morning to and from school! I'm just not sure what I can do. I can't just sit at home and wait until the strike is over. I have to go to class.

Man: Do you have any family or friends who live nearby?

Woman: Well, I do have an aunt, but she is 75 years old and doesn't like to drive when there are a lot of cars out on the road.

Man: Hmm. What other options do we have? Do you know Chris? He drives to school every day, and he might be able to help you out.

Woman: I know . . . but I think he already has three students he's giving rides to.

Man: It won't hurt to ask!

Woman: I guess.

Question: What do you think would be the best way for the woman to get to school during the bus strike?

Task 5

Location: Campus computer store. Issue: buying a new model computer versus an inexpensive older model

Conversation

Man: Hey! Did you hear about the sale on laptops at the campus computer store?

Woman: Yeah. But the sale is only on the older models.

Man: Really? Hm. You don't want an older model?

Woman: Well, it's $500 off, so it's significantly lower than the newer models. But I like the features on the new model.

Man: Sometimes I find the features to be useless. It just sounds nice, but I don't really use them.

Woman: But it has more storage than the older model, and just to upgrade that would cost me $200.

Man: But will you actually use all that storage space?

Woman: Well, probably not. But it's good to know I have more space.

Man: Even after the upgrade, the older model still saves you $300!

Woman: That's a good point. But sometimes you just want the newest one.

Question: The woman has a problem with the laptops that are on sale. Discuss her problem and explain the pros and cons that are mentioned in the conversation. Then explain what you would do and give your reasons.

APPENDIX B: ADDITIONAL RESOURCES

- The official ETS TOEFL Independent and Integrated Speaking Rubrics are available online at http://www.ets.org/Media/Tests/TOEFL/pdf/Speaking_Rubrics.pdfs

- Speaking prompts that we created with audio files, transcripts, and evaluation sheets are available online at www.danasaito.de/pages/teachers.htm

Reinforcing Grammar and Vocabulary Learning With High-Volume Speaking Activities

Kevin McCaughey

INTRODUCTION

Volume, according to Ur, is "the sheer amount of comprehensible language that is spoken, heard, or written in the course of an activity" (1987, p. 12). In other words, it is what English for speakers of other languages (ESOL) teachers want to get their students producing in class. All students in a classroom can read, write, or listen simultaneously. This ability is not so straightforward when it comes to classroom speaking. When a teacher elicits spoken responses for students—one at a time—it is hardly a speaking task at all. We would not ask just one student to listen to a recording, or one student to read or write while the others observed. Individual student talk is not an efficient use of class time.

As a new English teacher working overseas, I realized my speaking tasks did not offer learners much language practice. I had to reassess their design to increase the volume of language that students produced while maintaining accuracy. My goal was to create a set of focused high-volume speaking tasks. Through lengthy experimentation, I developed six keys for making a successful fluency task embedded in a focus on forms.

1. Put Students in Pairs or Small Groups

The only way to significantly increase talk time in class is to get students talking to one another. When students are arranged in pairs, half of the class can be talking simultaneously. A conversation between two people may be the most common or natural arrangement for language exchange (Norman, Levihn, & Hedenquist, 1986).

2. Scaffold Language With Prompts

The speaking tasks in this chapter employ prompts or cue cards that are distributed to each student. These visual references—whether in a handout or written on the board—function as speaking aids, providing students with content information and linguistic patterns to assist them when talking. Simply put, they *scaffold*, or guide, the conversation, thereby enabling most students to produce a satisfactory volume of talk focused on target forms.

3. Model Activities

Speaking tasks should be demonstrated in front of the whole class. A pair of students can run through a task together briefly. Modeling helps to avoid confusion about task requirements that can deflate motivation. That is, modeling acts as a secondary scaffold by clarifying the directions of the activity and, in turn, supports the linguistic and/or content cues that form the primary scaffold. Student modeling of activities allows teachers to spot potential problems before the task is underway.

4. Allow Students Time to Prepare

Students will benefit from some preparation time to examine the models on which they will base their speech. Once they receive their prompts, give them time to think them over, discuss any words they may not know with peers, rehearse language in their heads, or write notes. Folse (2006) finds that even the most reticent students are more likely to speak after they have had a chance to put something into writing.

5. Tell Students to Continue Talking

Students may be afraid of making mistakes or of learning bad habits from their partners. Emphasize that this speaking practice is primarily intended to make them more comfortable and confident in expressing ideas in English as they practice conversational usage of language introduced in class. One way to keep them talking is by setting time limits. Students in pairs or small groups can experience what Ur describes as "pleasurable tension" (1987, p. 23) when faced with a limited time. When they know their speaking time is limited, learners may push themselves to speak.

6. Encourage Variations

After running through an activity, teachers might wish to demonstrate variations of the model. Since high-volume speaking practice is the primary goal, do not discourage conversations that wander from the guidelines you provide. Students can learn a good deal by experimenting with the language. Time permitting, students should practice the tasks more than once with different partners, and the scaffold of language support can be taken away or scaled back. Remember that fluency is the goal of high-volume speaking practice, so avoid interruptions. As

Brown and Yule pointed out, even native speakers "don't produce ideal strings of complete, perfectly formed, sentences . . ." (1983, p. 21), so we should not insist our students do likewise.

CONTEXT

The critical incident that piqued my interest in the fluency–accuracy nexus in teaching English to speakers of other languages (ESOL) was a particular class session I taught in 1997. It was my first term teaching at a private school in the Republic of Moldova. I assumed that off-the-cuff exchanges were natural and useful in conversation classes and spent the entire 80-minute class eliciting individual responses from 16 preintermediate, young adult students. It was a "communicative" school, after all, and to me at the time, this seemed like a communicative lesson—based as it was on real talk, not on grammar or drills.

Reflecting on this, I cringe at the thought of those students sitting patiently through this teacher-centered exercise. I had provided absolutely no platform for students in the class to practice speaking English. Several extroverted students dominated the session, while those who were shy—or simply needed time to formulate their thoughts—were left out.

According to Cotton (2001), teacher wait-time—the pause a teacher allows after asking a question—is often a second or less, and students who are perceived as slow are routinely given the least thinking time of all. Furthermore, teacher-guided question sessions cause competition among certain students to perform for the teacher, and there is little indication in these cases that students listen to each other (Rowe, 1986).

In the lesson I describe here, many of my Moldovan students were content to nod, hoping I would take this as a signal of involvement. Later, I decided that if ever I was going to call something a "speaking task," it had better involve a lot of speaking time for all students. This decision resulted in a professional development challenge that started my experimentation with various speaking tasks.

CURRICULUM, TASKS, MATERIALS

Since the school in Moldova promoted the communicative approach, teachers were supposed to facilitate lots of talking. Yet, at the same time, our curriculum was based entirely on syntactic structures: Level 1 equaled present and simple past; Level 2 equaled irregular past, present progressive; Level 3 equaled present perfect; and so on. I thought that if I was going to give my students the confidence to communicate and practice specific structures, I needed speaking activities that targeted precisely those structures and offered students ample practice time. I soon discovered that increasing the volume of oral production using focused speaking tasks was more involved than simply putting students into groups.

I describe two sample activities in this chapter. The first targets a grammatical structure: the third-person singular. The second provides fluency practice focused on a lexical item, the verb *had better*. Linguistic targets for each activity are guided, or scaffolded, by cue card language prompts.

The Use of Prompts

Whenever someone asks me what my favorite film is, I draw a blank. That question is just too broad. If, however, someone handed me a list of 10 famous films, I am certain I would have opinions on all of them, comparisons and perhaps a ranking would emerge, and a conversation would begin.

As noted in the introduction, one key to increased speaking in the ESOL classroom is providing some form of written reference (prompts) on which students may model their language. These prompts may be handouts featuring unfinished sentences, questions, controversial statements, lists, charts, pictures, maps, or game boards. Once students have exhausted their ideas on the first question or topic listed on a prompt—and this may be only a matter of seconds—they can refer to it again for their next cue. The reference aids I have used can be described as one type of scaffolding for speaking tasks: the provision of visual and graphic language support for learners (Ovando, Collier, & Combs, 2003). With strong reference aids, students have the opportunity for "uninhibited practice" (Ellis, 1985, p. 161), free from close teacher monitoring. Ideally, as well, reference aids should develop from the shared interests of instructors and students alike, based upon common experience (Stewart, 1997, citing Bonwell & Eison, 1991).

The following sample activities that I outline are based on prompts that scaffold much of the language—both vocabulary and structure—that students will practice during the speaking task.

Activity 1: Name Three Things

Objective: Reinforcement of grammar structures

It is often the case that classroom grammar exercises (i.e., drills) are independent of speaking activities. Focused grammar practice through talking is rare, especially when it is high-volume speaking. Yet, it is possible, even simple, to take any syntactic form and provide models through which students can practice the structure orally. In the activity Name Three Things, students use a high amount of repetition by producing examples of the structure again and again (see Ur, 1987). In the following example, students speak in pairs, focusing on the third-person verb forms. Each partner receives one of the following two handouts (see Figure 1). After going over the instructions with students, the teacher should do one or two demonstrations with the entire class so that students are clear on the process involved.

Name Three Things is a noisy activity, where each student may produce up to 36 sentences using the third-person singular in 5 minutes or so—a high amount of repetition. Granted, at the basic level this is not particularly meaningful communication, but students are allowed to frame their own answers and use their imaginations. It can easily be made more communicative by encouraging students to ask for reasons ("Why do you say that?") to support their response.

Teachers should not monitor accuracy. The prompt cards themselves provide the focus on form, while the output produced allows learners to test hypotheses about how the target language works (Swain, 1985). The primary goal of these

---

Name Three Things a Person Does (Partner #1)

Directions: Face your partner. Take turns asking what a person does on these occasions or at these places. You may choose any square. Then say, for instance, "Name three things a person does in a movie theater."

Your partner will answer, "He watch<u>es</u> movies. He eat<u>s</u> popcorn. Sometimes he fall<u>s</u> asleep." Bravo. Your partner has completed that square. Mark an X through it. See which of you can get the most Xs in 5 minutes.

Note: Your partner has different subjects than you, so listen carefully.

in prison	on a cruise	at the circus
in Paris	at a picnic	when she's tired
in a train station	with a cat	at a wedding
on her day off	in front of a mirror	on New Year's Eve

--cut here--

Name Three Things a Person Does (Partner #2)

Directions: Face your partner. Take turns asking what a person does on these occasions or at these places. You may choose any square. Then say, for instance, "Name three things a person does in a movie theater."

Your partner will answer, "He watch<u>es</u> movies. He eat<u>s</u> popcorn. Sometimes he fall<u>s</u> asleep." Bravo. Your partner has completed that square. Mark an X through it. See which of you can get the most Xs in 5 minutes.

Note: Your partner has different subjects than you, so listen carefully.

when he's in love	at the beach	after dinner
when she has a cold	when she's angry	in a church
before he goes to bed	on Valentine's day	in fairy tales
when he's got no money	when she's scared	on an airplane

Figure 1. Oral Grammar Practice Handout

high-volume speaking tasks is to provide guided speaking practice that encourages students to think both in and about the language.

Activity 2: Checklist Talking—Had Better

Objective: Practice of lexical items

In the school where I taught in Moldova, auxiliary verbs such as *had better*, *supposed to*, and *would rather* appeared at a specific point in the curriculum. My upper-intermediate students in Moldova completed written drills on these forms handily. I felt frustrated, however, because there was never any textbook exercise incorporating these useful verbs into speaking practice. Given this materials gap, I wondered how my students could incorporate them into their own English. The answer I found was to create speaking tasks based on the target vocabulary.

Whether the additional speaking practice on targeted vocabulary hastened students' acquisition, I couldn't say. But the alternative of merely following the assigned text was not an option for me. I had come to believe in the retentive value that oral practice has for the acquisition of lexical and syntactic items. Ellis (1997a) supports the view that long-lasting effects may "occur only when learners have subsequent opportunities to hear and use the target structure in communication" (p. 83).

For this task, I wrote up a series of questions involving modals. The result is illustrated in Figure 2. The task is open-ended, meaning learners can express their own opinions using the targeted form *had better*. Understandably, teacher-created questions may not always be of equal interest to all students, so I try to supply more than they will need for the task. In this way, the Checklist Talking activity gives students a degree of choice.

REFLECTIONS

There's a reason people ask, "Do you speak English?" and not "Do you read English?" or "Do you understand English?" or "Do you know English grammar?" For most second language learners, the real reward to studying a second or foreign language is in speaking. My school in Moldova hoped to emphasize that aspect of language learning through a highly structured curriculum focused on forms. My job, as I saw it, was to facilitate fluency practice in lessons.

As an inexperienced teacher, my first attempts at fluency tasks involved broad topics and lots of time with students focused on the teacher. That was the arrangement in each and every foreign language class I had ever attended myself, so that was the image I had of classroom language instruction. Then, I shifted to having my students face each other, rather than the front of the class. I began to engage them in timed conversations that were simple but focused on forms.

The high-volume speaking activities that I described in this chapter do not always demand the use of high-order thinking skills, and they are not meant to replace other communicative speaking tasks. Their purpose is twofold: first, to

---

You'd Better Do It: Checklist Talking

Directions: Take a few minutes to look over the following questions. You will sit with a partner. Ask your partner *any* question on the list. You don't need to start with number 1. When you receive an answer, check the box. Then it's your partner's turn to ask you a question. You don't need to finish all 15 questions. You have about 5 minutes.

❑   1. If you owe somebody some money, what had you better do?
❑   2. If you feel sick, what had you better do?
❑   3. If you are tired before a test, what had you better do?
❑   4. If you need to wake up early, what had you better do?
❑   5. If you want to live to 100, what had you better do?
❑   6. If you want to get a raise at work, what had you better do?
❑   7. If you want someone to fall in love with you, what had you better do?
❑   8. If you want to be rich, what had you better do?
❑   9. What had you better **not** do when you're really tired?
❑ 10. What had you better **not** do when you're in love?
❑ 11. What had you better **not** say to someone when he has a new haircut?
❑ 12. You'd better **not** start whistling in what situations?
❑ 13. You'd better **not** start laughing in what situations?
❑ 14. You'd better **not** stay up late in what situations?
❑ 15. You'd better **not** leave home in what situations?

Figure 2. Lexical Practice Handout

supplement and reinforce written drills and themes covered in a curriculum and, second, to increase the volume of speaking in class.

Incorporating focused fluency tasks in lessons does not involve a new approach to teaching, or a restructuring of the curriculum. It can be done by pairing or grouping students and giving them appropriate prompts and models to keep them talking. Most students, like mine in Moldova, wish to become competent English speakers. To help them achieve this goal, I urge ESOL professionals to conceive more ways of building both fluency and accuracy through speaking tasks.

Kevin McCaughey has worked as a teaching English as a foreign language consultant throughout the former USSR and the Middle East, and in the United States. His Web site, English Teachers Everywhere (http://www.etseverywhere.com), offers a wide range of original English as a second language audio. Kevin plays the ukulele and writes songs for teaching English.

CHAPTER 5

Young Learners' Use of English: Imitation or Production?

Bärbel Diehr

INTRODUCTION

When compulsory foreign language teaching was introduced into German primary schools between 1999 and 2004, teachers faced a stiff professional challenge: How could they give their pupils the skills and encouragement to speak a foreign language? Thus, in 2002 a group of primary school teachers approached the University School of Education in Heidelberg, looking for a program of practical in-service training in assessing their pupils' spoken English. They were finding it difficult to elicit coherent discourse from young English as a foreign language (EFL) learners aged 6 to 10. In addition, assessing the texts produced by their pupils was even more of a problem because the texts were either very short (one- or two-word sentences) or just imitative (songs or rhymes).

Responding to this outcry for help from teachers, the Testing and Assessing Spoken English in Primary School (TAPS) study was launched. When it wrapped up in 2007, the conclusion was clear: If young learners are given the right kind of preparation and tasks to motivate them, they are capable not only of imitative, but also impressively productive use of English that significantly exceeds previous horizons of expectations (Diehr & Frisch, 2008). The insights gained in the German TAPS project are applicable to the teaching of young learners in any non-English environment where they are encouraged to speak the language for extended periods.

A Model of Speaking as a Basis for Encouraging Productive Speech

To establish productive use of English as a key aim of primary foreign language teaching, the tasks and materials in the TAPS project follow five strategies adopted from Levelt's (1989) psycholinguistic model of speaking (see Figure 1).

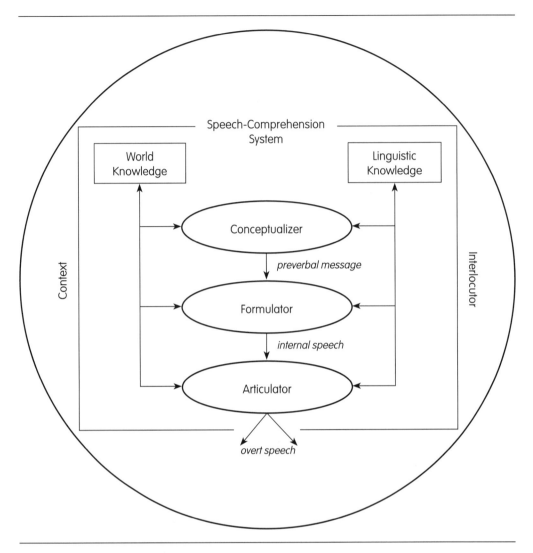

Figure 1. A Model Based on Levelt's Model for the Speaker (1989, p. 9)

These strategies (see Table 1) help teachers to carry out a scaffolded assessment in which learners interact with others and are supported in a structured way so that, eventually, they can take control of the task (Cameron, 2001, pp. 218–219; Pinter, 2006, pp. 56–58).

Levelt (1989) sees speaking as a productive process in which several components or modules transform an utterance, starting from a fragment of thought and leading to an audible sequence of sounds.

Practical Implications for Encouraging Productive Speech

The actual speech act begins in the *conceptualizer* when a speaker becomes aware of his or her speech intention. This initial process leads to a preverbal message, or speech plan. Since this speech intention plays a central role, the most important concern of teachers is to set a clear and appropriate goal (see Table 1). Young learners need meaningful tasks that provide them with a compelling reason to speak. In the course of the TAPS study, tasks such as *Make a date with your friend* or *Describe your favorite animal/hobby/book/TV program* consistently proved to give children positive motivation for talking because such tasks tap into pupils' real-life interests and needs.

According to Levelt's model, the speaker has recourse to a mental lexicon with integral phonological and grammatical information (see *Linguistic knowledge* in Figure 1). Because young learners are at an early stage of both language acquisition and acquisition of world knowledge, however, teachers need to provide them with appropriate support to meet the challenge of undertaking a task in English. Scaffolding strategies need to be aimed at activating existing conceptual knowledge (e.g., the concept of full hours when referring to time, as in *8 o'clock*) and extending it gradually (e.g., by halving the face of a large clock to expand the concept, as with *half past 8*). Scaffolding also covers language support in the form of activating familiar words and phrases, introducing new ones, and helping children notice structural features (e.g., "I *can't* play hockey, but I *can* swim and dive." or "I *like* swimming, but Peter like*s* cycling.") (see Table 1).

In drawing on Levelt's (1989) model, the preverbal message is further processed in the *formulator* (see Figure 1). The teacher's responsibility is to provide learners with sufficient and relevant processing material by demonstrating contextualised and focused language use on which learners can then model their own speech production (see Table 1). To enable the pupils to go beyond mere imitation of the model, teachers need to give sufficiently varied input. When talking about likes and dislikes, for instance, a choice of several verbs encourages learners to express different degrees of preference: I *adore* dark chocolate. I *love* fresh fruit. I *like* pasta. I *don't like* cauliflower. I *hate* cheese.

Table 1. Implementation of Levelt's Model of Speaking

Components involved in the generation of fluent speech (according to Levelt)	Scaffolding strategies to support young English as a foreign language learners' speech production
Conceptualizer	Suggesting a motivating purpose for speaking, setting a clear goal
Encyclopedic knowledge	Activating and extending factual knowledge
Knowledge about language	Activating familiar language items and introducing new ones, helping noticing
Formulator	Demonstrating language in context, providing a model for repetition and variation
Articulator	Providing audio equipment to tape oneself and time for joint listening

While the component processes of both the conceptualising and formulation systems are running, the *articulator* (see Figure 1) engages to convert the phonetic plan (or internal speech) into external speech. Although the articulator develops under the influence of the teacher model, it is very important to let children listen to their own spoken texts. Again, this is best done gradually, by the children speaking in chorus to begin with, but then moving on to using their "portable tape recorder" (i.e., by speaking into their own cupped hands to form a kind of receiver directing amplified sounds into their ears) (Wingate, 1993, p. 15). Finally, learner texts can be tape-recorded (see Table 1).

The teachers involved in the TAPS study unanimously confirmed that the step of being recorded and later being able to listen to their own voices had a powerful motivating effect on learners. Even though the children needed a couple of lessons to get used to the equipment and the recording process, their initial nervousness subsided and gave way to a heightened sense of achievement. The use of learner recordings in class also reinforces the development of a monitor or controlling authority (Krashen, 1988). Hearing themselves speak, the learners become aware of the correctness, appropriateness, and effectiveness of their texts.

CONTEXT

The Teaching Context: EFL in Primary School

In Germany, EFL in primary school has largely been hailed as a great success. Teachers and parents have welcomed it as an opportunity for language growth and cultural learning. Children are offered 90 minutes of English a week, sometimes taught as two separate 45-minute lessons, sometimes integrated into existing subjects, e.g., sports or mathematics, emulating the principles of immersive teaching. Both researchers' pilot studies (Doyé & Lüttge, 1977; Kahl & Knebler, 1996) and practitioners' reports (Bleutge & Obermann, 2004; Halder, 2005) concur that learners aged 6–10 embrace the new challenges enthusiastically. They excel in singing English songs or reciting English poems. Primary children love learning new sounds and rhymes and have a natural gift for experimenting with sound patterns. When a teacher assures them, for instance, that a new song is really not so difficult, that it is "easypeasylemonsqueezy," they respond with delighted giggles followed by immediate and prolonged repetitions of this eight-syllable word.

However, as teachers admit, despite children's admirable capacity for imitating spoken English, young learners do not often use the language communicatively, because they have problems producing extended and cohesive oral text. There is very little empirical evidence demonstrating what young German learners aged 6–10 can achieve in EFL. As a result, neither practitioners nor educational authorities know whether imitative language use is the most they can expect from primary foreign language learners, or whether they should strive for a more productive use of English in natural dialogue and extended discourse.

The Research Context: Action Research Into TEFL in Primary School

It seems reasonable to ask why educational authorities have not invested in more research to ensure a solid empirical basis for setting realistic standards for primary English. Comments made by authoritative researchers help explain the relative lack of valid and reliable research in this area: "Speaking is . . . the most difficult language skill to assess reliably" (Alderson & Bachman, 2004, p. ix). Fulcher (2003) suggests that testing second-language speaking may be more difficult than testing other second language abilities, "[p]erhaps because speaking is fleeting, temporal and ephemeral" (p. xv).

These difficulties are further complicated by the age, the language level, and the developmental needs of primary school learners. The study for TAPS was designed in the format of action research (e.g., Cohen, Manion, & Morrison, 2000, pp. 226–241) to address the practical needs of teachers attempting to function in such an underresearched area.

CURRICULUM, TASKS, MATERIALS

Although it is widely agreed that primary foreign language teaching should prioritize oral skills, educators cannot identify these skills precisely because not enough is known about the effects of foreign language learning in primary school (e.g., KMK, 2003, p. 7). Before the TAPS study provided its unexpected results, the researchers and practitioners working on this project had assumed that, in terms of language, primary English in German schools could produce only low to modest gains because of its limited time allocation of only two lessons per week, with each lesson lasting 45 minutes (Böttger, 2005, p. 155). Now that this study has illustrated just how well primary EFL learners can perform, teachers in non-English countries may want to follow the same route and try the task-based material that has been trialled in the TAPS project (Diehr & Frisch, 2008).

Materials used in German elementary schools before the TAPS project allowed only a secondary role for speaking skills, focusing instead on listening and reading. This was especially the case with the assessment material that came with the early course books (e.g., Bebermeier, Frederichs, Hartmann-Kleinschmidt, & Stoll, 2004; Becker, Gerngross, Puchta, & Zebisch, 2004; Karbe, 2004). Furthermore, the intellectual level of many existing exercises was still too low, that is, more suited to nursery school children than pupils aged 6–10. An early need was discovered, therefore, to design scaffolded tasks and age-appropriate materials that I will describe next.

A Speaking Task as a Stimulus for Language Production

The following task is aimed at primary EFL learners aged 8 and above who have been learning English for 2 years (approximately 150 hours of instruction). The idea developed from an observation made by two student teachers during a primary school practicum. They noticed that every day during recess children with a variety of minor problems—such as a stubbed toe, a grazed knee, or a mild headache—came to the staff room. After getting sympathetic attention from an adult and some comforting words from a classmate, the children relaxed and went away feeling much better. From this observation emerged the idea for a teaching unit that prepares young learners to talk about small ailments in English. The task they are given in the end is to comfort an unhappy friend.

Teaching Unit "Poor You!"

The unit (see Table 2) aims to boost young learners' productive use of English by enabling them to gain confidence in talking to another child, taking the role of either someone who has been unfortunate enough to hurt himself or someone

Table 2. Teaching Unit "Poor You!"

Teaching Unit: "Poor You!"		
Task: Comforting an unhappy friend		
1. Lesson Step	**Description of activity**	**Language in use**
1	**Noticing the problem**: Have a selected pupil (A) demonstrate a minor "accident," such as hurting his ankle or shoulder. Rush to his side to see if he is all right. Discuss the injury with child A.	[Miming a fall, a headache, etc.] A: Ouch! T: Oh no, what have you done? Or: Oh dear, are you all right? A: Ah, no, my head/shoulder/ hand/ knee/toe/etc. hurts. T: Poor you!
2	**Looking for a solution**: Ask the class what can be done to make child A feel better. If learners produce first-language (L1) responses, provide the corresponding second-language (L2) expressions. Encourage pupils to make some suggestions in English, too.	T: What can we do to make A feel better? Yes, we can sing her a song. Yes, we can give him a nice cup of cocoa.
3	**Noticing the language**: Practice expressing feelings of discomfort or pain using picture cards (Material I—The "Ouch" pack) and mime, speaking in chorus and/or individually.	Ouch, my head/knee/etc. hurts.
4	Sing the action song "Head, Shoulders, Knees and Toes" or "Hokey Pokey."	

Continued on p. 59

Table 2 (continued). Teaching Unit "Poor You!"

Step	Description of activity	Language in use
2. Lesson		
5	Welcome the class, asking individual pupils if they are all right. Sing the action song.	T: Hello, how are you? Ps: Fine, thanks. And how are you? T: I am fine, too. Let's sing our action song.
6	**Practicing the language**: Demonstrate mini-dialogue using the picture cards (Material I). Then distribute picture cards (Material I), and let pupils exchange question-and-answer turns in varying pairs.	T: Look, this is Linda. Hello, Linda. How are you? T/L: I'm not well. My shoulder/toe/ etc. hurts. A: Hello, Martin. How are you? B: I'm not well. My head hurts.
7	**Noticing the language**: Demonstrate mini-dialogue using picture cards (Material II—The "Comfort" pack).	T: Oh, Linda, poor you! Let me sing a nice song for you. Or: Let me give you a nice cuddle, etc. T/L: Oh, thank you. That's better.
8	**Practicing the language**: Distribute picture cards (Material II), and let pupil A comfort pupil B in varying pairs.	A: Oh, Max, poor you! Let me play the guitar for you. B: Oh, thank you. That's lovely.
3. Lesson		
9	Warm up with the action song. **Setting up the task**: Explain both roles (see 2. Lesson in this table). Have learners draw cards from either the "Ouch" pack (Material I) or the "Comfort" pack (Material II). To add more variety to the task, explain that the dialogues will be recorded to find out who is the unluckiest child and which friend has the best idea. Ask a pair of able pupils to demonstrate the dialogue, including dramatic simulations/mime (e.g., tripping, bumping into a door, falling).	T: Imagine one of you has a little accident. Ouch! But your friend is there to comfort you. A: Ouch! B: Oh dear, are you all right? A: Ah, no, my elbow hurts. B: Poor you! Let me read you a story. A: Thank you. You are so kind.

Continued on p. 60

Table 2 (continued). Teaching Unit "Poor You!"

Step	Description of activity	Language in use
10	**Performing the dialogue:** The entire class goes into pairs, practicing the dialogue. The task is made more productive by having learners draw different cards, practicing with different partners until they perform the dialogue freely without any picture cards and a completely new partner. The learners decide when to record a dialogue.	A: Ouch! B: Oh Frederic, are you all right? A: No, my head hurts. B: Poor you! Let me give you a nice cold drink. A: Oh, thank you. I feel much better.
4. Lesson		
11	Warm up with the action song. **Explaining the purpose:** Tell the class about the rationale behind the recording and the feedback round.	T: You all did an excellent job yesterday. We can now listen to your dialogues and find out who did a really good job, who is the "best" unlucky child, and who is the "best" friend.
12	**Discussing assessment criteria:** Ask the class what they think makes a good dialogue between an unlucky child and his best friend. Discuss criteria in L1 and introduce some terms in English.	For example: • good acting (e.g., a dramatic accident) • good ideas (e.g., a comforting suggestion) • the right words (vocabulary) • the right sounds (pronunciation) • speaking loud enough • speaking at the right speed (not too fast, not too slow)
13	**Assessing the recordings:** The class decides whose dialogue is the best one and discovers that two learners who can help and support one another can both benefit from this activity.	

who tries to comfort an unhappy friend. Within a short unit of three or four lessons, the children learn to express feelings, ideas, and suggestions, gradually taking control, at first of smaller parts (steps 6 and 8), and finally of the task as a whole (step 10). The picture cards illustrating body parts that can hurt (see Appendix A: Material I—The "Ouch" Pack) are to be used in steps 3 and 6, and the picture cards visualizing pleasant activities (see Appendix B: Material II—The "Comfort" Pack) are meant to be an aid in steps 7 and 8 when learners speak about ways of comforting a friend.

Focus on the Task

Although the unit described has been classroom tested in German primary grade 3, teachers who intend to try it in their own classes should compare the task-specific demands with the support the children in their class normally need. Realistically, they might expect each dialogue to last half a minute and 8-year-old learners to produce approximately 12–15 words each. At first glance, that may not seem like much, but the TAPS study has revealed that tasks requiring interaction between L2 learners pose far more difficulties than does extended monologue. A single speaker can prepare his presentation beforehand and, up to a point, control his interaction with the audience. Dialogue tasks, however, are more complex, requiring flexibility and "awareness of how to cater for other participants in discourse" (Cameron, 2001, p. 52). Even with mature 3rd graders, teachers should remind pupils of the need to listen carefully to a speaking partner before they begin the first pair work (step 6). Teachers will find that, in this respect, steps 12 and 13 can effectively raise children's awareness of their own role in making a brief chat smooth and enjoyable.

Task Demands and Task Support: Comforting an Unhappy Friend

The interactional demands of this task are intensified by its language demands as L2 learners have a much smaller lexicon at their disposal than L1 children. As a result, the L2 learners may be mature enough to respond flexibly or even sympathetically to a faltering speech partner in L1 but may lack the vocabulary and grammar to encourage their partner to speak out in L2 (e.g., using phrases such as "Hey, what's wrong?" "How can I cheer you up?" "Let's sit down and talk."). The other child may lack the language to describe a quite complicated ailment.

Related to this point, it is vitally important that the teachers themselves speak English fluently and naturally, using idiomatic expressions and a rich vocabulary. They need to offer learners alternative ways of saying the same thing, thus providing them with two or three ready-to-use chunks that can easily be retrieved from memory and avoid overmonitoring in unexpected situations. The authentic context of the task (*Comfort your unfortunate friend* or *Let yourself be comforted by a good friend*) and the unpredictability of the outcome may pose a challenge for children. But such realistic situations actually afford increased opportunities for productive language use. This challenge is best supported by a balanced approach offering both *repetition* (e.g., through speaking the new lexical item "It hurts!" in chorus) and *variation* (e.g., through describing several aching parts of the body, such as "My head/tooth/jaw/ear/etc. hurts"). Once the learners have grasped just one pattern, "possessive pronoun + noun (part of the body) + inflected verb (*hurts*)," they can express many different sensations.

Despite the difficulties that the task presents, it has turned out to be exceptionally popular with learners, because it involves them physically, socially, and emotionally. Children love acting out accidents and crashes or faking exaggerated clumsiness. Dramatic demonstrations also have a novelty factor and grab the audience's attention. At the same time, this task links language practice to children's real-life interests and concerns: Everybody feels low when they have a headache. Everybody appreciates a helping hand when they are injured. The children's familiarity with the concepts of injury, accident, and distress engages them with the task and makes it cognitively accessible. They need to listen carefully to their partner's complaints, develop empathy, feel with them, and use their creativity to come up with a truly comforting suggestion. Thus, this task gives them the chance to learn a valuable social skill and practice it in English.

Adapting the Teaching Unit "Poor You!"

To suit the needs and abilities of less advanced or more advanced learners, the entire unit can be simplified, shortened, or expanded. In an attempt to reduce the language demands, teachers can, for instance, restrict the number of misfortunes and ailments to two or three, and introduce just one standard phrase of consolation in steps 3–8. Also, the teacher may want to leave out step 12, which requires a metalinguistic discussion about the criteria that make an exchange between two speakers a good dialogue.

In an attempt to upgrade the unit, it is precisely in steps 12 and 13 that more advanced learners aged 10–12 can be challenged. They should be encouraged to reflect upon qualities of good communication, acquire the technical terms in English, and use them in peer assessment.

Teachers who are required by a course syllabus to include reading and writing in their classroom work can easily add word cards to the picture cards in steps 3 and 6–8 and have learners write the script for their dialogue to be used in a later performance.

REFLECTIONS

The TAPS project's key aim was to develop a set of tools with which to assess the English spoken by primary EFL learners, and to test and evaluate the tools' viability. To further this aim the study incorporated several research questions of which the first two are relevant in the context of this chapter:

- What tasks and elicitation techniques can best support L2 learners in grades 3 and 4 (i.e., aged 8–10) to produce extended and coherent discourse, and what kind of tools (e.g., charts, scales) can teachers use to assess learners' performance?

- To what extent can L2 learners in grades 3 and 4 produce complex oral texts that can be classified as extended and coherent discourse?

As the study followed the key transformational principle of action research, that is, directly involving "those responsible for action in improving it" (Cohen,

Manion, & Morrison, 2000, p. 229), the teachers themselves completed a trial of the tasks and materials inside their classrooms in the course of regular lessons. After the trial process from September to December, a questionnaire study was distributed to the participating elementary school teachers. Then a formal discussion about the entire assessment cycle was held to enable participants to reflect on their experiences. Both the discussion and the questionnaire evaluation clearly showed that, first, the task-based materials were successful in encouraging young learners to speak English and, second, the assessment tools had proved feasible, fair, and reliable. This result was confirmed in a thorough test of interrater consistency, in which the individual assessments of each of the three independent raters were closely compared. The results showed conclusively that the TAPS assessment tools proved altogether reliable in the objective assessment of oral competence (Diehr, 2006, pp. 36–40).

While trialling the assessment tools, the spoken texts of 216 pupils were video-recorded, digitized, and transcribed, providing unexpected answers to the second research question: *To what extent can L2 learners in grades 3 and 4 produce complex oral texts that can be classified as extended and coherent discourse?* The sample consisted of 10 primary groups (seven classes in the 3rd year and three in the 4th). A fine-grained analysis of the children's spoken texts was made on the phonological, lexical, grammatical, and pragmatic quality of their performance. The analysis disclosed surprisingly extensive text production that exceeded the standards spelled out by most primary school programs of study in the country. At most, primary EFL learners are expected to speak in very short and simple sentences (Ministerium BW, 2004, p. 78). The TAPS learners, however, produced far more than one-, two- or three-word utterances. On average, the third graders spoke 18 words each in mini-dialogues, 30 words in performing a part in a role-play, and 70 words in describing a picture showing a wild animal. Fourth graders produced an average of 263 words in narrating a story, with individual children reaching an impressive 353 words (see the Soresi chapter in this volume for more on speaking rates).

What makes these results so remarkable is that most of the pupils produced speech beyond mere repetition and rote learning. This is particularly noticeable in those utterances where the children improvise on and deviate from expressions in the original source text. Pupil texts consistently exceeded expectations, not only in quantitative terms, but also qualitatively by using complex syntactical patterns (e.g., relative clauses, clauses of cause and effect, combinations of reporting clauses and direct speech).

Conclusion

The speech data in the TAPS corpus show how primary learners in their first years of learning EFL are capable of developing their oral skills to such an extent that they can use the small amount of L2 at their disposal productively, gradually expanding their vocabulary, grammar, and interactional expertise. The results of the TAPS study thus confirm and even expand Swain's output hypothesis (Swain, 1995). The learners' monologues and dialogues produced in the course of this study suggest that requiring young learners to produce coherent and communicative utterances in L2 fosters the development of syntactic and textual structures as well as pragmatic skills. It is my hope that analysis of classroom-tested tasks like "Poor You!" will inspire primary school teachers in EFL contexts to make oral practice an integral part of their classroom teaching. If they are to foster productive language use, they need to find meaningful, communicative, and enjoyable tasks for young learners.

Bärbel Diehr is a professor of teaching English as a foreign language at Bergische Universität Wuppertal, Germany. She was formerly a faculty member at the University of Education, Heidelberg, and Ruhr-Universität Bochum, both in Germany. Her previous experience as a teacher trainer and grammar teacher is reflected in her research.

APPENDIX A: MATERIAL I—THE "OUCH" PACK

The "OUCH" Pack
- picture cards -

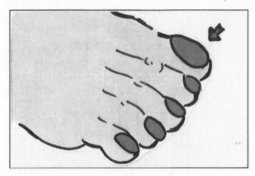 

 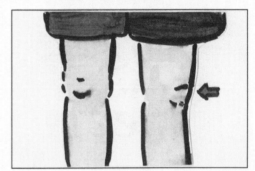

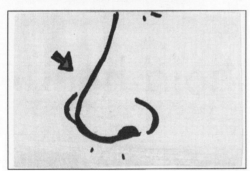 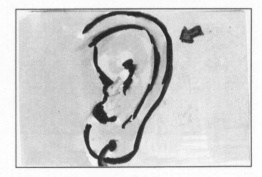

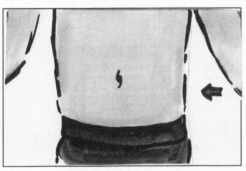 

APPENDIX B: MATERIAL II—THE "COMFORT" PACK

The "COMFORT" Pack
- word cards -

sing a song	play the guitar
give a sweet	cup of cocoa
give a cuddle	hold hand
read a story	?

CHAPTER 6

Reframing and Reconstructing Situational Dialogues: Scaffolding Speaking Tasks for English for Occupational Purposes

Yoshihito Sugita

INTRODUCTION

In Japan, high school and university entrance examinations have a huge backwash effect on English language instruction. Because these are very high-stakes exams, secondary school teachers feel a deep obligation to their students to teach English as an examination subject. The classes are taught mostly in Japanese because using English as the medium of instruction slows down the process of accumulating knowledge required for these high-stakes exams. As a result, most Japanese students receive little exposure to English, have little interaction with the language, and have low oral proficiency after 6 years of study in junior and senior high school.

In this chapter, I describe a classroom practice in second-language instruction for developing nursing students' oral production skills in the context of Japanese English as a foreign language (EFL) classes. There is an increasing awareness in Japan of the communicative uses of spoken English. *The Japan Times Online* (Asami, 2007), for example, reports that a rising number of medical societies in Japan have adopted English as the official language for presentations at conferences, so now medical researchers and practitioners feel the need to learn to speak, as well as read and write, the language.

This chapter focuses on the use of the Dynamic Listening and Speaking (DLS) method. The original DLS method was devised for training simultaneous interpreters with the goal of enhancing skills in comprehending a spoken foreign language. The method centers on trainees attempting to understand a speaker's oral English and recasting the main idea in English, as well as explaining the meaning in their native language (e.g., Japanese). In the DLS method adapted for the EFL classroom, however, learners listen to a certain length of text, and they are asked to summarize in their own words the gist of the content while listening. The main goal of the practice is to enhance students' skills of self-expression in which they use English to convey their understanding (Shinzaki & Takahashi, 2004).

I decided to adopt the DLS method under the notion of *scaffolding*, based upon the sociocultural theory of mind (Vygotsky, 1980). Scaffolding is defined as a process in which students are given support until they can apply new skills and strategies independently (Rosenshine & Meister, 1992). Scaffolded instruction is "the systematic sequencing of promoted content, materials, tasks, and teacher and peer support to optimize learning" (Dickson, Chard, & Simmons, 1993, p. 12). The scaffolding in the DLS method described here incorporates the following features. First, the method requires the participation of students as speakers of English in the classroom. This motive promotes interacting with the language in the form of self-expression through English. Second, the reframing and reconstructing approach involves a focus on meaning, in which participants are concerned with message and communication. This approach encourages students to use the language as much as possible to communicate. Third, the method meets the nursing students' needs for oral production skills. Situation-based activities engage them in meaningful, authentic language use that promotes motivation and develops communicative skills through the situational practice. Furthermore, I believe that the scaffolded speaking tasks create conditions for promoting learning that work particularly well in the context of English language classes for Japanese learners, and potentially for other kinds of instructional environments as well.

CONTEXT

The Faculty of Nursing at Yamanashi Prefectural University in Japan has approximately 300 students. The nursing context in some regions of Japan has been changing in accordance with the recent influx of foreigners and the return of Japanese who grew up overseas. According to the report released by the Immigration Bureau under the Ministry of Justice (2005), the number of foreign residents in Japan was 2 million in 2005, up from 1.36 million in 1995. Obviously, the more people from abroad who visit a Japanese hospital as outpatients or inpatients, the more need there is for specialized English education for healthcare professionals. My aim for the nursing students in our program is to help them feel competent in situations where they must understand and speak to foreign patients in English. Therefore, the course Oral Communication for Nursing Students was developed with the following goals:

- Teach students strategies for communication with foreign patients in situations where they must interact with patients in English.

- Introduce students to key expressions they will need to communicate with patients through English.

- Encourage students to communicate meaning by using their own English rather than focusing on a fluent command of the second language (L2).

To achieve these aims, relevant situations are highlighted in the course: working in the lobby of the hospital, working at the registration desk, checking the registration card, helping visitors find their way around the hospital, asking about symptoms, checking blood pressure and weight, dealing with laboratory specimens, and administering medicine. The underlying assumption of adopting such a situation-based approach is that learning activities in which language is used for carrying out meaningful and authentic tasks promote learning, and language that is meaningful to the learner supports the learning process (Littlewood, 1992; Richards & Rodgers, 2001). A focus on communicative and situational factors in language use also requires teachers to consider how well communication tasks engage learners in meaningful, authentic language use rather than merely mechanical practice of patterns. In my course, therefore, tasks are designed to avoid controlling students' language by requiring specific grammatical or lexical items. Thus, my students have opportunities to use all the language they know in order to complete the tasks.

The DLS method is a type of meaning-focused activity where students listen to a relatively short text, take notes, and then try to reconstruct the text they have heard. In Japan this type of notetaking skill is readily taught at interpreter training courses, but it is seldom taught to secondary school students. Japanese students generally have difficulty with notetaking in English; therefore, I redesigned the unit sequence of the DLS method in order to facilitate more active student involvement through notetaking. The unit sequence in each class (see Figure 1) is as follows: listening comprehension of the dialogue, taking a cloze-type dictation, reading aloud and repeating practice, writing the summary of the dialogue, and giving an oral presentation.

The following considerations justify the use of this procedural sequence in the course. As contended in Krashen (1982) and Long (1983), comprehensible input is necessary for L2 acquisition. According to Ellis's computational model (see Ellis, 2000), parts of the input are attended to and taken into short-term memory so that they become *intake*. Some of the intake is stored in longterm memory as L2 knowledge that is used by the learner to produce spoken and written output. After a global listening to focus on meaning, intensive listening, such as partial dictation, may facilitate students' noticing of a form (e.g., Ellis, 2001; Rost, 1991; Schmidt, 1992). Before attempting to reproduce the text, learners may confirm their understanding and get the gist of the text through reading aloud

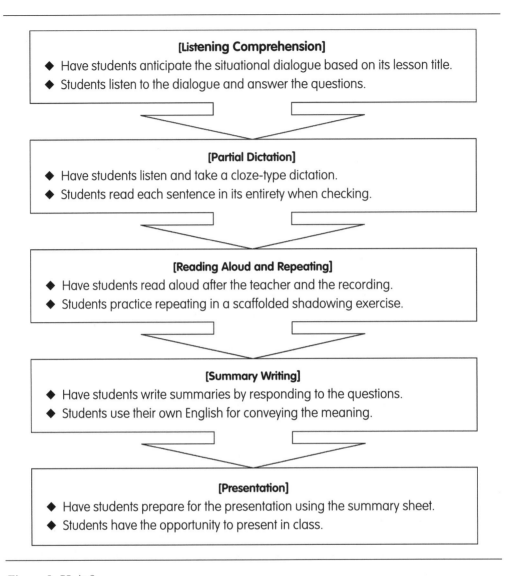

Figure 1. Unit Sequence

and repeating activities. It would follow from Swain (1985) that when learners have the opportunity to produce target items they are more likely to acquire them. Furthermore, according to Reid (1994), successful oral summaries are brief and clear descriptions of original materials that allow the listener to easily understand the main ideas of the longer material. This seems to activate writing processes that facilitate reconstruction of the text and generate a document for the oral presentation step of the sequence.

CURRICULUM, TASKS, MATERIALS

Oral Communication for Nursing Students is a 30-hour course that meets over a 15-week term. There were eight female students registered in the fall semester of 2005. All eight of the participants had taken General Tests of English Language Proficiency (G-TELP) Level 4 (max = 60), and their scores ranged from 31 to 39 with a mean score of 35.125, indicating a preintermediate level of language proficiency. At the beginning of the course, the students were informed of the course objectives, content and materials, unit sequence, and evaluation. After the explanation of the syllabus, each student took an information transfer test, which provided data on their speaking proficiency. They were asked to describe the picture shown in Figure 2 after 1 minute of preparation. The advantage of this test method is that the task does not require the students to read or listen, and thereby it is useful for eliciting the students' ability to speak (Weir, 1990). The final class was a posttest session in which the students were asked to describe the same picture again. After the test, I asked the students to write their overall impression of the course.

All classes during the term followed the procedural pattern outlined in Figure 1. In each class, I used the book *How Are You Feeling Today?* published by Seibido (Sukegawa & Harrington, 2006). The authenticity of course material is one of the key issues concerning a communicative orientation to language teaching. I chose the textbook mainly because it is characterized by focusing on language as discourse rather than sentence-level language. This focus is relevant to the point made by McCarthy and Carter (1995, p. 214) about the features of

Figure 2. Picture Used in the Information Transfer Test

their corpus of spoken English as "a use of texts rather than invented sentences, being based on scrutiny of real spoken data, and including tasks and questions." In addition, the textbook includes tasks and questions designed to enhance the relevant situation-based activities. Although I cannot say for certain whether the textbook is based on scrutiny of real spoken data, I agree with Widdowson (1996, p. 67) that the language presented in textbooks does not need to be "real" English, but rather "appropriate English for the classroom."

Example of Classroom Activity

During the instruction period between the pre- and posttests, all lessons followed a familiar template based on the procedural pattern, so that students repeatedly practiced a sequence of activities as indicated in Figure 1. In this section, I give a more complete description of an entire class using the dialogue in Figure 3. Before starting with listening comprehension, I incorporated a top-down processing approach to the lesson; I wrote the theme of the lesson on the whiteboard and had students anticipate the content of the dialogue in order to activate their background knowledge. Then, I played the audio recording of the sample dialogue twice. After the students listened to the dialogue, they chose possible answers to each question. There were five questions about the dialogue (see Appendix A). I supplied answers to the questions and checked the students' understanding of the content. I consider this listening activity to be the first scaffolding stage supporting the students' reconstruction of the situational dialogue.

I played back the tape with a short pause between sentences, allowing the students to take a cloze-type dictation (Appendix B). When checking the dictation, the students were asked to read each sentence in its entirety. After they completed the dialogue, chorus reading was done as a class. Later, in pairs, they practiced

---

(Mr. Stevens' registration card is now ready.)

Clerk: Thank you so much for waiting. Here's your registration card.

Mr. Stevens: Thank you very much.

Clerk: Please check that your name and birth date are correct.

Mr. Stevens: Let me see. Yes, everything is correct. Is there any other information that you need?

Clerk: Yes, one more thing. Who should we contact in an emergency?

Mr. Stevens: My wife. My wife's telephone number at her office is 3014-8765.

Clerk: Now everything is complete. Please give this card to the receptionist in the Internal Medicine Department.

Mr. Stevens: Thank you very much. You've been very helpful.

(Sukegawa & Harrington, 2006, pp.12–13)

Figure 3. Checking the Registration Card Sample Dialogue (Lesson 3)

repeating in a scaffolded shadowing exercise with one student reading a sentence and the other student listening and then repeating the sentence. During these activities, the students were encouraged to memorize as much of the content and language forms as possible. Students were motivated by the process because they knew that they were not allowed to look at the dialogue in the textbook while reconstructing the text at the end.

Next, I distributed the summary writing sheet (see Appendix C) to each student. I asked the students to write summaries by responding to the questions individually. I made it clear that they did not have to write the same sentences as the text. They were encouraged to use their own English for conveying the meaning, and students were allowed to use dictionaries for support. Upon completing the summary, each student used it to prepare for the presentation. As they prepared, the students incorporated all additional knowledge of the linguistic items to clarify meaning. No time limit was set, but the process of the text reconstruction and the eight students' presentations did not take more than an hour.

REFLECTIONS

I believe that this scaffolded approach proved to be effective partly because students developed their productive skills in the established language aspects: vocabulary, complexity, accuracy, and fluency. Realization of these language aspects was measured using an information transfer test (i.e., description of a picture), as illustrated in the previous section. Adopting a longitudinal method, I administered the information transfer test twice in a pre–post design, before and after the training. In addition, I calculated the degree of improvement in vocabulary, accuracy, fluency, and complexity of learners' oral production based on each objective measure. When comparing outcomes from two related samples, a paired *t*-test is generally used as a statistical test. In this analysis, however, a signed-rank test, which is a nonparametric alternative to the paired *t*-test, was chosen because there were just eight learners in this study.

Despite the small number of subjects, some interesting findings emerged. First, both the number of edited spoken words and variety of words used for describing the picture showed statistically significant differences, more in the posttest than in the pretest ($p < 0.01$). This means that learners progressed in their use of vocabulary. Next, the learners' utterances were divided into *communication units* (c-units), which are described by Pica, Holliday, Lewis, and Morgenthaler (1989, p. 72). The c-units are "utterances, for example, words phrases and sentences, grammatical and ungrammatical, which provide referential or pragmatic meaning." An example of a c-unit might be "Please this seat." The number of words in c-units (i.e., "Please this seat.") that were not complete, or lacked a verb, but that provided pragmatic meaning, increased markedly ($0.05 < p < 0.10$). This indicates an improvement in syntactic complexity. Furthermore, accuracy in utterances was improved because the number of errors decreased significantly ($p < 0.01$). Finally, the marked increase in the number of spoken words per minute demonstrates that speech rate was ameliorated ($p < 0.01$), whereas repetition of the same words or phrases, which provides an indication of hesitation, caused a hindrance to the development of oral fluency.

The results I have presented here are not conclusive in a statistical sense, and I do not claim to have demonstrated the benefits of this approach in general. I may draw some tentative conclusions based on the discussion with respect to the effects of task characteristics and task repetition, and in terms of their implications for further research, however. First, in a text-reconstruction task learners listen to or read a text and process it for meaning. They store the propositional content but not the linguistic forms used to encode the content, so they draw on their own linguistic resources when they reconstruct the text (Ellis & Barkhuizen, 2005). In the same way, through reframing and reconstructing situational dialogues, the learners are concerned with paying more attention to the content than the forms. As a result, they learn to use their own language for conveying the meaning of a text; therefore, the amount of output as well as speech rate may increase (for more on speech rate, see the Soresi chapter in this volume).

Regarding this point, one of the two students who made surprising progress in oral fluency (12.9 wpm → 360.0 wpm; 14.3 wpm → 43.8 wpm) commented that in every class she had to explain about the dialogue, so she considered its content and strived to speak. Another student felt released from concern about grammar while speaking because she thought that conveying the meaning was most important during the presentation. Second, having done the same pattern of lessons repeatedly, the learners seemed to perform better in terms of accuracy and complexity. This change is likely because repetition of tasks may enable learners to move their attention towards improving their language formulation (Bygate, 1996). As such, the student with the highest G-TELP score commented that she gradually grew accustomed to writing summaries of the dialogue because the conversational pattern between the nurse and patient was very similar in each unit. By the end of the course, she reported being able to attend to the language form as well as the content.

My experience teaching this course showed me the importance of giving students time to write and plan for speaking tasks. It also confirmed for me the importance of repetition when doing language-learning tasks. Repetition resulted in simplifying the original task and controlling frustration. The implication of these points is that, particularly for beginning and intermediate students, scaffolding serves as a means of achieving a task and furthers student learning. That is, an approach that incorporates scaffolding features makes it possible for learners to perform beyond their existing developmental level. To this end, the one-way text reconstruction task I adopted greatly benefited by providing appropriate scaffolding throughout the unit sequence. An alternative approach I could have adopted would be communicative information-gap exercises wherein learners ask each other for missing information that is reported later either orally or in writing.

Information-gap tasks would have been rather difficult for the low-proficiency learners in the course to accomplish, however. I believe that such two-way information-gap tasks would not have offered my students the same benefits of the scaffolding features they relied on through the one-way text reconstruction tasks.

Several problems came to light as a result of the analysis, however. First, regarding fluency, verbatim repetitions probably occurred because the learners may have paid more attention to deciding what meanings to express than to finding an appropriate word to express the selected meanings. Therefore, I suggest that it is worthwhile to explain to students how to plan their talk and how to revise and edit their summary for improving their presentation.

Another problem may be related to the small class size. There were only eight students in the course, so each student had the opportunity to present in every class. This alone may have led to the improvement of their oral production skills. Typically at Japanese universities, classes have 40 students. Such a large number of students in a class would require much more time for the culminating presentations. One suggestion is to divide students into groups of four or five, and have them present in their groups (see the McCaughey chapter in this volume for more on group work).

The text reconstruction process I have described in this chapter incorporates scaffolding features and seems to create conditions for promoting the learning of English with Japanese learners. Providing scaffolding throughout speaking tasks is what I consider to have been a critical aspect of student learning in this course. Further research should be undertaken to develop procedures for scaffolded instruction and to show if it indeed facilitates and increases long-term learning in different English for speakers of other languages contexts.

Yoshihito Sugita is an associate professor at Yamanashi Prefectural University, in Japan. He is now working on his doctorate in English education through Waseda University. He is especially interested in research and pedagogy in second-language writing and in language-teaching materials and methods.

APPENDIX A: QUESTIONS FOR LISTENING COMPREHENSION

1. What did the clerk give the patient?
    (a) his registration card
    (b) his ID card
    (c) his application card

2. What information did the clerk want the patient to check?

    (a) his address and telephone number

    (b) his identification number

    (c) his name and birth date

3. What other information did the clerk need for registration?

    (a) the person to contact in an emergency

    (b) the person to refer him to

    (c) the person to take care of his child

4. What telephone number should the hospital call in an emergency?

    (a) 3104-8765

    (b) 3014-8765

    (c) 3041-8765

5. To whom should the patient give his registration card?

    (a) the nurse on the patient unit

    (b) the receptionist in the Internal Medicine Department

    (c) the cashier at the next window

(Sukegawa & Harrington, 2006, pp. 12–13)

APPENDIX B: PARTIAL DICTATION FOR INTENSIVE LISTENING

Clerk: Thank you so much for 1) _____ 2) _____ your registration card.

Mr. Stevens: Thank you very much.

Clerk: Please 3) _____ that your name and 4) _____ are 5) _____.

Mr. Stevens: Let me see. Yes, 6) _____ is correct.
Is there any other information that you 7) _____ ?

Clerk: Yes, one more thing. Who should we 8)_____ in an 9)_____?

Mr. Stevens: My wife. My wife's 10) _____ is 11) _____.

Clerk: Now everything is 12) _____. Please give this card to the
13) _____ in the Internal Medicine Department.

Mr. Stevens: Thank you very much. You've been very helpful.

(Sukegawa & Harrington, 2006, pp. 13–14)

APPENDIX C: SUMMARY WRITING SHEET

Summary Writing [Lesson 3]

Mr. Stevens' registration card is now ready.
1. What did the clerk give Mr. Stevens?
The clerk gave . . . .
2. What information did the clerk want Mr. Stevens to check?
She wanted him to check . . . .
3. What other information did the clerk need for registration?
She needs the information about . . . .
4. Who should the hospital contact when Mr. Stevens is involved in an emergency situation?
5. What telephone number should the hospital call?
Mr. Stevens says that they should contact . . . .
6. To whom should Mr. Stevens give his registration card?
He should give the card to . . . .
7. What does Mr. Stevens think of the clerk?
He thinks the clerk . . . .

CHAPTER 7

An Experimental Application of the Problem-Posing Approach for English Language Teaching in Vietnam

Hoa Thi Mai Nguyen

INTRODUCTION

In many countries today, English-language education for tertiary students ultimately aims to develop communicative competence together with critical thinking skills. This idea seems to be new, however, particularly where I teach, in Vietnam. The methodology used in education in general and English-language education in particular in Vietnam is described as the knowledge-imparting process, or teacher-centered approach (Le, 2007; Nguyen, 2003). Students at secondary schools are taught using rigid drills for the memorization of vocabulary and grammar rules. Their English lessons do not attempt to link language study with their life outside the classroom. From a critical perspective, this pedagogy raises basic questions about inequality and change in education: What is the purpose of education? Does our society want to produce passive or active citizens? Concerning this problem, Fairclough (1992) claims:

> People cannot be effective citizens in a democratic society if their education cuts them off from critical consciousness of key elements within their physical or social environment. If we are committed to education establishing resources for citizenship, critical awareness of language practices of one's speech community is an entitlement. (p. 6)

Yet, several researchers (e.g., Atkinson, 1997; Pennycook, 1999) argue that even in countries where educational planners espouse a concern with developing students' ability to think critically, the teaching of critical thinking still seems to be a challenge because of requirements for new teaching skills. This challenge is said to be especially problematic in the context of English as a foreign language (EFL) settings, such as Vietnam, where teaching and learning are generally limited to knowledge transfer from the teacher to the students.

This situation inspired me to consider how to transform teaching methodology in the hope of improving opportunities for my students' critical thinking development. During my graduate study abroad, I was introduced to critical pedagogy in teaching English to speakers of other languages (ESOL). I believe that this pedagogy offers a means of developing my students' critical thinking. What attracts me are the joint goals of fostering English communicative abilities, as well as the ability to apply communication in tasks designed to develop a critical awareness of the world and to seek solutions to social problems (Akbari, 2008; Crookes & Lehner, 1998; Walsh, 1991).

The critical pedagogy of Paulo Freire (1972, 1973) provided me with food for thought for implementing an alternative approach in second-language teaching in Vietnam. His is a problem-posing approach that gives people language to express their critical opinions and take action for social change. Graman (1988) believes that Freire's critical pedagogy, which is based on problem-posing, is particularly appropriate for learning a second language. It creates a learning community in which students are free to express their ideas and contribute their own knowledge and skills to shape the classroom experience. This chapter sheds light on the application of the problem-posing approach in teaching speaking skills for tertiary students in Vietnam. More specifically, it focuses on:

- describing the context of tertiary English language teaching (ELT) in Vietnam and the need for applying problem-posing education

- describing problem-posing education and its applicable framework in language education

- reflecting on the application of problem-posing education at the tertiary level in Vietnam, including challenges and suggestions for its use

CONTEXT

During the past decade, English teaching has been a part of an energetic nation-wide reform program in language teaching in Vietnam. Currently, English is introduced at all levels of schooling, from as early as grade 3 (Nguyen & Nguyen, 2007). However, the methodology used in English language teaching in Vietnam, especially at the secondary level, seems to treat learners as passive recipients. Lessons do not include anything that may require learners to think for themselves. In classes, the students play passive roles by receiving knowledge while the teacher acts as an authority of knowledge. At the tertiary level, the situation improves somewhat as students are provided opportunities to practice the four language skills. However, the issue of how to link language lessons with the world outside is often ignored by English for speakers of other languages (ESOL) teachers in Vietnam. English language education in Vietnam shows characteristics of the banking, or transmission, model of education (Freire, 1993), which implies an expert teacher in control and a strong hierarchical relationship between teachers and students (also see the Brandt chapter in this volume).

In the pattern of banking education, knowledge is not usually critiqued; rather, it celebrates the status quo and prepares students to accept the authority of standard syllabi, required textbooks, or other teaching materials (Freire, 1993). This style of pedagogy raises many issues for teachers engaged in reforming English teaching in Vietnam to focus more on developing students' communicative abilities and cultural knowledge. Even after studying English for years at the secondary and tertiary levels, Vietnamese students often do not acquire the ability to communicate in English. That is, they seem to be structurally competent but communicatively incompetent. Besides, in Vietnam, none of the language courses focus on problem-solving exercises. Vietnamese students are not familiar with a style of teaching that persistently asks them to examine the reasons for their actions and question themselves, their peers, and experts.

Now that the country has joined the World Trade Organization (WTO), new opportunities and challenges have emerged for Vietnam as its exposure to the outside world expands. As a result, government officials and business people now deal with a large amount of new information in English that needs to be comprehended and analyzed quickly. To accomplish this, they not only need to master English but also develop their ability to deal effectively with the world outside the classroom. This great social change has inspired me to look for ways of teaching that can meet these new student needs. The problem-posing approach offers one possible solution to Vietnamese teachers.

I applied this approach to design supplementary speaking activities for my class of 25 2nd-year students who are enrolled in a preservice EFL teacher education program in Vietnam. Following the course book, I integrated these activities into lessons with the aim of developing the students' abilities to reflect and act on the social issues around them.

Problem-Posing Education

In arguing about the need for a problem-posing approach to education, Freire (1972) stated:

> whereas banking education anesthetizes and inhibits creative power, problem-posing education involves a constant unveiling of reality. The former attempts to maintain the submersion of consciousness; the later strives for the emergence of consciousness and critical invention in reality. (p. 62)

Problem-posing education opens all subject matter to be questioned rather than merely accepted. The responsibility of the problem-posing teacher is to diversify subject matter and to use his students' ideas and experience as the base for developing critical thinking: "In this democratic pedagogy, the teacher is not filling empty minds with official or unofficial knowledge but is posing knowledge in any form as a problem for mutual inquiry" (Shor, 1992, p. 32).

Wallerstein (1983), and Auerbach and Burgess (1985) highlight the importance of identifying students' experiences to the process of learning language. In short, students are likely to develop intellectually and linguistically when they analyze their own experiences and build on their own words to describe and better understand these experiences through engaging in *problematizing* the status quo. Critical and problem-posing approaches to teaching ESOL go beyond communicative language teaching and engage students in discussions of oppression and social justice. Therefore, the problem-posing approach requires that the teacher ask students to express what they think, to make inferences, generalize, and evaluate (also see the Perry chapter in this volume).

The course book for my class is unimaginative. The speaking activities in the book do not connect students with the social issues in their lives. The purpose of the course book is narrowly limited to developing students' speaking ability. It does not address students' critical thinking about the social issues they confront daily. In addition, Vietnam is changing rapidly due to the globalization of production. My students wonder about the direction that social change should take in their country, and I believe that the ultimate purpose of education is to prepare students for the real world.

To address my concerns with the simplicity and lack of intellectual stimulation in the course book tasks, I designed experimental supplementary activities for each topic. This limited experiment in materials development was designed to see how university students in Vietnam would react to a problem-posing curriculum.

CURRICULUM, TASKS, MATERIALS

Framework for a Problem-Posing Approach in Language Teaching

Based on Freire's idea of three stages in education: *listening,* which begins before teaching; *dialogue,* which takes place in the class; and *action,* which extends to consequences outside the classroom, Wallerstein (1983) suggests five main steps in a problem-posing activity. These five steps are especially important guidelines for English-language teachers to structure problem-posing activities successfully. The following is a detailed description of each step, with examples and accounts of classroom interaction.

Step 1: Literal Description

In this first step (Freire's *naming the problem*), students must respond to a text or visual by describing what they see. The principal idea behind this approach is that the starting point for learning should be a problem, query, or puzzle that the learner wishes to solve. Thus, the purpose of Step 1 is to raise students' awareness of a problem. This step begins with reflection and description of the text. Neutral description is the way to find out what students perceive about teaching materials. "What do you see?" is commonly asked at this step. At this descriptive level, students learn vocabulary, language structures, and grammatical rules, and they become interested in the discussion content. Topics are normally controversial and evoke discussion and reactions from students. The teacher selects and presents the problem-evoking situations by using pictures, videos, questions, readings, and stories.

Step 2: Affective Response

Students raise questions about the text or visual to explore Freire's step of inquiring about their feelings about the problem. The questions generated often identify a problem that can be further explored. The purpose of Step 2 is to identify what is problematic in the literal descriptions of situations in Step 1. At this stage, the teacher prompts some questions that relate the situation to the students' experience. Students are given opportunities to use English to freely express their views and explore the questions about what they have described. "What is the problem here?" is the common question at this step. The successful posing of problems requires teachers to accept the role of facilitator. The teachers' role is to pose the problem, encourage different perspectives, tolerate different opinions, participate in the learning process, and avoid imposing any ideas related to the topic or presenting solutions. This step starts moving students to an analytical level, asking them to say what they think.

Step 3: Inferences

Students are asked to relate the issues to their personal experience by making a connection with their own life (Freire's *why* questions, asking for cause). The purpose of this step is to ask each student to reflect personally on the problem under consideration. Common questions at this step are:

- Is this your problem?
- Do you also experience it?
- How is this the same?
- How is it different?
- How do you feel about it?

At this stage, the teacher tries to link the topic of discussion with the students' real-life experiences. In other words, this step asks them to make inferences. Students are given opportunities to explore topics that are emotionally charged for them while at the same time practicing language skills through listening and conversing.

Step 4: Generalization

If a problem has engaged the students, they can think about it in a larger context (Freire's *social context*), exploring historical, social, political, or other background that illuminates it. The products of the first three steps—descriptions, questions, and personal connections—provide important data for situating the problem in its larger context. What happens at this step depends on what has been achieved in the previous steps. "Why is there a problem?" is the common question at this step. The teacher tries to promote inquiry by posing questions to lead discussion in a larger context. Critical thinking begins when students have opportunities to link their individual lives with social conditions.

Step 5: Application and Evaluation for Other Situations, Exploration of Solution

Depending on the themes that have emerged from the discussion, participants may wish to apply and evaluate the solution and, more importantly, take action to address the problem (Freire's step of *what should be done*). "What can you do?" is the common question at this step. The teacher tends to design questions or tasks that make students act on the problems they identified in the previous stages. Application or evaluation activities may include writing a letter to authorities, discussing solutions to the problems, or participating in a project outside class.

Based on the philosophy of problem-posing education, I designed 13 problem-posing activities for English majors in Vietnam, using the five-step framework outlined above. I integrated additional problem-posing activities based on the course book topics. Basically, for each of these activities, I designed related questions to encourage students to discuss a topic according to the problem-posing framework. Students participated in several activities that led them to describe the situation, identify the problem, relate the problem to their life, analyze the causes of the problem, and seek solutions. Next, I outline one example.

Example of Problem-Posing Materials: Traffic in Hanoi

The theme of this unit is traffic congestion in Hanoi. The issues for discussion concern the current traffic situation in Hanoi, its causes, and solutions. The activity begins with a picture that poses the problem. I showed the photograph that I took to prompt discussion among my students (see Figure 1).

Based on the framework for applying the problem-posing approach to language teaching, I created the unit plan shown in Table 1. Through the five steps of the development of these units, I established the context that helped my students to develop their language skills and their ability to react to the social issues in their lives. To explore the developmental questions in the unit, the students must acquire the language input needed to discuss the topic in English. For the traffic example, students might need to learn the present verb tense in order to describe the photo. They learn the English language by considering the material through the five steps as part of an authentic situation. The underlying assumption of this approach is that students can develop their communicative competence through listening and conversing, not drills or memorization (Wallerstein, 1983).

Wallerstein (1983) also emphasizes that the five-step procedure will liberate energy that can stimulate creativity and raise motivation for using English if it presents a problem situation that is "immediately recognisable to students" (p. 20). In other words, the situation should identify challenges of the society in which students live. In addition, he added:

> The problem presented should not be overwhelming to students. There should be room for small actions that address the problem even if they don't solve it. Local community issues usually provide opportunities for students to have an impact with small-scale actions. (p. 20)

Problem-posing activities are not free conversation or discussion. To coordinate these activities, I had to plan carefully and organized class sessions to allow students to explore the problems that guide the activities at each of the five steps. These activities can help students use English to raise their voices in the classroom and in society to help them "become more fully human and transform the reality around them" (Hones, 1999, p. 27).

REFLECTIONS

Students' Feedback

I interviewed 15 of the 25 students in my class about their opinions and experiences participating in these problem-posing activities. In general, students were satisfied with their experience. Most of them reported that they enjoyed

Figure 1. Photograph to Prompt Discussion

Table 1. Problem-Posing Unit on Traffic in Hanoi

Steps	Questions
1 Literal Description	The teacher asks students to work in pairs to describe the photo: • *What can you see in the photo?* • *What types of vehicles are used?* • *Are these people travelling during rush hour?* • *Can you guess where this photo was taken?* During this step, the teacher can provide students with linguistics input if necessary.
2 Affective response	The teacher asks students to work in small groups to discuss the following questions: • *What problem(s) can you identify in this photo?* • *Is the problem common in Hanoi?*
3 Inferences	The teacher asks students to write individually to answer the questions: • *Have you ever experienced this?* • *How do you feel about it?* • *What are your thoughts about this situation?* • *What questions does it raise for you?*
4 Generalization	The teacher passes out copies of questions and issues that the students have written anonymously and asks for comments on their friends' opinions before discussing these questions: • *Why is there a problem in Hanoi?* • *What are its causes?* • *Why do you think so?*
5 Application and evaluation for other situations, exploration of solution	The teacher asks students to work in pairs or groups to answer or discuss these questions: • *What do you learn from the photo?* • *Do you want to change your situation as you have described? Why?* • *What solutions do you suggest to change the situation?* Then, the teacher asks students to write a letter to the authority to suggest some ways to improve the traffic in Hanoi and gives them the option to mail it or not.

discussing topics related to their lives. These activities gave them opportunities to express their opinions and learn from other students. Two students in the class stated, "Participating in these activities makes me think more about my responsibility to improve the current situations." These activities seemed to help the students gain confidence to state their opinions in English and make changes in their lives outside the classroom. Most of the students reported that these activities not only helped them to develop their language competence in discussion but also made them aware of the social issues surrounding their lives, encouraging them to take action. Five of the students said that they were particularly interested in the last steps in the activities, which focused on how to improve the situation they had experienced. One of the students said that he learned much by exchanging ideas with his classmates rather than hearing ideas from his teacher. He felt that his classroom had become a forum for exchanging ideas. Interestingly, two other students said that they continued to discuss the issues with people outside the class. Five of them reported that after completing these activities they thought more often about controversial issues and felt like they could contribute to change the current situation. Two students reported sending their solution letters to authorities.

Regarding the challenges of participating in these activities, some of the students said that they sometimes found it hard to express their ideas because of their limited language proficiency. Some topics required advanced terminology. Related to the issue of language proficiency, two of the students added that their friends sometimes took the floor from them because of their hesitation and lack of linguistic confidence.

My experience shows that a problem-posing approach can be very useful in developing students' critical thinking. There are noticeable challenges to applying this pedagogical approach in ESOL classes in Vietnam, however. Throughout the 13 weeks of the course, the following challenges were identified.

First there was the cultural challenge. Kubota (1999) also critically looked at cultural differences in ELT. She contends that Western culture and Eastern culture

> have given labels such as individualism; self-expression, critical and analytic thinking, and extending knowledge to Western cultures on the one hand, and collectivism, harmony, indirection, memorization, and conserving knowledge to Asian cultures on the other. (as cited in Pennycook, 2000, p. 14)

Kubota criticized this artificial cultural divide, but I believe this cultural difference should be taken into consideration in applying Freire's philosophy about education because it can be regarded as the product of Western culture. While it may be stereotyping, these characteristics of Asian culture actually do challenge English teachers when introducing problem-posing activities in Vietnam. Vietnamese culture is certainly influenced by the Confucian heritage, which highly praises the role of the teacher in transmitting knowledge because it emphasizes hierarchy and the mutual obligation of group members rather than equality and individualism (Bond & Hwang, 1986, as cited in Sullivan, 2000). Freire's ideas about education stem from a value placed on individuality, freedom, and choice, however. This tension between Vietnamese culture and Friere's philosophy presented me with significant challenges.

Second, traditional teaching methods have been popular in Vietnam for a long time, leading to passive learning habits. In Vietnam, learning is considered the job of the students. In other words, learning is what students do. Many of my students explain that the most important reason to go to class is to learn from the teacher because "he knows a lot and can give us answers." The teacher adopts the role of the "father/mother" in class and is responsible for his students: "Everyone must obey the teacher" (Vu, 1995, p. 227). That traditional attitude toward the teacher and learning cannot be changed in a short time. Therefore, the application of a problem-posing approach in ELT in Vietnam will take time and depends much on the teacher in finding the most suitable ways of incorporating critical thinking in English lessons. It is necessary for the teacher to find ways to alleviate the resistance and overcome barriers to this change. Concerning this issue, I briefly introduced students in the course to the philosophy of problem-posing education before actually applying it. I played the role of facilitator and encouraged them to question and speak out. The students were clearly interested in learning about problem posing because it seemed so novel to them.

Third, Vietnam is a one-party state. Some educators might think that a one-party-led government may not appreciate teachers using critical pedagogy. This is not currently the case in Vietnam, however. Today, the government of Vietnam needs well-qualified citizens who can make serious contributions to the country's development. Besides, the use of a problem-posing approach in English-language teaching does not aim at producing dissidents, but citizens with competence in foreign languages and ability with critical analysis and application. Still, teachers need to be sensitive and tactful when using critical approaches.

Finally, this approach challenges my role as a teacher. In Vietnam, traditionally "the teacher presents the lesson, almost reading the lesson he prepares" (Vu, 1995, p. 227). In problem-posing education, the role of the teacher shifts; he is no longer the answer provider and becomes, instead, a facilitator. I have applied traditional teaching methods for a long time, so when I first began using this approach I felt fearful of engaging in discussions in which ready-made answers were missing. This clearly threatened my authority and status. My responsibility as a teacher is to study to improve not only my English, but also my social knowledge. Yet I must be realistic, so I am aware of the fact that the students will resist new teaching and learning methods because they are comfortable following the Confucian path of accepting authority and traditional pedagogy that emphasizes the role of teacher as a knowledge transmitter.

There are many difficulties in applying Freire's ideas about problem-posing education in ELT in Vietnam. It is obvious to me, however, that the problem-posing approach is worth doing for the benefit of the students. I believe that it possibly can be considered as an alternative approach in ELT. Despite many challenges faced by both teachers and students, applying the problem-posing approach can be effective for ELT in Vietnam.

To make the approach work in EFL contexts, teachers can provide students with linguistic input. They can guide discussions so that quieter students would have a chance to participate. More pair work and group work should be carefully planned and organized (also see the McCaughey chapter in this volume). In other words, the teacher needs to help students listen to one another and try to understand the different positions that other people in the class speak from.

By providing carefully planned pair-work and group-work activities, the teacher creates a safe place for problem posing to happen. In group work and pair work, students will have more chances to use English to interact with one another and then to express themselves in their group, class, and, ultimately, in society. As facilitators, teachers provide any necessary information that will move the discussion to a higher level of thinking and "must be careful not to impose their worldview, but to encourage students in their own critical thinking" (Wallerstein, 1983, p. 19). This shift in discussion involves changing classroom discourse patterns from IRE (teacher *initiates*, students *respond*, teacher *evaluates*) into dialogue.

Apart from encouraging dialogue, in selecting "text" for problem-posing activities, teachers are advised to first try to discover students' issues or problems, and then select and present the familiar situations by using pictures, videos, questions, readings, and stories. Obviously, the situations should be somehow problematic in the local context.

Conclusion

I have highlighted the fact that English-language education at the tertiary level should not only aim at developing students' communicative competence but also their ability to engage with the world around them. Freire's vision of problem-posing education is a process of creating a learning community in which students are free to express their ideas and contribute their own knowledge and skills to shaping the classroom experience. I have found that by following the steps for teaching laid out in this chapter, a sense of empowerment was created in my classroom not only for students, but for me as the teacher. More importantly, this approach gives teachers a broader view of what they can contribute to the linguistic development, as well as to the critical thinking development of their students. Also, it gives a broader view of what they can learn from students: "If teachers are not learning much from their students, it is probable that their students are not learning much from them" (Cummins, 1996, p. 4). I would argue that this idea of teachers learning from students is very new to many Vietnamese. To contribute to changing the current situation in ESOL classrooms in Vietnam, it is necessary to explore different approaches; problem-posing education is one.

I attempted this small-scale classroom research project as an exploratory investigation into the potential for problem-posing education in Vietnam. I believe that this Western culture-oriented approach, if carefully planned, can work well for students in Vietnam or in a similar context where there is significant dependence on the teacher. The results of my investigation show that the problem-posing approach is applicable to non-Western ELT contexts. The Vietnamese students in my English conversation class found the approach challenging and beneficial. It entails a good deal of work and coordination by the instructor, but I believe the results warrant the effort. I am encouraged by my students to continue experimenting with this transformative pedagogy.

Hoa Thi Mai Nguyen has worked as an EFL teacher, teacher trainer, materials writer, and researcher at the College of Foreign Languages at Vietnam National University, Hanoi, for several years. She has published mainly in the areas of language teaching methodology and EFL teacher education. She is currently working toward her doctorate at the University of Queensland, in Brisbane, Australia.

CHAPTER 8

From Podcasting to YouTube: How to Make Use of Internet 2.0 for Speaking Practice

Robert Chartrand

INTRODUCTION

Computer-assisted language learning (CALL) has the potential to provide language learners with vast resources of authentic written, audio, and video materials to supplement lessons. Through the World Wide Web, educators can find materials for their students to study during class or for independent learning outside of class to encourage learner autonomy. Ellis (2003) claims that listening tasks provide an excellent means for measuring whether learners have acquired the target language. Recent advances in technology mean that today learners of a language can listen to podcasts for listening practice, as well as produce their own podcasts for speaking practice. I have found that such speaking–listening tasks often motivate students to engage with the online community in meaningful communication. That is, tasks like these can significantly raise students' potential to generate meaningful output and stimulate their interest in speaking. When using podcasting and social networking Web sites, learners can choose to listen to audio podcasts and view video podcasts on a specific Web page or through specialized software such as iTunes (http://www.apple.com/itunes/).

Why is podcasting so popular? One of the main reasons for the popularity of podcasting is the automated downloading of episodes. It is not only a way to download audio files from the Internet, it can also be thought of as a form of expression, interaction, and community building. An increasing number of educators and learners are starting their own podcasts and producing their own radio programs, language courses, lectures, and a variety of other audio and video programs. Because these podcasts are always associated with a Web page,

91

podcasting remains a unique way to share information with the audience and for the audience to provide feedback to the producers through the Web site, if so desired.

Furthermore, generating language is also an important part of the language acquisition process. Creating student-generated materials such as podcasts or videos is interesting to students and helps them to learn and acquire the language. According to Swain (2007), "The output hypothesis claims that the act of producing language (speaking or writing) constitutes, under certain circumstances, part of the process of second language learning" (p. 5). Thus, encouraging students to speak and experiment with the language is an integral part of learning. A Web-based learning environment can promote constructivist learning through authentic activities related to the vast amount of information available on the Internet. Instructors can provide students with access to a substantial variety of tasks available in a combination of formats, such as text, graphics, audio, and video. Moreover, these multimedia resources can contribute to an increase in students' motivation (Woo, Herrington, Agostinho, & Reeves, 2007).

This chapter describes a podcast that I developed with a colleague to produce materials for our university students in Japan. I discuss how we used the podcasts with our students, and I share ideas on how teachers can set up their own podcasts. After outlining some classroom projects that make use of this medium, I report on classroom research and the theoretical support for using podcasting and student-generated materials. Moreover, I explore recent developments that have emerged on the Internet, in particular with social networking sites such as MySpace (http://www.myspace.com) and YouTube (http://www.youtube.com), and I suggest some activities for language learning.

CONTEXT

I am currently employed at a 4-year liberal arts college and medical school in southwestern Japan. Having been involved in teaching English conversation classes for the past 24 years, I have often felt constrained by the lack of reading and listening materials that students have access to and the acute lack of opportunities in English as a foreign language (EFL) settings for students to practice their English speaking skills in a meaningful way. In Japanese universities, for example, students can commonly take one class (90 minutes) of English conversation per week over a 15-week term. Normally, there are two terms per academic year. This is scarcely enough time for students to significantly improve their speaking skills.

The Internet has helped to alleviate this restriction. More recently, due to the incredible processing power of modern computers and the fast transfer speeds provided through broadband Internet connections, sharing sound and video files has become a reality. Whereas just a few years ago Internet users were limited to reading and writing messages in text, the World Wide Web has come of age, and it is now routinely possible to send and receive the huge amounts of data required for audio and video files. This fact, as well as the vast improvement in easy-to-use software, has made it possible for English for speakers of other languages (ESOL) educators and language learners to make full use of the Internet to assist students with improving language skills.

CURRICULUM, TASKS, MATERIALS

My university classes meet once a week for 90 minutes. As is typical in Japanese universities, most of the undergraduate students are busy with other classes, part-time jobs, and socializing with their friends. Therefore, it can be challenging to encourage students to practice their English language skills—especially speaking—outside of class. To motivate our students, my colleague and I sought to produce materials that are relevant to our students' levels and needs. The result was that Bill Pellowe of Kinki University and I embarked on a project to produce our own podcast, ELT Podcast (http://www.eltpodcast.com/). The home page of the podcast is shown in Figure 1.

Two approaches can be used by a language teacher who is interested in using

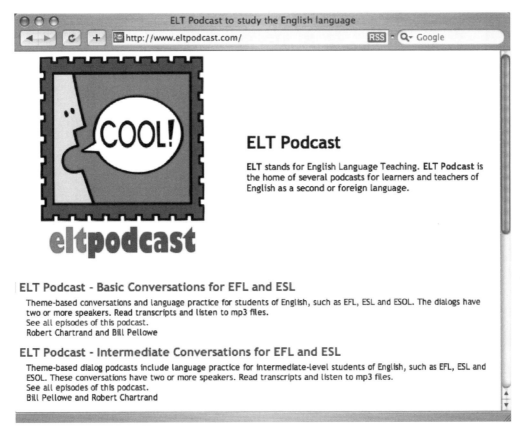

Figure 1. Home Page of ELT Podcast (reproduced and used with permission of Robert Chartrand and Bill Pellowe)

podcasting as a tool for learning. The first is to create a podcast and the other is to use a podcast that is freely available on the Internet. I will describe both possibilities here.

Creating an Original Podcast

First, I will explain how teachers may create their own podcasts. We created our own podcast Web site because of our desire to design the site to our own specifications, and we wanted the ability to control it in the future. A user can access this site from a computer that has an Internet connection and view three main areas: Basic Conversations for EFL and English as a second language (ESL), Intermediate Conversations for EFL and ESL, and The Teacher's Lounge.

Automated Podcast Web Site Solution

It is beyond the scope of this chapter to describe in detail how to create a new Web page for podcasting; however, there are a number of ready-made Web solutions that are available for the novice user. Use a Web site that will assist you in easily creating a podcast. For example: http://www.clickcaster.com, http://www.mevio.com, http://www.podomatic.com, or http://www.audioblog.com. These Web sites allow the user to record a podcast using a computer connected to the Internet without having to purchase additional software. The only requirement is that the computer must have a microphone so that the user's voice can be recorded directly to the computer (Geoghegan & Klass, 2007). The voice is digitized automatically on the Internet through the Web site and then uploaded and generated for display on the World Wide Web. The instructions are easy to follow, and the level of technical expertise required is minimal. I call this the *automated podcast Web site solution*.

Commercial Software Podcast Solution

Another way to create a podcast is to use commercially available software. The following two listed software applications allow the user to have more control over the podcast and design of the Web site. This solution requires more technical knowledge than the automated Web site solution, however. Moreover, the user is required to have a Web site host that will accept the audio data from the podcast to be uploaded. Examples of software that will assist you in the process are iWeb, part of the iLife software package for the Mac operating system, (OS) from Apple Inc. (http://www.apple.com/ilife/iweb/), and ePodcast Creator for the Windows OS from Industrial Audio Software (http://www.industrialaudiosoftware.com/products/epodcastcreator.html).

Using iWeb, for example, a podcast is fairly easy to produce. The first step is to create a Web site. The user chooses a template from the list provided by the software application, inserts the text and pictures that will appear on the Web site, chooses an audio file that has been prepared previously, and finally uploads the data to a Web server. In the case of iWeb, Apple Inc. has a commercial Web hosting solution, which is called MobileMe, and allows the data to be published easily to the Web with minimal effort. Other services are available from Internet service providers, and the costs vary. This is what I call the *commercial software podcast solution*. This solution is not difficult, and most users who are comfortable using a computer will be able to produce their own Web sites with podcasts fairly quickly and easily.

Recording an Audio File

In order to create a podcast, it is necessary to record an audio file. This can be done in a variety of ways:

- Record directly onto a computer. This option provides the best quality audio. The audio recording occurs in a quiet room with a computer and a good microphone. For best results, use a USB audio interface such as Fast Track USB (http://www.m-audio.com/products/en_us/FastTrackUSB .html).

- Record via a computer communication network, such as Skype (http:// www.skype.com/). This option is preferable when there is more than one person being recorded, but in a different location. For instance, if one person is in Fukuoka, Japan, and another in Tokyo, such as in the English Language Teaching (ELT) Podcast Teacher's Lounge (described later in this chapter), then the recording can take place via Skype. The podcasters log in to one main user account, and several people can talk at the same time, as in a conference call. The recording of the conversation occurs live by way of software such as Audio Hijack (http://www.rogueamoeba.com/ audiohijackpro/) for Mac OS X or Replay Music for Windows (http:// www.applian.com/replay-music/index.php).

- Record directly onto an MP3 portable audio recorder, such as an iPod. This option is convenient when the audio recording occurs in a location where computers are not available or in a situation where the recording takes place while moving. This method can be useful when interviewing someone at a meeting, talking to someone while walking outside, or in a classroom where computers are not available.

The quality of the audio and the time length of the recording are directly related to the size of the data file. Better quality audio will have a larger data file. It is preferable that the data file be kept small, without hindering the overall quality of the audio, which is where audio editing software can help. Several good programs are available. One of the most popular software programs available today for recording and editing sound is Audacity (http://audacity.sourceforge .net/download/), a free application for Mac OS X, Windows, or Linux. For the editing of our ELT Podcast, we used SoundStudio 3 (http://www.freeverse .com/) by Freeverse and GarageBand by Apple Inc. We found that SoundStudio 3 produced better quality sound for our needs, and GarageBand, with its wide assortment of copyright-free jingles, was useful for mixing voice with music.

Using Podcasts in the Classroom

Developing a podcast is like planning a syllabus (Chartrand, 2006). There are quantitative elements to consider, such as how many lessons, how much time per lesson, and how much material to cover. There are qualitative elements as well: What level of language is appropriate for the learner? What are the goals, objectives, and needs of the learner?

Therefore, questions that might be asked when producing a podcast may include: How many podcast episodes will be produced? How long will each episode last? Who will do the recording? These were some of the questions that we asked each other when my colleague Bill Pellowe and I developed our original podcast, ELT Podcast. For this podcast, we anticipated producing English conversations for beginner-, intermediate-, and advanced-level learners, respectively. We had planned to develop 10 different conversations for each of the three levels and include different topics for each one to ensure that there would not be too much repetition of expressions and phrases. As of this writing, however, we have yet to complete the advanced level. Nevertheless, we have added a section to our podcast, The Teacher's Lounge. This is an area for teachers to discuss issues relevant to teaching ESOL. We hope that teachers will find the discussions relevant to their classroom experiences as well as other issues related to the profession.

Next, I describe the beginner and intermediate levels of our ELT Podcast site and how they can be used in a language classroom. I follow up this description with a short discussion of the Teacher's Lounge.

Beginner Level

We anticipated that at the beginner level, English learners in our classes would not have good listening skills, therefore we opted to play each conversation three times: the first time at normal speed, the second time at a slow speed so that the learners could hear each word pronounced clearly, and the third time at normal speed again. We made this decision to facilitate the student's understanding before they go on to the next step.

I introduced this podcast in two of my conversation classes last year, with about 30 students in each class. This class was held in a language lab with computers connected to the Internet. After completing their self-study of the beginner conversations, I asked students verbally what they thought of this type of learning exercise. Most of their feedback was positive (i.e., "I appreciated the chance to listen at slow speed," "It was interesting to listen to my teacher's voice on the Internet," and "This is a cool way to study English"). Some of the students had an MP3 player, such as an iPod, and they downloaded the podcasts to their players for listening when they had time. Next, I describe how I used the podcasts to teach English during class time.

I use podcasts in the classroom as supplementary material. As shown in Figure 2, all of the recordings from the beginner and intermediate conversation podcasts have been written down in the Podcast Notes section. Students can read the scripts for practice and refer to the "Let's practice" drills for building their own original short conversations. These notes are also accessible through iPods. Here is a brief synopsis of what I have done in the past.

1. I ask the students to listen to one podcast for homework.

    - Students can read the script on the ELT Podcast Web page if they like, or they can listen to the conversation without reading the script. Giving students the choice on reading the script reinforces their learner autonomy.

    - Students can also download podcasts through the iTunes application.

2. At the beginning of the next class, I play the recording in the classroom.

    - Students listen without reading the script.

3. After listening to the dialogue three times, as described in the previous step, I ask some questions.

    - Questions may include:

        ♦ Where is Robert going next week?

        ♦ Where is Tampa?

        ♦ Why is he going there?

        ♦ When is he going?

        ♦ When is he coming back?

    Solicit answers from students.

4. I distribute scripts for this conversation to the students.

    - Students practice reading the conversation a few times in small groups.

        ♦ Students do not need to memorize the whole conversation.

        ♦ Ask students to look up at their partner when speaking.

        ♦ They may look at the script again before saying the next line.

5. After the students have practiced this dialogue a few times, I introduce them to the Let's Practice section (see Figure 2).

6. In this section, students have to come up with their own answers.

   - Provide a few examples for students to see; however, ask them to think of their own answers.

   - Give students a few minutes to think of their answers, and encourage them to write answers down if they can't remember them.

   - Ask students to mix with other students in the class, and ask a few students the questions noted in step 3.

   - The original answers are provided by the students, so most answers will be different.

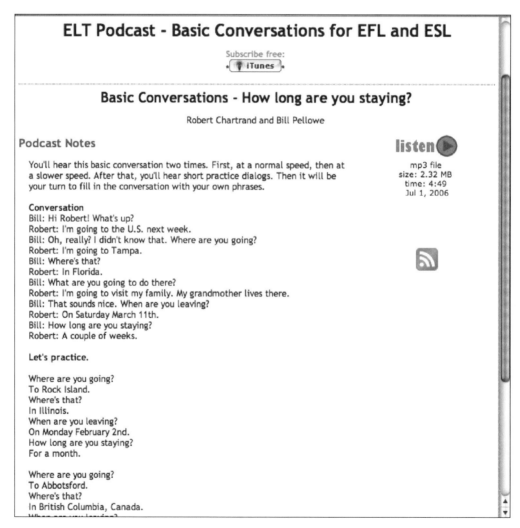

Figure 2. ELT Podcast Basic Conversations for EFL and ESL (reproduced and used by permission of Robert Chartrand and Bill Pellowe)

- Circulate in the classroom at this time to encourage students to stay on task and to speak to as many students as possible.

7. One alternative activity is to write down the answers for a fixed number of students.

   - This will encourage students to ask a minimum number of classmates the questions.

   - Students produce answers on paper to show that they have completed the task.

These activities are very popular with my students, so they willingly practice the target language without hesitation. In the classroom, I use the podcast as preview material, and once the lesson is finished, my students can review it as often as they like. They know that the material is always available on the Internet for them to access outside the classroom.

The beginner conversations on our ELT Podcast site include a short model conversation and a practice section to encourage learners to explore the language beyond the demonstrated model. Each podcast is not long and does not take up

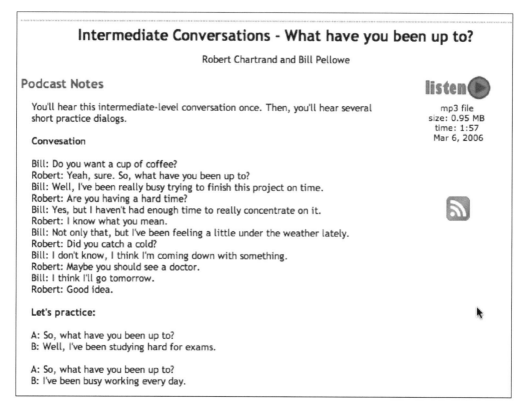

Figure 3. ELT Podcast Intermediate Conversations for EFL and ESL (reproduced and used by permission of Robert Chartrand and Bill Pellowe)

much class time; I like to use this as a warm-up activity in my lessons. Figure 3 shows intermediate conversations available on the Web site.

Intermediate Level

This level is more advanced than the beginner level in that the focus is more on use of the language rather than on form. The intermediate level contains more idiomatic expressions such as, "You get what you pay for," "I'm tied up all week," "It's been raining cats and dogs," and so on. We also focus on specific oral expressions that may come up in real-life situations. "What have you been up to?" is one example of this type of practice. Also, at this level the dialogue is spoken only one time at a normal speed. When recording these conversations, we were aware that our students would be listening to us, so we made an effort to pronounce words clearly. If the students want to listen to the conversation again, they can do so as many times as they wish by pressing the play button. Therefore, we felt it was not necessary to record the same conversation more than once. We purposely focused more on the practice activity, to encourage the students to be involved in their learning and come up with their own answers. The classroom activities can be done in the same way as outlined for the beginner level; however, teachers may need to focus more on teaching the meaning of the idiomatic expressions.

The Teacher's Lounge

More recently, we have focused our attention on creating a podcast for language teachers to talk about experiences teaching English in Japan. The participants in this podcast include Kevin Ryan, from Showa Women's University in Tokyo and the University of Tokyo; Dominic Marini, from Fukuoka International University in Japan; Bill Pellowe; and me. We discuss issues that are varied and of interest to the ELT community. These podcasts are produced with teachers of English in mind, so we talk in natural English about subjects of interest to teachers. Some of the topics include regional accents and English language teaching; attendance policies, motivation, and enforcement, student expectations; and seating arrangements in the language classroom. These podcasts are 16 to 35 minutes long, much longer than the beginner and intermediate conversations. There is a link on the ELT Podcast homepage to access The Teachers' Lounge.

Podcasts Available on the Internet

Not everyone has the time or technical inclination to embark on the task of creating podcasts. There are, however, a large number of podcasts that could be used in ESOL classes for language input and speaking practice. I will introduce a few of the sites here and then discuss one podcast in particular that I have used in my class.

- http://www.breakingnewsenglish.com/
  This podcast specializes in current events. It contains excellent materials for use in the classroom, such as warm-up activities, before and after reading–listening activities, a survey, discussion questions, and a writing task. It is read in British English.

- http://www.voanews.com/specialenglish/
  This Web site from Voice of America contains many news items containing audio files read by a VOA announcer in slow American English, so it is easy to understand for English-language learners.

- http://a4esl.org/podcasts/
  This is a collection of links to the 30 newest podcasts for ESL learners. It contains good source of information to see what's new in this field.

- http://iteslj.org/links/ESL/Listening/Podcasts/
  This is another good collection of links to podcasts for ESL learners.

- http://www.shambles.net/pages/learning/EnglishP/eslpodcast/
  This is another good collection of links to podcasts for ESL learners.

- http://abcnews.go.com/Health/
  This is a good source for health information. Users can view the Medical Minute podcast, which is more easily accessible through the iTunes software by searching ABC News Medical Minute.

Teaching Medical English

I teach at the Medical School of Kurume University once a week, and I have been using the Medical Minute podcast (ABC News) as a resource to encourage the students to speak about health issues in English. When I first showed the medical students this podcast, they were surprised that I expected them to understand this material. It is fair to say that most of the students understood less than 10% of the podcast at the beginning of the course. Following is the lesson plan that I have used for this material.

- Task objectives
  - to help students understand the listening material
  - to discuss the medical issues included in the material

- Begin by writing down some key vocabulary on the board.
  - Key words are some of the difficult expressions that are discussed in the podcast.
  - Teach the vocabulary needed.

- Watch the podcast to familiarize the students with the vocabulary.
  - This podcast is available as a video through iTunes, the ABC News Web site, or the Odio Web site.

- Assign the podcast as a dictation.
  - ◆ Show the students how to access the podcasts on their own.
- Check the dictation with a script.
  - ◆ Keep track of the students' progress.

The podcast lasts for only 1 minute and utilizes commonly used expressions with some medical terminology. The Medical Minute Podcast uses the right combination of language, recording length, and difficulty level to support ESOL students in acquiring the new language they will need in their professional careers. According to the Input Hypothesis (Krashen, 1982), language learners must receive comprehensible input through listening or reading activities that are slightly above their current ability. Following is an example of the language used in the podcast:

> As the summer comes to an end and vacations are over, a new survey links long hours at work to high blood pressure. Researchers surveyed more than 24,000 California workers aged 18 to 64 about their life styles, their work habits, and whether they had high blood pressure. People who packed more hours into the workweek were more likely to report having high blood pressure. Those who worked 40 hours a week were 14% more likely to report high blood pressure than people who worked 11 to 19 hours per week. (ABC News, 2006)

In my experience, after 2 months and 10 podcasts, I noticed a remarkable improvement in the dictations recorded by my students. Their listening skills improved dramatically, and they also began to speak about the content in the podcasts with more confidence. At this stage of the learning process, the students were able to learn on their own. One key point is that I had chosen the material at a slightly higher difficulty level than I thought they could understand, and I encouraged them to write down the words even though they had no confidence in doing so. It became clear that they could gradually write down more vocabulary, and their understanding of the content was also increasing. Eventually, after correcting their dictations, the students were able to have medical discussions about health-related topics in English, whereas 2 months earlier this was not possible.

Social Networking Web Sites

Social networking Web sites, such as YouTube, MySpace, and Facebook, have become extremely popular among Internet users who wish to share their ideas, videos, and other activities online (Dieu & Stevens, 2007). This contemporary phenomenon has led the World Wide Web in innovation, and the term *Web 2.0* specifically applies to these types of services. These Web sites can be accessed easily; they are free and interesting to users.

These are new tools for learners of English to express themselves in authentic ways. Teachers can support students with this type of social networking activity by having them practice a speech that they want to record before sharing it with the rest of the online community. Following are two teaching ideas.

Activity 1: Watching and discussing videos

- Go to the YouTube Web site (http://www.youtube.com).
  - ◆ Look for a specific video that would be useful for students.
  - ◆ Introduce it to students.
  - ◆ Discuss the video in class.

Activity 2: Post a video on YouTube

- Go to the YouTube Web site and register (no charge).
  - ◆ Ask students if they would be interested in posting videos on YouTube.
  - ◆ If the students agree, discuss what kind of videos they would like to make.
  - ◆ Choose a topic with the students.
  - ◆ Film the video with a digital camera.
  - ◆ Edit the video.
  - ◆ Post videos on YouTube.

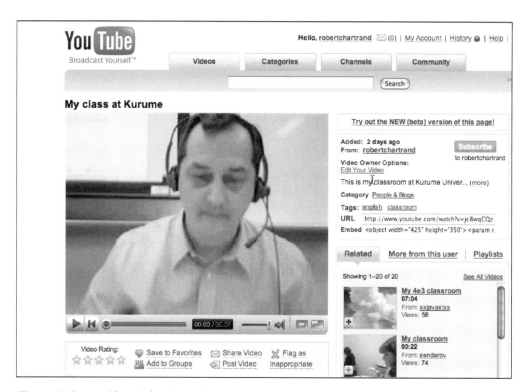

Figure 4. Screen Shot of the YouTube Page Displaying the Video Information

A search on YouTube will reveal a number of ESL-related videos posted by teachers and students (see Figure 4 for an example). These can be shown to students who are not confident about posting their videos on the Internet. The videos can also be used to promote discussions in class. Posting a video is not as difficult as it sounds, especially if computer resources are available to the teacher and students. It is beyond the scope of this chapter to go into details on how to make a video and upload it to the Web; however, many Web sites and books on this topic are available (also see the Yeh chapter in this volume). For example, http://www.Boutell.com offers an online resource for making a video podcast (Boutell, 2008), and *Podcast Solutions* is one of the most useful books on how to produce podcasts, including video podcasts (Geoghegan & Klass, 2007).

REFLECTIONS

In this chapter, I have outlined some ways to use podcasting and social networking Web sites to encourage ESOL students to listen and to produce their own materials to share on the Internet. This type of activity used to be very difficult to integrate into ESOL lessons due to costs and technical limitations; however, these barriers have slowly been fading, and it is now possible to use these online tools to improve students' English ability.

After having used these tools with my ESOL students, I can say that this method of learning is useful, but challenges remain. There is a certain amount of time needed for teachers and students to learn how to use Web 2.0 technology. If a teacher is not familiar with computers and the Internet, then this type of task may seem to be very exotic and difficult. Also, even if one is familiar with computers, there is still a need to learn how to use iTunes, to search for podcasts, and listen to a number of podcasts to determine which ones are suitable. Additionally, the actual process of producing a podcast can be time-consuming. When one of my colleagues recently expressed interest in making podcasts, however, I introduced him to the PodOmatic Web site (see Commercial Software Podcast Solution). He found that the process was straightforward. His students expressed satisfaction in being able to listen to the teacher's voice at home. Without this type of technology, the teacher would have had to produce tapes or CDs for each individual student, which would have meant more time and expense than producing a podcast.

Some of my students have told me that this method of learning is appealing to them because they are familiar with computers, and they appreciate the fact that it does not cost them any money. Also, they can learn at their own pace. A small minority of students does not enjoy learning with computers and does not attempt to study outside the classroom. But this is likely true no matter what medium is used for instructional delivery.

In this chapter, I have described just a few ways for ESOL teachers and students to use the Internet, especially podcasting, for speaking practice. This ability to use computers for the benefit of language learners has appeared relatively quickly, so it is sometimes difficult to keep up with all the latest trends and techniques. I do believe, however, that this is a very positive trend for both teachers and students of languages, and learning how to use this technology will allow learners to develop communicative language skills more effectively. Motivational, pedagogical, and affective factors have persuaded me to believe that meaningful output can be produced by language learners through new technologies such as podcasting. They are easy to use, inexpensive, and readily available through the Internet. By making an effort to experiment with this technology, ESOL teachers can contribute significantly to their learners' progress in speaking English.

Robert Chartrand has a master's degree in teaching English to speakers of other languages from the School for International Training, Brattleboro, Vermont, in the United States. His current research interests include CALL and using the iPod for language teaching. He is cocreator of the Web site ELT Podcast. He lives in Japan and teaches full-time at the Kurume University Institute of Foreign Language Education.

CHAPTER 9

(Re)Cycling Speaking Tasks on the Road to Pedagogical Renewal: Drama in the ESOL Classroom

Tim Stewart

INTRODUCTION

Choosing language teaching as an occupation can involve individuals and families in a great deal of movement—institutionally, geographically, or both. Specifically in this field, there has been an extended discussion about whether or not teaching English to speakers of other languages (ESOL) is a profession and if ESOL educators can have professional careers (Johnston, 2003, pp. 106–110; Maley, 1992; Ur, 2002). My own experience tells me that the answer is *yes*. I have taught in a wide range of programs, from assembly line conversation schools to graduate-level ESOL. And, like many ESOL educators, I have moved. I have changed institutions and continents a number of times. In this chapter, I describe how entering a new institution several years ago reinvigorated my teaching. The chapter is focused on one course in particular, how it was designed, and why.

Change is inevitable. It often causes anxiety. It can be frightening. It can be exciting. But teachers always hope that, in the end, it is for the best. Since the work of teaching flows according to unmistakable rhythms, seasonal and scheduled, teachers are creatures of habit and routine. Teachers and students begin a term with nervous excitement. Eventually, patterns get set as courses develop, and before long the cycle ends with the relief of closure. Then the process begins again. The regularity of teaching schedules results in a degree of comfort for teachers.

What does this have to do with teaching speaking? Before describing the tasks I developed for one course, I consider the advantages and disadvantages of professional routine. My chapter is framed by the contention that from a certain pedagogical perspective it might be possible to look at long-term employment at one institution as too much of a good thing. I realize this is an extravagant position to take in a field plagued by perpetual short-term contract work without benefits. I also recognize that curricular reform within a school or a system can serve the same professional development function I will describe. My chapter highlights potential benefits of career change for classroom teaching. I believe that my career moves from one institution to another have helped me to become a better teacher. That is, by being forced to respond to new and unfamiliar professional circumstances, unexpected possibilities for pedagogical development can open up. This chapter describes a recent experience while developing a new course focused on speaking.

CONTEXT

I enjoyed working as a founding faculty member at a new and dynamic teaching institution in Japan for 10 years. I have written extensively about the dedication to pedagogy at that institution (e.g., Perry & Stewart, 2005; Sagliano, Stewart, & Sagliano, 1998; Stewart, Sagliano, & Sagliano, 2002a, 2002b). Ten years is a long time, though, especially in an English as a foreign language (EFL) context, and many colleagues eventually left the school. Due to concerns about the long-term viability of that new private university, I decided to accept an offer to move to a well-established Japanese public university. Unbeknownst to me, this was the starting point for a renewal of my pedagogical development.

At the time I accepted the new position, I did not realize that aspects of my teaching practice had actually begun to stagnate. Paradoxically, the vigorous teaching environment in which I was working might have lulled me into a state of self-satisfaction. The spirited faculty and the unique interdisciplinary team teaching pedagogy made the university very dynamic. My practice was fundamentally transformed by the experience. Many faculty members working there had the feeling that, for 10 years, we were on the cutting edge in Japanese higher education. I didn't see it until later, but the fact was that I had gradually limited my practice by anchoring myself to teaching routines built around particular sets of materials. Others, notably Richards (1998), have remarked on the positive benefits of routines for teachers. By teaching the same courses for several years, however, teachers could become susceptible to a form of professional stagnation that might be expressed as falling into a rut.

Moving meant giving up familiar routines in exchange for the unfamiliar. My former institution was experimental, with 1st- and 2nd-year courses meeting two or three times each week for a total of 5.5 hours. At the large public university I was entering, however, the traditional Japanese *koma* system was firmly entrenched. This meant meeting students in courses just once a week for 90 minutes, which was extremely frustrating for me. Once I accepted that unfamiliar circumstance, however, it became an opportunity to reinvigorate my pedagogy.

This was when the realization hit me that I had begun to coast in my teaching. I was relying too much on the tried and true activities and techniques I had developed over the previous 10 years. The result was that I had automated my teaching to a greater degree than I wished to admit.

By the end of the first term at my new institution, I had the distance to see all of this and began to make adjustments to my pedagogy. The current situation in tertiary education in Japan is that the most capable students vie to enter the 87 national universities. For me, this meant that the students at my new institution were, overall, more proficient and tended to be significantly more motivated and autonomous. I found that if I assigned work, it was completed and often to a much higher standard than I had come to expect. With this in mind, I set out in the autumn of 2004 to challenge my students and myself by developing a new course with a speaking focus that integrated materials and tasks in a kind of cyclical design.[1]

CURRICULUM, TASKS, MATERIALS

The overarching theme that I used for the 2nd-year speaking course was human conflict. My choice was inspired by two colleagues at my former university (Gene Pleisch and Mundoli V. Narayanan). The culminating activity in the literature course they were team teaching was a play called *Us and Them* by David Campton (1977). While watching their students present this powerful play about xenophobia, I was gripped by the emotional impact of the drama. I had used skits and short plays, including student-authored material, in courses off and on, but I realized then that I had forgotten about drama as a technique in teaching. By the end of the moving performance, I had decided that I wanted to explore the use of drama again in lessons. I explained my intention to my colleague and asked if he would share some materials with me. He did so gladly.

Drama in ESOL

Why use drama in ESOL? Surviving in modern societies requires people to create a series of masks to don in accordance with daily interactions. At times, all people become actors in their own lives, which may appear to play out in a narrative style, like a series of stories or dramas. People are interested in stories. Some stories are acted out in dramas. By watching these stories unfold, audience members can learn about themselves. Viewed from the perspective of the ESOL classroom, students and teachers can learn many things through drama.

Wessels (1987) believes that drama is a potent technique that ESOL teachers can use to improve proficiency in the *four skills*. In particular, she claims that drama helps students with pronunciation, rhythm, and intonation. Wessels

---

[1] I subsequently team taught this course with Professor Terry Laskowski from 2005–2008.

presents a good case for drama being a forceful communicative agent in the classroom because it is an activity that can be structured as more genuine communication than the A–B paired conversations found in most textbooks, involves emotional output, teaches nonverbal language, and motivates students. The motivational pull of drama for teaching is further explained by Via (1972):

> We get involved with putting on a play rather than with the task of learning English, and so we do what everyone who teaches English really hopes to do—that is, to have the students learn by doing. (as cited in Wessels, p. 13)

Maley and Duff (1982) stress that the value for teaching of dramatic activities "is not in what they lead up to but in what they *are*, in what they bring out right *now*" (p. 6). They further claim that using drama activities for ESOL:

> will certainly release imagination and energy—and this is hard to do in language teaching. Indeed, this is one of the purely *educational* objectives that takes us well beyond the limitations of teaching the foreign language as a subject. (p. 6)

Cycling of Tasks: Variations on a Theme

The points made above about the desire to move beyond teaching English "as a subject" (Maley & Duff, 1982), and how engaging with tasks naturally allows students to learn language, and other things, "by doing" (Via, 1972), are central precepts of content-based language instruction. Content-based language instruction (CBLI) can be described as "the integration of particular content with language-teaching aims" wherein "the activities of the language class are specific to the subject matter being taught, and are geared to stimulate students to think and learn through the target language" (Brinton, Snow, & Wesche, 1989, p. 2). Theme-based teaching is widespread in ESOL and, as such, is the most popular approach to CBLI used in the field. The particular theme selected determines the range of language items and activities. As these are cycled throughout a course, a scaffold is built to support "higher levels of language processing" (Brinton, Snow, & Wesche, p. 15). The curriculum I outline in this chapter was created around one major theme and requires a high degree of coordination, particularly with regard to materials. Brinton, Snow, and Wesche state that the recycling of topic-related language and concepts through various tasks in a course can help students increase their communicative fluency. This was the basic pedagogical rationale for the cyclical design of the curriculum.

The Course and Secondary Tasks

The curriculum in question was developed for an intermediate-level 2nd-year speaking course taught at a Japanese public university. The curriculum extended through two required courses that were taught in tandem over 1 academic year. The Speaking I course concentrates on the writing and performance of a variety of public speeches. The following tasks that I describe were introduced in the second course, Speaking II. While teaching Speaking I, just after taking up my new post, I did not stray far from materials and techniques that had served me well at my previous institution. It took me a semester to get my bearings institutionally, as well as personally, with the students. Before the start of the fall semester in October 2004, it was clear to me that I needed to reinvigorate my practice.

The development of effective presentation skills in both English and Japanese is strongly promoted by the department in which the students were enrolled. In Speaking I, students organized and presented various kinds of speeches in English. The main objective for Speaking II was to introduce students to a wider range of public speaking tasks: short oral reports, debates, poster presentations, and drama.

Although the students were in the Communication and Information Studies Department, and many were interested in finding media-related jobs after graduating, few of them reported following the news regularly. I responded to this situation by requiring the students to present summaries of current news stories to their peers. These were presented at the start of each lesson based on a model that I demonstrated on the first day of class (later done as podcasts; see the Chartrand chapter in this volume). The students were given a notetaking form (see Appendix) that they filled in while listening to the news reports. Whenever students were unable to fill in all of the boxes on the notetaking form, I expected them to get the necessary information by asking the presenter questions. One advantage I found with this form was that the boxed sections allowed me to quickly spot which students needed to ask questions and what kind of information they needed, so I was able to encourage and direct hesitant students to question presenters. It is significant that many, if not most, of the questions teachers ask students tend not to be genuine questions, but *display questions* (Lynch, 1996c). These are referential questions to which the teacher already knows the answer. University students need time to devise, ask, and respond to genuine information questions.

Speaking II also incorporated debate in English. In fact, this was the only aspect of the course that was required by the department's curriculum. There is not enough space to discuss debate for ESOL students in this chapter, but I have given this pedagogy some thought (see Stewart, 2001, 2003; Stewart & Pleisch, 1998). Teachers can introduce a wide variety of tasks that integrate the four skills during preparation for a debate event. By introducing debate in Speaking II, I was able to recycle aspects of public speaking from the previous course (Speaking I), including organization, language, and the use of visual aids. I am calling debate a secondary task here because I chose not to integrate it into the thematic unit. The built-in danger to a thematic curriculum is that the theme might not appeal to learners, and even if it does, basing an entire course on one theme risks the onset of thematic burnout.

The Primary Tasks: Poster Presentation, Essay, and Play, with Background Music

The play was the culminating course task, with a performance scheduled for the final class session. The theme of *Us and Them* (Campton, 1977) is the repetition of pointless conflict in human societies. In the play, two groups simultaneously arrive at a wonderful land and plan to settle. They get along well at the start but soon decide that they need a borderline to mark their land. Appreciation for the line promotes calls for a fence and then a wall: "Good walls make good neighbors!" But once walled in, their suspicion and distrust of the Other gets the best of both groups. Violent conflict ensues as the buildup of fear and mistrust leads them to decide that the wall must be torn down in order to expel the Other. What began as peaceful and prosperous societies end up destroyed. Throughout the play, the recorders of history observe and comment while dutifully recording human activity for future generations.

The wall theme inspired me to consider real-world conflicts that my students could investigate and present through posters. I felt that the one that most closely paralleled the play was the Israeli–Palestinian conflict. The controversial barrier being constructed by Israel situated the metaphorical wall of the play in a real-world context. I chose poster presentations for several reasons: They are creative displays of content knowledge, the visuals on posters serve as public speaking aids that wean students off of written scripts, and the carrousel presentation activity is an intensive small-group interaction that encourages notetaking and information exchange on content (see the Carduner & Rilling chapter in this volume). What follows is a description of how I organized these linked units.

This was new territory for me, so the first thing I did was read. I read more about drama in ESOL and about the long conflict between the Israelis and Palestinians. After that, I reconfigured the play so that the number of roles matched the number of students in the course. I also edited the language where appropriate. Another thing I did was to search for credible and readable sources of information for my students on the Israeli–Palestinian conflict and the barrier being erected.

The material I found regarding the Israeli–Palestinian conflict could be divided fairly neatly into four categories: historical background leading to the building of the barrier, Israeli views of the barrier, Palestinian views of the barrier, and international views of the barrier. I distributed this material amongst four groups of students. The poster preparation was done first in these four expert groups, followed by a jigsaw speaking exercise (Slavin, 1989) and then a poster carrousel activity. From the information that they gathered during these integrated classroom tasks, the students wrote a multidraft essay. The entire unit took approximately three to four 90-minute class sessions. Table 1 describes the sequence of the activities, and Figure 1 shows the poster carrousel small group presentations.

The cyclical nature of the curriculum should be evident by this point. To begin

Table 1. Jigsaw, Poster Presentation, and Essay Sequence

1. For homework, each member of an expert group reads and summarizes a section of the group's materials and brings the summary to the next class.

2. Students explain their summaries in their expert groups. Each group decides on the main points to use in its presentation. The teacher checks these points.

3. Four cooperative (or jigsaw) groups are formed, consisting of one member from each of the four expert groups. Students explain the key information from their group's reading to members of other groups. Students take detailed notes.

4. Students use the information gathered from this jigsaw exercise in the first draft of an essay on the topic of the barrier erected between Israelis and Palestinians.

5. Each expert group creates a poster with visual images representing its main ideas. Students practice their presentations. The teacher returns draft one of the essay.

6. The four posters are displayed in different parts of the classroom. Four cooperative groups are formed (one student from each expert group). As the groups rotate in carrousel fashion around the room, when a student comes to his poster, he must present it.

7. Listeners take notes and ask questions. They are told at the start that the purpose of the poster carrousel is to gather more information for their essay.

8. Draft two (and subsequent drafts) of the essay is assigned.

with, students recycled the presentation skills covered the previous term in Speaking I. They identified main ideas and supporting details from readings and discussed these with the other members of their expert group. Then they explained this information in jigsaw groups and later in a poster presentation. The use of visuals such as posters was emphasized as well in the earlier Speaking I course. The objective was to have students talk about key aspects of their poster, rather than rely on a prepared script that they read (also see the Brandt chapter in this volume). With the essay, the jigsaw, and the poster presentations, I encouraged students to merely report the views expressed in the reading. In other words, I told them to follow the same pattern that they had used in the news reports and not to editorialize. The content of the jigsaw and poster activities formed the basis of the essay. The essay was divided into six sections: introduction, historical background, Israeli views, Palestinian views, international views, and conclusion. Once again, they merely reported the various points of view. Students did not write a conclusion until the very end of the course when, in the third draft, they stated their opinion about the barrier dividing Palestinians and Israelis. When writing the conclusion to their essays, I asked the students to consider all of the viewpoints noted, as well as to consider the message of the play *Us and Them* (Campton, 1977) and their experience performing it. A further recycling of skills occurred since the same students were in my academic writing course. That is, through the essay assignment in the Speaking II course, they were able to transfer their knowledge from the writing class to another context.

Once the poster presentations were completed, class activity turned to the

Figure 1. Poster Carrousel Small-Group Presentations

play. As a transition between these two major tasks, I introduced the students to the song *Us and Them* by Pink Floyd (Waters & Wright, 1973). We did some listening comprehension exercises, and then the students, in groups, considered possible interpretations of the song. Later, I solicited ideas and added information where it seemed appropriate. This is just one example of how a theme can be recycled throughout a unit or a course using various materials and media (see Brinton, Snow, & Wesche, 1989; Kasper, 2000a, 2000b).

The stage was now set for the play. I will not describe the practice exercises we did in detail, as there are good books available on uses of drama in language teaching (e.g., Maley & Duff, 1982; Wessels, 1987). As I pointed out above, drama can be a powerful technique for ESOL educators in building motivation, confidence, fluency, vocabulary, cultural understanding, intonation, and rhythm, among other things. I assigned different groups of students to a scene. They worked in their groups saying lines and putting the words together with actions. A nice thing about the play *Us and Them* (Campton, 1977) for ESOL students is that lines are short and repetitive, so memorization is not burdensome. We practiced for about three class sessions before the final performance in front of invited faculty and students. Our version of the play took about 30 minutes to complete. Figure 2 shows the students performing the play.

Alternatives

Naturally, the speaking tasks used in this course could be ordered in a variety of ways, but it seems to me that drama is a nice way to end. By the conclusion of the play performance, there was a real sense of accomplishment and fellowship in the class.

An alternative to the course design presented in this chapter would be to expand the drama section and possibly have student groups write and perform skits or short plays. Depending on the time, technology, and expertise available, these could be recorded and edited with a movie software program for a professional look. But Maley and Duff (1982) are right to downplay a focus on performance while emphasizing the affective and creative benefits of using drama activities for ESOL.

With the play and theme that I chose, different real-world conflicts could be investigated, such as Northern Ireland, Kashmir, North and South Korea, or the issue of Mexican migration to the United States. Local issues could be researched as well. The topic of Us and Them (Self and Other) is one that resonates deeply with ESOL students and teachers.

Although I mentioned earlier the potential for thematic burnout to occur, teachers working with this curriculum might consider adopting the theme of

Figure 2. Students Acting in the Play

the play into the debates and news reports, too. Students could be directed to choose news items that focus on social and cultural conflict, for example. Debates could be conducted on topics such as: Should Japan accept more immigrants? Or, should visitors to the United States (and Japan) be fingerprinted and photographed?

Thematic organization of curricula allows for flexibility regarding materials (see Ellis, 2003, pp. 218–221; Nunan, 2004). Teachers can tailor exercises for any number of discrete or integrated skill focuses using newspapers, music, movies, Web sites, stories, poetry, and other materials related to a particular theme. To do this, good forward planning is essential.

REFLECTIONS

I will reflect from several angles on the practice I describe in this chapter: the perspectives of pedagogical values and beliefs, student reactions to the curriculum, and professional development. The first angle considers the use of controversial topics in the ESOL classroom—that is, to use them or not to use them. Introducing serious social and political issues into ESOL lessons has some critics (e.g., Santos, 2001), but to me this position is terribly naive. I do not mean that teachers should turn language classes into forums to indoctrinate students according to some wider political agenda, but I firmly believe that educated people need to be informed in order to fulfill their role as citizens (and not just consumers). A democracy without an informed populace is a borderline democracy at best. At the very least, university students should be aware of history, follow the news, and learn to be skeptical consumers of what they watch and read through media literacy education.

There is always some risk when introducing controversial issues into lessons, but with proper planning and a sincere attempt at maintaining balanced coverage, I believe that teachers can help students develop and express their own opinions on important issues (see the Hoa and Popko chapters in this volume, and chapter 7 of Johnson, Johnson, & Smith, 1991, for example). Informed and purposeful dialogue, instead of shouting down and freezing out opponents, is sorely lacking in public forums today. Pretending that the world outside of the classroom does not exist is highly patronizing, especially at the postsecondary level. Kubota (2002) sums up some very poignant arguments in this regard by challenging the deception that underlies efforts to maintain a "nice," politically correct profile in the profession of ESOL. Although it could be an uncomfortable revelation for some colleagues, politics is everywhere, even in "a nice field like TESOL" (Kubota, p. 84; also see Edge, 2006).

Next, I will consider the curriculum design from the point of view of students. In the anonymous end-of-course survey, the 18 students in my winter 2007 course expressed overwhelming enthusiasm for this curriculum. Drama activities were rated the most enjoyable (16 students), followed by the debate and poster presentations. Students reported a very high level of satisfaction with all five major course tasks in terms of helping them develop English proficiency. The top three rated tasks for English practice were: the multidraft essay, followed by the debate and the news summary presentations, with the poster presentations and drama activities just behind.

The survey also asked students how they felt about the topics and the curriculum design linking the topics for the poster, drama and essay. Only four students wrote that they felt the topics were too difficult. Most students said it was important to learn topics like these and seemed to appreciate the spiral gradation in the presentation of material. One student wrote in the conclusion to his essay: "I majored in world history in high school but this is the first time that I could learn the Israeli-Palestinian conflict this deeply. . . . Through the play, I could think about the wall as if it was my own problem." This quote sums up what many students wrote. They described the poster presentations as challenging but interesting. Drama was clearly enjoyable: "We had so much fun!," "It was most enjoyable activity," "It was a unique experience," "There is nothing like this in other classes in the university. It was so interesting." The linked essay assignment was rated as being highly enjoyable by only three students. However, 17 of the 18 students rated it as being very useful for their English study. Several students commented on the usefulness of the process of writing three drafts for the essay. All of the students wrote very positive comments about how the materials were recycled throughout the poster presentation, essay, and play. One student wrote: "I think it was a good way to understand this topic and preparation for our play." And another commented: "Knowing about the Palestinian-Israeli issue helped us with the play."

Finally, what motivated me to get my practice moving and evolving again? Here I wish to make an important distinction between what is referred to in the literature as *teacher burnout* (e.g., Zemach, 2006), and what I call *stagnation*. This is important because "burnout" might actually be an overused term in education. I certainly do not downplay the widespread affliction and serious nature of burnout, but I think there is a case to be made that many veteran teachers might experience bouts of stagnation in their practice at various career junctures. The symptoms of a stagnating practice are not nearly as dramatic as those associated with burnout, but some of the longer-term effects could be similarly damaging in terms of professional development. For vital professional development, teachers need to stay active in their fields. It is easy, and perhaps simply human nature, to become complacent after teaching the same courses for 5 or 10 years. This is why we need to challenge ourselves in our teaching, and that should involve challenging our students as well.

The materials that I described in this chapter required a higher level of processing than I likely would have used with students at my former university. Indeed, there were audible gasps from students when they first saw the 15 pages of the play. And some students wondered aloud if they were capable of explaining in English a small portion of the complex issues surrounding the barrier now erected between Palestinians and Israelis. After teaching these students in the first semester, I had anticipated such reactions. For this reason, I carefully designed the curriculum so that the materials and skills were recycled throughout the course. This is what Richards (2001) calls *spiral sequencing*: "the recycling of items to ensure that learners have repeated opportunities to learn" (p. 151). The challenge of creating this complex curriculum was energizing for me and resulted in a spin-off effect as I generated ideas about new materials for other courses. I imagine that after using them for several years, I will look for other ways to reinvigorate my practice. Meeting challenges like this gets to the fun of teaching.

Reflecting back, there were different levels of drama in my classroom that semester several years ago. One was the drama of students working together to construct knowledge, improve communication, and develop their understandings. Underlying the curriculum I describe in this chapter is a simple objective: I wanted students in the course to have the opportunity to think and talk about their ideas. Drama activities gave them a valuable opportunity to put themselves in someone else's shoes—that is, to momentarily separate from the Self and to become the Other. The Japanese students in my classes want to investigate serious issues, they want to be challenged, and they want to express their opinions about sophisticated topics.

Another drama that started before the first class session was playing out in my practice. I saw the need to develop my professional practice in light of the opportunity that arose following my move to a very different university environment. Some ESOL educators might view the topics I introduced in this class as too complex for a foreign language course. To scaffold the vocabulary, grammar, and concepts, I reintroduced items throughout the course in a cyclical gradation (Richards, 2001). Students read, spoke, wrote, and acted out materials, each time reinforcing their learning. I see my primary role in the classroom as that of a facilitator, helping students to develop their linguistic proficiency. But as educators, don't ESOL practitioners have a greater role to play? Social and political problems in the world require attention and action. I believe that teachers can facilitate and educate by carefully laying out contrasting perspectives on complex and vital issues and allowing students to develop their own understandings. This is one way to give students a real voice. Barriers can be overcome and walls can come down. Building bridges is the work of ESOL.

Tim Stewart was the editor in chief of the TESOL serial publication Essential Teacher *in 2006 and 2007. He has moved again to join the faculty at the Institute for the Promotion of Excellence in Higher Education of Kyoto University, in Japan.*

APPENDIX: NEWS REPORT NOTES (TRUNCATED SAMPLE)

Presenter: Date:

Source Information:	Main Points:
Title:	
Questions:	Opinion:

Missing information? ASK A QUESTION!!!

Focus on
Public Speaking

Data and Donuts: Preparing Graduate Students in Language Education to Speak at Conferences

Jessie Carduner and Sarah Rilling

INTRODUCTION

In preparing for their future professional lives, graduate students in many fields need to acquire not only content knowledge but also the skills to conduct classroom and other research, as well as disseminate findings through public forums such as conferences. Opportunities to share with colleagues abound, and professional conferences in many fields use English as a *lingua franca* for international researchers to share and discuss findings.

Graduate students—and, for that matter, many professionals (Connor, 2006)—vary in their presentation skills and confidence. Second-language presenters can face additional challenges in executing public speeches in culturally appropriate ways because they may be unfamiliar with audience expectations, especially if their presentation experience has been limited to the classroom. Students are often less practiced in speaking from a position of authority or power, since it is normally the teacher who holds this position (Diaz-Rico, 2008; Morita, 2004). Inaccurate pronunciation, sentence structure, or vocabulary may hinder smooth communications, and these language-related issues are often complicated by a lack of familiarity with the discourse structure of conference presentations (Ferris, 1998). Additionally, speakers may not use an appropriate level of formality (register) to address fellow professionals, be practiced in fielding questions, or fully understand the expected format of conference presentation genres.

Students and other novice public speakers do not always recognize the need to clarify specialized terms or concepts, or, conversely, they may unnecessarily dedicate too much time to explaining information already familiar to the audience. They are often not practiced in pacing a talk and pausing for effect or reflection, and they may transition poorly between topics, causing their presentation to appear fragmented or disorganized. Worse still, inexperienced presenters often read from their notes or slides rather than using these as prompts, consequently disengaging from their audience, or if they read too quickly, rendering the content incomprehensible. Public speaking strategies such as using humor and anecdotes to maintain the audience's attention are often noticeably absent. In sum, novice presenters, especially when working in their second language, may be inattentive to audience needs; they may lack discourse-management strategies; and they may be unaware of how to use hesitation markers, recasts, or rephrasing, and stalling devices to work around these gaps to keep the discourse flowing.

To assist English for speakers of other languages (ESOL) and foreign-language pedagogy graduate students in preparing for professional speaking tasks, we have integrated what we call Data and Donuts conferences into master's courses at our university, specifically into two courses: Pragmatics and Language for Specific Purposes (LSP). Data and Donuts sessions began as informal gatherings at a local coffee shop where interested faculty and students discussed recent research projects in applied linguistics while enjoying donuts and coffee. Later, we adopted this title for our students' formal course presentations of classroom and sociolinguistic research. Through these Data and Donuts sessions, we sought to create a formalized platform for student presentations that was casual yet professional in nature. Data and Donuts conferences allow our students to showcase their work and provide a venue for peer and faculty feedback in a supportive environment through a process Morita describes as "discourse socialization" (2000, p. 287). In this chapter, we begin by describing the context in which Data and Donuts was conceived and first implemented. Next, we provide a detailed account, along with handouts, of how we train graduate students to give conference presentations using two common formats: a talk or lecture followed by questions and answers, and a poster session. The chapter concludes with recommendations and ideas for expanding Data and Donuts.

CONTEXT

Communicative Competence and Conference Presentations

When speakers present at a conference, even during an informal presentation such as a poster session, they must draw not only on their content expertise but also on their understanding of their potential audience's needs and expectations. This understanding requires communicative skills that extend beyond linguistic competence or knowledge of grammar and vocabulary. Celce-Murcia, Dörnyei, and Thurrell (1995) propose a comprehensive model of communicative competence that includes, in addition to linguistic competence, discourse competence, sociocultural competence, actional competence, and strategic competence. Appendix A describes selected components from this model and highlights features graduate students in language education need to develop in order to prepare and execute professional conference presentations.

Students in Our Language Education Programs

Our graduate programs in language education (teaching English as a second language–English as a foreign language (ESL–EFL) and foreign-language pedagogy) combine core and elective courses to provide students with a broad understanding of the profession and allow them to engage in focused advanced study. Our students come from various educational and national backgrounds. Currently, about 40% are U.S. citizens, while 60% are international students from Eastern and Western Europe, Africa, the Middle East, and Asia. In recent years, a special arrangement has brought cohorts of graduate students from Taiwan. Students' undergraduate majors reflect a wide range of disciplines, such as second–foreign languages and language pedagogies, physical and social sciences, and business. Many students have already taught or tutored English or a foreign language. Although they have all made oral presentations as part of class projects, either as undergraduates or in other graduate courses prior to entering our programs, many have limited or no background in research techniques or conference presentation experience. In fact, many have never attended a professional conference.

Graduate students in our programs must be able to demonstrate academic prowess in both literate and oral practices. When students struggle to meet the expectations of graduate-level study, we advise them to seek appropriate support (writing and tutorial centers are available to students at our university). Our ESL Center, an intensive English program (IEP), provides a range of courses for second-language students who do not meet admissions standards, and some of our graduate students first take courses there prior to admission to our degree programs. International students who have completed IEP courses, and other second-language students who have attended U.S. high schools and universities, have often had explicit instruction in preparing and producing oral reports and other types of oral academic and professional presentations (see also Morita, 2000). These students often have a better understanding of formal and informal presentations as discourse structure (discourse competence) with certain audience expectations (sociocultural competence). They may be more advanced in applying language functions (actional competence) and in negotiating their own linguistic deficits (strategic competence). Graduate students who have not attended conferences or experienced explicit training in oral presentation skills need additional support in successfully conveying research processes and products orally, especially for successful class and conference presentations.

Data and Donuts Presentations Within the
Graduate Curriculum: A Genre-Based Approach

Students are expected to give many oral presentations in our classes. In the past, graduate students, and especially our international students, tended to read directly from their own handouts, computer-projected slides, or posters. They made little attempt to gauge their listeners' understanding and interest, and made only minimal, if any, eye contact (see also Connor, 2006). We soon realized that requiring students, particularly ESOL students, to give oral presentations without preparing them better for the task was counterproductive and would neither motivate nor ready them to present in professional out-of-class venues. While oral presentation assignments were failing to socialize our students into the profession as we had hoped, Data and Donuts, our out-of-class coffee house conversations about scholarly activities, was successfully doing just that. Consequently, we decided to adapt Data and Donuts into two courses in our graduate programs: (a) Pragmatics and (b) LSP. Near the end of these courses, we invite faculty and graduate students from the English and Modern and Classical Language Studies (MCLS) departments to attend a Data and Donuts simulated conference, with our students as the conference presenters. Light refreshments (donuts, coffee, and an array of international snacks and deserts) are provided prior to the start of the sessions and during an intermission between sessions.

The presence of guests creates a supportive yet semiformal environment for our students to present their culminating course projects. Since peers and faculty in English and MCLS attend, the simulated conference takes on a truly professional atmosphere, complete with an informed audience. Members of the audience often challenge our graduate students to answer difficult questions, to provide more context or background, or to give illustrative examples. Thus, presenters need to engage in both rehearsed and unrehearsed discussions about their research as happens in actual professional conference settings. By participating in Data and Donuts conferences, our students get valuable practice for presenting at professional gatherings in the field while gaining confidence and experience in public speaking.

One has only to look at a recent catalog of events at a Teachers of English to Speakers of Other Languages (TESOL) convention to note that there are a number of presentation formats, from colloquia to papers to video and poster sessions. We tie specific oral presentation genres to the content of our courses. In the Pragmatics course, for example, students present quasiexperimental research processes and results, so the paper format, or traditional conference paper followed by question-and-answer (Q & A), seems to fit well with our goal of developing advanced oral discourse competence. Our challenge has been to discourage students from merely replicating and reading sections from their written paper and to encourage them to select and highlight findings and make pedagogical recommendations that they believe will be of particular interest to Data and Donuts attendees. In the LSP course, students present the results of discourse analyses and appropriate teaching materials they create, both of which lend themselves to multimodal presentation formats. Posters are an appropriate genre because they combine textual–visual information with oral interactions. During poster presentations, typically, individuals, pairs, and small groups of attendees circulate freely among the displays. This means that the oral complement to the poster is often a series of Q & A sessions directed by the interests of the viewers, with the presenter explaining the important features and findings represented on the poster.

The Pragmatics course has three broad goals: (a) to introduce major issues in the field, (b) to help students develop strategies for applying pragmatic theories to language teaching (and to their own language learning in the case of our second-language (L2) graduate students), and (c) to give students experience in the professional and scholarly approach to pragmatics through an original, albeit small-scale, research study with an oral presentation component. Through the course textbook (LoCastro, 2003) and recent representative research articles (e.g., Alcón Soler, 2005; Yu, 2005), the instructor introduces pragmatic theories such as speech acts, methods of data collection and analyses, and teaching and learning of pragmatic skills in a second language. Practice activities in class include: role-plays, discourse (or dialogue) completion tasks, pragmatic judgment tasks, discourse analysis, and student-prepared microteaching demonstrations, all of which serve as preparation and practice for the final Data and Donuts presentation. Additionally, students have a chance to pilot data-collection methods. Peer and instructor support of each individual's research project strengthens the overall quality of the students' research, writing, and final presentation (Data and Donuts) by providing multiple opportunities for them to articulate their studies.

LSP draws heavily on the field of discourse and genre analysis of language use (see Dudley-Evans & St. John, 1998; Orr, 2002). Research on texts from specialized domains, focusing on rhetorical and linguistic patterns, can inform the LSP practitioner and provide models of language use the learners may encounter or need to master. LSP professionals prepare specialized tasks for language learners using resources found at the workplace or education–training site to address learner needs. Students in the LSP course learn discourse analysis techniques for genre study, which they apply in the preparation of two posters (based on their reading of Wennerstrom, 2003) demonstrating (a) a personal genre (e.g., restaurant menus or household notes) and (b) a professional–academic genre (e.g., an annotated bibliography or professional *curriculum vita*). Each poster contains a synopsis of their discourse analysis research, identifying particular learner needs, and samples of the teaching materials that they created to address specific needs. In addition, research on the genre of conference presentations in a variety of formats (e.g., video theater, individual paper) is demonstrated so that students might better understand the genre of poster sessions.

CURRICULUM, TASKS, MATERIALS

In the past with our in-class oral presentations, many students have simply patched together bits of written text and read these aloud in a rote and unintelligible fashion with little visual or textual support. The lack of cohesive devices to draw arguments together and students' inattention to audience needs has rendered dull many a graduate student presentation (by domestic and international students alike). We have found that preparing our students to present within two different conference genres (paper presentations and poster sessions) raises their awareness of varying types of public discourse and provides them with opportunities to learn how to tailor their presentations for specific audiences, thereby increasing competence in disseminating information both for class and conference presentations.

Pragmatics Paper Presentations

Data and Donuts presentations are the culminating event in the Pragmatics course. During the last two class meetings, students make a 15–20 minute professional-level talk on their own empirical research study, according to the guidelines in Table 1. The talk is given to an audience of classmates, faculty, and student guests. Throughout the course, students are given substantial peer and

Table 1. Guidelines for the Pragmatics Course Presentations

Data and Donuts Presentations
• The presentation should be 15–20 minutes long.
• Before preparing and giving your presentation, read Baugh (1997), Chapter 9, "Giving an Oral Presentation" and *Convention Tips for Presenters* (TESOL, n.d.-a).
• Expect faculty and student guests from English and MCLS.
• This is to be a *talk*, not a reading exercise. Tell us about your research. Do not read to us. Consider using note cards rather than a written essay.
• Your audience will want to know the following:
♦ What did you study?
♦ What did you want to find out through your study?
♦ Did you have a theory or hypothesis you wanted to test?
♦ Why did you choose the topic you did? What is interesting or important about it?
♦ How did you collect and analyze your data? What instruments or techniques did you use?
♦ What did you find out? Did you get the results you expected? Why or why not?
♦ What can we conclude from your study, or what pedagogical implications are there?
• Provide handouts or visual support of your data collection instruments and *primary* findings.

instructor feedback on their research study, portions of which must be submitted every few weeks.

As preparation for this major presentation, it is important that our students gain confidence in discussing their research topic well in advance. They must acquire the vocabulary related to the theories and research techniques they will employ, as well as practice fielding questions by giving examples and clarifying technical jargon in class. Several activities throughout the 15-week semester (as outlined in Table 2) require students to talk about their research study to a partner or the whole class spontaneously and with preparation.

The speaking practice activities related to the students' research study are generally informal, often with the class seated in a large circle. Twice during the semester, each student must "teach" an aspect of pragmatics to peers as if teaching. The microteaching topics are related to students' research topics. For example, a student studying how nonnative speakers learn to apologize in English may teach a lesson on how to apologize in English for the microteaching demonstration. Following the microteaching demonstrations, students give an account of the lesson objectives and rationale for their pedagogical choices and invite questions and comments from classmates and the instructor. Again, this activity simulates the type of interaction expected during Data and Donuts and professional conference presentations. Feedback is meant to encourage reflection on speaking style, ability to engage an audience, clarity of the lesson including appropriate

Table 2. Preparatory Activities for Pragmatics Course Presentations

Scheduling for Preparation of Data and Donuts Papers
1. Students submit a paragraph describing their pragmatics research topic and motivations for choosing it to an electronic discussion board. (week 3 of 15)
2. Students ask each other questions and submit suggestions for each others' studies via an electronic discussion board. (weeks 3–5)
3. Students are asked to tell the class orally, in *impromptu* fashion, about their research topic. (week 5)
4. Students bring a copy of their introduction, initial literature review, and data-gathering methodology and instruments for peer review in dyads. (week 7)
5. Students pilot their data-collection instruments with the whole class, after which they engage in a whole-class discussion of strengths and weaknesses of the instrument. (week 7)
6. Students discuss their research study with the instructor in individualized appointments. (weeks 8–9)
7. Students are invited each class to ask questions or seek opinions concerning their study. (weeks 8–14)
8. Students give presentations on their research projects. (week 15 and final exam week)

vocabulary and register for the intended audience (ESL students), and effectiveness of visual aids and support materials. A critical benefit of microteaching is that students observe a variety of presentation styles and techniques that they can later apply (or reject) to the preparation and performance of their final presentations (Data and Donuts).

Until recently, audience feedback has been gathered only orally and anecdotally. We are currently piloting an evaluation form similar to one that might be used at a professional conference (see Appendix B) as part of the routine so that students get feedback on their presentations not only from the instructor but also from their audience of faculty and peers.

Language for Specific Purposes Poster Sessions

During the LSP course, students prepare two poster sessions, each representing an original discourse analysis and including language teaching materials developed through the study of a personal and a professional–academic genre (see Appendix C). Points are awarded for clarity of discourse analysis, as well as poster design and quality of oral interactions during the Data and Donuts conference. In preparation for the discourse analysis projects, we study Wennerstrom (2003, p. 74), who follows a seven-step process in teaching L2 learners to analyze and produce genre-specific texts: (a) initial discussions, (b) genre collection, (c) genre analysis, (d) project design, (e) drafting, (f) review, and (g) revision. This process trains students as both analysts and informed writers of a variety of text types.

We have students read convention presentation tips to consider design issues, such as tips related to TESOL's poster sessions (see, for example, *Preparation Guidelines for Poster Sessions*, TESOL, n.d.-b). While TESOL's size specifications for the displays are irrelevant to our classroom goals, the tips provide good ideas for both content display and for interactions with visitors at the poster session. We focus additional preview activities throughout the semester on discourse analysis in materials and curriculum development for meeting specific learner needs. Project preparation activities allow students to talk both formally and informally in class about their own genre studies in terms of methods of data collection, analysis, findings, and teaching applications.

Students prepare a mock-up of their posters on paper and discuss their design choices in groups. Form follows function, so students often select a design mirroring content, such as a threefold standing poster of a menu they created to display analysis and teaching applications of a corpus of restaurant menus. In preparing posters, students practice multimodal writing by combining text (in appropriate sizes for a poster audience) with graphic images, text samples, and teaching samples. By having students share their developing projects orally in class throughout the semester, our objectives are two-fold: for them to gain insights into discourse analysis from their peers, and to collect ideas for poster design, display, and presentation. Figure 1 shows a student poster project that features analysis of comic strips.

Figure 1. Poster Session About Teaching the Language of Comic Strips

Poster sessions for the Data and Donuts Conference are conducted carrousel style with about half of the class displaying posters and half acting as viewers at one time (see Lynch & Maclean, 2001, for a detailed description). While the presenters remain at their posters, viewers participate as audience members. Audience viewers rotate through the poster displays asking questions at each station and interacting with the presenter. During our Data and Donuts forums, faculty from other courses (both English and MCLS) and graduate students from our programs join the event and circulate around the carrousel display. Visitors provide a wider audience with slightly different needs and objectives than class-mates who have also prepared poster sessions. Audience members ask questions about the content of the poster and the teaching ideas associated with the genre that the student researched, including choice of texts, methods employed with the discourse analysis, and so on. Rather than giving a formal talk, the presenter prepares to answer questions about the genre, provide additional information about the discourse analysis he conducted, and talk about the teaching ideas even if not asked, since poster presenters often initiate talk. After the first group of poster viewers have circulated to all posters, classmates swap roles, and a new carrousel round begins. As the carrousel of viewers moves around the display, the presenters have opportunities to refine what they say to each successive visitor or group of visitors, which Lynch & Maclean (2001) have shown improves language learners' professional poster presentation skills.

REFLECTIONS

In our programs, Data and Donuts forums have served an apprenticeship role (Morita, 2000), giving students firsthand experience in using research and presentation skills that are valued by applied linguists. Short of taking students to a regional or international conference, a practice we encourage and support, Data and Donuts conferences provide a venue for this important professional practice: effectively presenting original research to an audience of peers. Our graduate program further supports these goals through a series of spring semester (January–May) professional development workshops on, for example, conference proposal writing, during which we inform students about departmental and other institutional funds for conference presentation.

Data and Donuts conferences help to professionalize our graduate students' experience by building their confidence in making presentations. Students gain knowledge of different presentation genres and an understanding of audience expectations, especially by using such resources as conference guidelines and tips and by making their own observations on the performance of others. With continued mentoring by faculty, several students have presented at regional and national language teaching and graduate student conferences. We find this accomplishment very gratifying because it is a sign that we have succeeded not only in showing students in our program how to prepare a research study with concomitant teaching applications, but also in giving them the confidence to take the next professional step as conference presenters. One former student recently published her study in a prestigious teaching journal, another sign of the professionalizing potential of Data and Donuts.

As a curricular innovation, we believe that incorporating Data and Donuts into our graduate classes has provided our students opportunities to increase their awareness and practice of the discourse management and strategic competence essential to becoming practicing professionals. In the future, we hope to explore integrating Data and Donuts more widely and more systematically so that each graduate course might provide students with an opportunity to present their learning processes and products to wider audiences. This might include other conference presentation genres to parallel course content such as video theater in our computer-assisted language learning course or demonstrations in curriculum and teaching courses. We also plan to add components to current Data and Donuts procedures, including:

- **Conference proposals:** Currently, students are required to submit topic proposals to their instructor for feedback and suggestions. In the future, students will be required to fill out a "conference proposal" form to make the conference simulation more complete. We may even institute a blind reading by the class of the proposals to demonstrate the value of careful attention to detail at the proposal phase of conference participation.

- **Videotaping for reflection:** Video can be used effectively in teacher development, especially since it documents behaviors and interactive strategies (or lack thereof) that might not otherwise be noticed by speakers (Bailey, Curtis, & Nunan, 1998). Through videotaping, and reviewing and reflecting on their own presentations, students can improve their presentation techniques. Alternatively, faculty and students can watch and discuss the videotapes together.

- **Regional student conferences:** Most Data and Donuts attendees are known to the student presenters. In order to make the simulation more realistic, we might participate in a wider university forum or invite students and faculty from other universities in our region to a regional student conference to widen our audience.

We urge other teacher educators and ESL instructors working with graduate students to consider the wide benefits of the practice we have described in this chapter. The tasks for public speaking training that we have outlined above, including open discussions of ideas prior to class presentations, can readily be adapted to other presentation formats. Consider holding some course content discussions outside of class and in different venues. It is amazing how sharing a cup of coffee or tea with students can help them relax. So go ahead: Pour the coffee, and share research insights along with teaching applications. Simulated conferences like Data and Donuts have the potential to professionalize students' speaking for effective classroom presentations, conference presentations, and demonstrations at teaching forums.

Jessie Carduner is an assistant professor of Spanish and foreign language pedagogy in the Department of Modern and Classical Language Studies at Kent State University, in the United States. Her research interests are in the acquisition of speaking and writing proficiency in a second language, interlanguage pragmatics, and career advising for foreign-language majors.

Sarah Rilling is an associate professor of English at Kent State University, teaching applied linguistics courses such as ESP, World Englishes, L2 writing, and Task Research and Design. Her teaching, research, and language learning take place predominantly in the United States, Japan, and Germany.

APPENDIX A: BEYOND LINGUISTIC COMPETENCE— COMMUNICATIVE COMPETENCE AND CONFERENCE PRESENTATIONS

I. **Discourse competence**—knowing how conversations and speeches are organized. Students gain practice in working with different:

    A. *genre structures* that occur during a poster or conference presentation such as introduction, presentation of the content, use of audio visual aids

    B. *conversation management techniques* such as turn-taking, establishing or redirecting topics, answering questions, and taking or relinquishing the floor

II. **Actional competence**—indicating intent. Language functions emphasized include:

    A. *interpersonal exchanges* such as identifying oneself and reacting to others' speech

    B. *information functions* such as giving information, reporting, explaining, and discussing

    C. *expressing opinions*

    D. *suasion* or suggesting and persuading

III. **Sociocultural competence**—using cultural and social knowledge to convey messages. In this category, students learn to make linguistic adjustments based on:

    A. *social and contextual variables* such as assuming a role of an authority or "expert"

    B. *stylistic factors* such as the need to use a scholarly tone in a conference presentation

    C. *nonverbal communicative factors* such as enhancing the presentation through facial expressions, gestures, voice modulation, silence, pausing, eye contact, and use of physical space

IV. **Strategic competence**—using strategies to enhance communication and prevent breakdowns. Some strategies that learners may use include:

    A. *stalling or time-gaining strategies* such as fillers and hesitation devices

    B. *self-monitoring strategies* such as rephrasing, or self-correction

    C. *interactive strategies* such as checking the listeners' comprehension

(Categories adapted from Celce-Murcia, Dörnyei, & Thurrell, 1995).

APPENDIX B: AUDIENCE EVALUATION FOR DATA AND DONUTS IN THE PRAGMATICS COURSE

Presentation Evaluation Form

Paper title: _____   Presenter: _____

> 5 = Strongly agree;   4 = Agree;   3 = Neither agree nor disagree;
> 2 = Disagree;   1 = Strongly disagree

The presentation was well organized.   _____

The speaker's content was clear.   _____

The speaker read aloud a written paper.   _____

The speaker was engaging.   _____

Audio-visual (AV) aids were high quality.   _____

The speaker used AV effectively.   _____

The presentation was professional.   _____

The speaker should propose this study for
presentation at a regional or national conference.   _____

Please comment on additional items, such as the speaker's pace or delivery, use of definitions and new terminology, etc.

_____

_____

_____

_____

_____

_____

_____

APPENDIX C: PREPARING DISCOURSE ANALYSIS POSTERS FOR THE LSP COURSE

Data and Donuts: Poster Presentations

During the semester, you will present two discourse analysis posters: (a) a Daily Discourse Analysis Poster, and (b) an Academic Discourse Analysis Poster. Each poster analyzes one particular genre (with samples) and demonstrates an understanding of the genre linguistically, rhetorically, and visually. The posters also present teaching materials for the genre. Posters should be visually appealing and pedagogically sound. Classmates and invited guests will view your posters.

The Daily Discourse Analysis Poster represents a genre from daily life (e.g., prescription labels; job application forms; car insurance or registration documentation). Present your discourse analysis findings, and devise teaching materials following Wennerstrom (2003). The Academic Discourse Analysis Poster reflects your analysis of a collection of academic artifacts (e.g., reports, academic journal abstracts, introductions to research articles). Include text samples, your discourse analysis, and instructional materials.

Tips for Preparing Your Poster:

- Let your poster tell the story. You will be available to answer questions, but you will not give a formal presentation. Information should be clear from the poster itself—make it as informative and self-contained as possible.

- Use poster display boards with fonts large enough to read from 2–3 feet away. Consider ease of use in a small space with an audience of 3 or more people at a time.

- Prepare a combination of graphic and textual elements to clarify your content.

- Make sure to include pedagogical materials based on sound practices.

- Don't forget to include your name and e-mail address somewhere on the poster!

Tips for Presenting Your Poster:

- Consider what your audience may or may not know about your topic. How common is the genre you have analyzed? Has your audience likely produced or consumed the genre?

- Consider teaching applications. What ideas do you have that are not listed on your poster?

- Ask your audience questions as to how this genre supports their students' learning.

- Poster presenters often initiate interactions with the audience. Provide additional information orally to clarify each section of your poster.

Tips for Audience Participation at Data and Donuts:

- Study the content of the poster and ask questions related to how the presenter selected and presented content information.

- Study the poster and ask two or more questions.

- Consider the genre and the teaching materials in light of the language learners you teach. Discuss your ideas with the presenter.

- Think of your own poster. What did this presenter do more effectively than you did? Tell him so. What advice do you have for this presenter? Tell him.

CHAPTER 11

A Holistic, Humanistic Approach to Developing Public Speaking Skills Through Speech Mentoring

Amanda Bradley

INTRODUCTION

English speech contests are an institution in Japan. Annual speech contests are held from elementary school through university, gathering students to showcase English prowess at special community events.

Traditionally, speech contests in Japan are characterized by formality and proceduralism, and while, ideally, autonomously drafted speeches are prized, most speeches are clearly the work of coaches. The college where I taught differed from the Japanese norm because English was the language of instruction with active learning and critical thinking explicitly promoted. Such instructional goals contrasted with the general situation, where memorization and reproducing teachers' content are valued.

For the college's annual public speaking contest, interested students were asked to work with a teacher of their choice. Two instructors committed to mentoring students volunteered to help prepare them and formed the Speech Event Steering Committee in order to ensure optimal coordination. Moreover, in terms of pedagogy, mentoring (as opposed to coaching) focused on drawing out the unique initiatives of each individual and fitted more closely with the institutional mission of providing a broad liberal arts education.

The basic challenge in preparing students for the contest was for them to spend enough time in the process. Once students committed themselves and set up regular mentoring sessions, the second challenge was to enable them to express their own ideas. We discovered that helping our students to express their own ideas could best be achieved through an intensive process of mentoring that included careful empathetic listening and facilitation. After years of experiment-ing, the Speech Event Steering Committee settled on starting speech prepara-tion approximately 5 weeks before the event. This timeframe was decided upon because students had shown a greater tendency to procrastinate over the longer periods previously used for preparation.

In this chapter, I will share the speech process developed with colleagues and students over 7 years and its outcomes. Student experiences and feedback direct my exploration into the notion that speeches can be used to promote a *deep approach* to learning.

I was first introduced to deep approaches at the London Scholarship of Teach-ing and Learning Conference in May of 2004 and felt inspired to submit a paper for the conference proceedings. At that time, I read Paul Ramsden (2003), a major exponent of deep approaches to learning, and discovered that this concept fit my learner-centered approach to teaching. Ramsden asserts that quality teach-ing implies recognizing that students must engage with the content of learning tasks to reach understanding. Because I was working in a content-based learning program, the explicit focus on meaning coincided with my existing teaching goals.

A Working Definition of Deep Approaches

Deep approaches to learning focus on grasping meaning, organizing ideas, and relating content to other subjects and to the student's own experience. They are typically contrasted with surface approaches focused on memorizing or picking out discrete items to pass tests, for example.

Scholars at the University of Gothenberg, Sweden (Marton & Saljo, 1976), first distinguished between deep and *surface* approaches in their research into university students' reading ability, finding that more effective readers grasped the main point and overall meaning of academic texts as they examined them critically. They classified such students' approaches as deep. Conversely, students who tried to rote-learn information they considered important rather than seek understanding of the overall meaning, and attempted to memorize details they felt might serve to recall specific information teachers would later ask about were classified as surface learners. Ramsden (2003) provided practical guidelines for teaching based on the original research in his seminal work, *Learning to Teach in Higher Education*. Table 1 lists the principles of a deep approach to learning.

CONTEXT

The students I mentored were enrolled in an English-immersion liberal arts program in which teaching English to speakers of other languages (ESOL) educa-tors team teach with discipline-area faculty. The program differs substantially from conventional curricula in Japanese higher education because English is the

Table 1. Principles of a Deep Approach to Learning

Students:

- have the intention to understand
- have vigorous interaction with content
- relate new ideas to previous knowledge
- relate concepts to everyday experience
- relate evidence to conclusions
- examine the logic of arguments

(adapted from Entwistle, 1984).

language of instruction. The content-based English instructional design model employed at this university effectively integrates language learning and academic development.

The students ranged from beginners to high-intermediate learners who were fairly proficient across the skills. All students were eligible to join college-wide speech events, and they were able to select mentors. The number of candidates for any one speech contest ranged from 10 to 15, with mentors sharing duties equally. Candidates were divided into two categories, junior and senior, with students who had spent 6 months or more in an English-speaking country placed in the senior category.

During the process, I wanted my students to express themselves in natural, spontaneous English, pay attention as listeners and speakers, grasp and convey meaning, ask questions and relate content to their experience and the broader world, and be able to describe their learning process. If students rose to those challenges, it would mean that they were applying deep approaches to learning.

There was a tendency among my Japanese university students toward surface learning. In my classes, some students initially indulged in extensive dictionary work and focused on vocabulary, rather than meaning. They sought pat answers rather than using critical thinking and showed little awareness of their learning process or the role of their written and oral expression as part of their development. This learning behavior was at cross-purposes with the academic goals of the institution, which focused on active learning and critical thinking. I believed this surface learning was likely to reinforce a spiral of low self-esteem and poor learning habits for some students. In addition, observing students over the years had shown me that, over and above success in discrete activities such as winning a speech contest, young people also sought to educate themselves in a broad sense. They acquire knowledge and awareness in one class and apply it to other classes and disciplines, as well as to social and other interactions outside of school and later in life (also see the Hoa chapter in this volume). I held that deeper educational goal for my students.

English speeches offered a number of features to counteract students' unconscious preoccupation with surface learning. I believed that success would depend on my ability to create a facilitating environment for students and to encourage deep approaches to learning through my teaching (see Ramsden, 2003, p. 146).

CURRICULUM, TASKS, MATERIALS

Innovations

By assessing the quality of speeches over several years, the Speech Event Steering Committee decided to change the conventional speech format used in Japan from first-person accounts of personal experience to narratives derived from other sources, including the students' own creations. We also encouraged participants to use the third person to gain a new perspective. In one speech assignment, I asked my students to craft a narrative from the point of view of one or more inanimate objects. They chose things such as items in a pencil-box, a new football, and an old pair of football boots in a drawer.

Given the liberal arts program at the college, students were also invited to make speeches related to their discipline courses. The aim was to encourage a deeper approach to course content by applying it to another context. This innovation encouraged students to base speeches on their psychology, political science, history, American literature, Japanese literature, and education courses, among others.

Approximately 1 month before the event, public speech orientations were led by two mentors, with the help of former speech contestants. Table 2 outlines the preparation process that we followed.

Table 2. The Speech Preparation Process

1. The process was explained and experiences shared, including questions and answers.
2. Students chose mentors.
3. Mentoring was scheduled outside class hours.
4. Students met mentors in their offices, chose topics, and began the drafting process.
5. Students and mentors negotiated schedules and met regularly (15–20 hours on average).
6. Final drafts of speeches were proofread and submitted (450–500 words).
7. Individual delivery mentoring took place in the mentor's office.
8. In the final week, plenary rehearsals were held.
9. Speech contestants were invited to perform in relevant classes.
10. The speech contests were held.

The following aspects of the speech process contributed to deep rather than surface learning approaches:

- engaging in free oral and written expression, not repetition of teachers' words

- developing well practiced, but spontaneous, delivery, not memorization

- using a written draft as a support for delivery, not seeing delivery as a test of memorization

- perceiving writing and speaking as a means of self expression and intellectual development, not merely as an academic requirement

- selecting content that does not necessarily reiterate teachers' or source text words

- understanding the task to convey a message to an audience, rather than seeking to fulfill requirements for a grade

- finding one's own voice in English and interacting in English voluntarily with the mentor, not using English because it was required

- listening to the mentor; understanding, reflecting, choosing, and following a course of action; not waiting to be told or unquestioningly obeying the teacher

- applying speech skills to other purposes outside of the speech contest

A Whole-Person Model

For the speech process, I followed a whole-person model by inviting students to take part using both body and mind (Curran, 1977). Bearing students' affective needs in mind, I wanted them to know that all contestants were winners and the performance was a continuation of their study, rather than a trial. I wanted them to feel accepted and appreciated. For the speech event, I encouraged them to relax their bodies to dissolve stage tension. I also stressed the notion that the voice is an instrument for individual expression.

Mentoring

Mentoring was essential to the speech process. Students chose mentors for affective reasons, such as trust and rapport. My mentoring was based on a Counseling Learning model (Stevick, 1990) entailing the following assumptions:

- The mentor is not in a position of power or infallibility.

- The learner is unconditionally accepted.

- All candidates are able to achieve the stated goal of creating and delivering an appropriate speech.

While mentoring, I practiced the following skills:

- listening actively and accurately

- observing and reflecting back

- empathizing

- giving information

- questioning

- challenging

- giving feedback and summarizing

It must be said that these mentoring techniques, particularly the ability to know students without judging them, to refrain from displaying infallibility or engaging in long-winded teacher talk, took me many years to hone.

Sessions took place in my office. The setting was aimed at providing a welcoming, relaxed, yet academically focused environment. The two mentors had different approaches, although in both cases the process was organic and based on drawing out individual students' ideas through careful empathic listening, questions, and feedback. All students worked part of the time with the other mentor to gain an alternative perspective. Although the process focused on the goal of delivering a final speech, it was also holistic (Forbes, 2003). It included skills such as time management, interaction with different teachers and peers of different ages and ability, and the development of a sense of individual competence. English was used throughout as a means of communication between mentors and students. The skills practiced throughout the speech process were applied to other contexts, including classes, assignments, and different public speaking contexts. In classes, I highlighted speech contestants' work, recycled their written speeches, and asked them to repeat performances for in-class audiences to emphasize the continuous nature of the process.

The Distinction Between Coaching and Mentoring

A high school speech contest highlighted the difference between traditional speech coaching and mentoring for me. As a judge, I found it difficult to choose three winners, since more than three exhibited similar qualities. Winners were finally decided by mathematical averaging. One student considered herself a failure when passed over for the second time and was inconsolable, a very unpleasant consequence of the win–lose nature of coaching for very specific goals (Wylde, 2005).

Mentoring, in contrast, reinforces the humanistic view, accepting and catering to individual learning stages. It is a process entailing greater affective involvement, choice, and long-term rapport (Brockbank & McGill, 1998), whereas coaching may be seen as more of a surface process entailing training candidates for a finite goal. One student saw mentoring in this way:

> I go to my mentor because I want her to hear what I'm thinking. She doesn't show she's busy. She's never shown that kind of anger, that kind of edginess, with fingers on the computer, head turned away. She knows that she has to show a certain behavior and body language. She never forgets she is a mentor.

Metacognition

A primary function of my mentoring process was to introduce the speech contestants to the concept of metacognition (i.e., the student's understanding of how he learns) (Flavell, 1976). Metacognition was a leap for my students from the familiar mode of high school speech coaching, driven by teachers' instructions. Also, there was no template for it. It is based on the learner's awareness and facilitated by my feedback and questions as their mentor. At the drafting stage, a student might say he was not satisfied with a paragraph, and I would ask "Why not?" If he did not know, I would base a question on my perception, such as "Do you think this paragraph fits here?" to facilitate an understanding of cohesive and coherent discourse. For him to grasp a sense of the appropriateness of content, I might say, "Would you like the whole college to hear this?" To encourage an awareness of audience, I would tell the student that he knew his topic but his audience might not, and ask for more details to provide the speech with clarity and audience appeal.

Whenever students were unable to answer, I chose whether to give them time or to answer for them. How much help to offer a student is an individual assessment made by each mentor, with the understanding that every student is unique. My goal was for all students to develop and express as much self-awareness as possible.

First-year students expressed differing metacognitive awareness of their speech project:

- I think that my writing is improve because I could write without dictionary.

- I don't think the speech project made me feel more confident actually because I noticed many points to improve. I cannot improve all things.

- I learned it is important to charge my whole heart because the speech isn't interesting without my heart. I didn't write the speech except this class. I learned a different way to tell my content.

Choosing Topics

In recent years, the general speech theme was "stories from which we learn." The theme was presented with examples during an orientation, and students were given several days to reflect on it. Many came up with the idea of a description, including "My favorite English teacher" or "I was bullied in school." We asked them first to tell the story then to interpret it to create a message to give their audience, such as "Good teaching is caring teaching" or "If you have been bullied, your job is to let victims know that they are not alone." Students were invited to take a deeper approach to writing by going beyond basic description because they maintained an appropriate balance between story and interpretation.

Drafting

The voluntary nature of the speech process made it highly learner centered, and students perceived the need to write multiple drafts to improve their work. I tend to follow an organic process, guiding individual students according to ongoing needs. Table 3 demonstrates the teacher's and learner's roles in drafting speeches.

Because narrative structure creates excitement and appeals to audiences, I encouraged students to base speeches on stories structured with characters, a problem, a climax, a resolution, and a moral. The stories were inspired by literature, folk tales, nonfiction, or personal experience.

One student, Seigo, told the story of his name, both in real life and according to legend. The moral was that facing life's challenges makes us develop and mature. Figure 1 shows the first and final drafts of his speech introduction.

Table 3. Guidelines for Drafting Speeches

Mentors need to:
- be available and respond soon to e-mail messages
- show acceptance of students at their stages of academic development
- make sure students know the purpose is learning
- convey the notion that all contestants are winners
- focus on the overall task
- guide revision through questions:
  - *What is your main point?*
  - *Is this point important in your story?*
  - *Which phrase(s) could you omit?*

Students need to:
- take the initiative to meet the mentor regularly (e.g., three times weekly)
- write a first draft
- write subsequent drafts incorporating insights from the mentoring session
- refrain from self-deprecation
- self-monitor
- view the teacher as a resource
- ask questions

First Draft

When we go to the course of life, we have a lot of troubles and challenges which are disaster, money, trouble, sickness, prejudice, human relations and so on. What can we do about it?

My parents named me Seigo. Seigo means "sea bass child." Seigo is promotion fish. Promotion fish means getting on in years, the name is changing. In case Seigo changes Fukko, next Suzuki. My parents thought they could help me name by giving me an auspicious name.

I heard another promotion fish story in Japan. I am going to tell you.

Final Draft

As we go through the course of life, we meet with troubles, disasters, money problems, sickness, prejudice, human relations, and so on. What can we do about it? To give me a chance in life, my parents chose for me an auspicious name, Seigo. My name is the name of a "success fish," the young Sea bass which grows into the powerful deep-sea adult Suzuki. Let me tell you the time-honored Japanese story of "Success fish."

Figure 1. Drafts of a Speech Introduction

These draft introductions illustrate the development of cohesiveness by focusing on the central theme (i.e., that bass fry develop into strong and "successful" fish). Curran (1977, p. 20) makes the point that an accepting teacher will enable the learner to feel valued and free him to learn, since he is no longer held back by self-doubt. In a session with Seigo, I asked him, "How could you focus your topic more?" and Seigo was able to assess his own writing and edit out irrelevant points. Later, he asked me how he could make it more appealing, and I suggested questions to interact with the audience. This prompt led him to insert: "What can we do about it?" Seigo improved his draft after one discussion on the impact the Japanese word *fukko* might have on non-Japanese judges. He realized that non-Japanese listeners might not automatically grasp the meaning (a kind of fish), but might merely note *fukko* as another Japanese name or word. As a result, Seigo focused more on the central point, omitting distracting or excessive detail such as the words *fukko* and *promotion*.

Delivery: Mentoring the Learner's Voice

Initially for many students, the classroom seemed to evoke a threatening past, when they were judged negatively if they spoke spontaneously. In presentations, or speaking when called on, I found that many students mumbled or droned, making meaning difficult to follow and listening tedious. They needed to understand their voices as a vehicle for their expression and their personal identity. To make that point, I shared with students what Socrates reputedly said when meeting people for the first time: "Speak so that I can see you!" Because voice is the deep carrier of language (Stengel, 2000) and is consequently central to the process of expressing meaning, I encouraged students to develop their English-speaking voice by speaking in class and in public events and to enjoy doing so.

I found lessons to be learned from voice therapy where therapists work one-on-one with clients. A degree of transparency is needed between the therapist and client, and the client must engage of his own will (Stengel, 2000). My students needed to develop vocal self-esteem. I thought it might best be achieved through individual mentoring following these three steps:

- The student read the speech out loud as the mentor listened and took notes.

- The mentor read the speech out loud and students chose to make notes or transcribe the mentor's version.

- Phonological comparisons were made and differences, including arbitrary changes such as intonation, and fixed-word stress, were discussed.

I discovered that for some of my students, writing had contained an element of threat, perhaps because of past experiences. Once drafts were completed, students expressed relief as they shifted to delivery practice. English was largely limited to the classroom and, for many students, used only when teachers called on them to speak. The speech process, however, necessarily demanded interaction in English and a focus on phonology.

Stress and intonation based on emotion was often a new concept for students. Most contestants initially tended to chant their speeches. In fact, *sound meaning* is part of a deep approach to speaking, and focusing on sound in mentoring sessions appeared to be liberating for students. This was particularly significant for so-called weak students who found that they could make accurate and appealing sounds. I offered my students a recording of my version of their speech as a resource, with the understanding that a speech is the expression of the student's voice. They were free to copy me or not. Students gave feedback after the process. Following are some examples:

- I changed to take care of my voice better than before.

- I improved my speaking because I could say what I wanted to say.

- I don't know if my speaking improved, but I tried to speak so that audiences could hear my voice.

- The speech project improved my speaking. Because I talked of my experience such as Subjective and Objective to everyone in the room. I could tell my opinion more than before.

Rehearsal

A week before the performance, the hall was open for students to practice together. The hall was for celebratory events and created a special atmosphere. The president of the university would attend the event.

The normal Japanese hierarchy based on students' English proficiency, age, and experience was abandoned because all the students keenly observed and critiqued one another. The work of previous weeks crystallized, and transformations took place as students honed their speeches. Students used a podium and microphones, practicing turning and making eye contact around the hall while using body language and projecting their voices. Peers and mentors spread around the hall to give speakers focal points for eye contact.

Mentors observed from various positions to gain different perspectives. I took comprehensive notes, explained them, and usually demonstrated the speech. Then, I asked students to compare both performances. They practiced again to incorporate desired changes. The process took about 20 minutes for each participant. Despite a common view that last-minute changes are confusing, our students were able to incorporate them because they had not programmed themselves to rigid memorization.

When there was a rhythm problem, I would transcribe the stress on the board, mark time with a pen, or have the student move in time with the phrases for the kinesthetic element to assist retention. In addition, I found a useful and student-friendly book with a teacher's guide that graphically shows good posture and other performance skills (Le Beau & Harrington, 1998).

As a result of the nonthreatening, cooperative environment and the sense of time being maximized, energy became focused on the task at hand. A student who felt threatened by the cavernous room full of people removed his contact lenses; as the faces blurred, his fear dissolved. The activity connected to a real-life event, and the enjoyment was palpable. These are all hallmarks of deep approaches (Ramsden, 2003).

The Performance

However much time students spend on preparation, the quality of final performances is an unknown. In keeping with a deep approach, I did not require memorization. The all-or-nothing nature of memorization limits the scope for learning and renders it a less useful skill in real life. I believe the problem-solving approach of recovering from a memory slip is more valuable.

My students worked from a copy of their texts typed in 18-point font. They had been taught to move their index fingers down each side as they spoke. The focus of such practice was on ownership of the speech (also see the Chernen chapter in this volume) and the ability to mold it in the moment, skills that could be recycled for academic presentations.

REFLECTIONS

I believe that speeches provide students with an opportunity to apply deep approaches to learning language and content. The process hinges on engagement. From the pedagogical standpoint of mentoring, once a student has decided to engage he is more likely to succeed because he seeks out the assistance that he feels necessary to develop skills for improved learning.

Are most students willing to engage in deep approaches? What distinguishes speech work from other kinds of study is the intrinsic motivation of participants, involving the learner's self, his choice, his will, and his voice. Intrinsic versus extrinsic parallels the essence of deep compared with surface approaches. The outcome for those I mentored was that they invested in their topics so that they discussed them in depth, saw them from different angles, and used English as a vehicle for their authentic expression. One student described his intrinsic motivation: "If I have to find my own direction, writing makes me think more. I notice the sense of judgment in myself rather than the teacher." This is an indication of the student's metacognitive awareness that through process writing, he was able to assess his own work rather than depend on a teacher's judgment.

Former speech performers tended to be more at ease with oral English in class and to sign up for public events. As evidence of the deeper bonds mentoring creates between teachers and students, performers often returned to the same mentor with different endeavors until graduation and even afterwards. A graduate reflecting back on her speech 4 years earlier commented:

> The speech process was totally different. It was a creating job. When class required me to do assignments, I wrote about what the professor wanted, but the speech I wrote about was what I wanted to deliver. Doing assignments is not pleasant, just required. Speeches are voluntary, from my heart, more smoothly and easily. The quality was better too because I seriously thought about it. Assignments, I just had to do them. I didn't think about how I can persuade my professors better, but audiences are diverse, so I thought about it seriously.

English Speeches in Other Contexts

The English speech process described here may be adapted to contexts other than the conventional speech contest. For instance, I set shorter 300-word speeches for students with an option of extending the length to the conventional 450–500 words. Students of higher proficiency took that option. Additionally, some classes held exhibitions rather than contests. There were other competitions in which I taught the students criteria for judging and they collectively acted as judges. In some cases, the students voted on whether to hold competitions or exhibitions.

The logistics of in-class projects did not allow for sustained individual mentoring for all students. Since I was the class teacher, however, there tended to be a trusting rapport, and students willingly engaged in the task, worked cooperatively, and generated considerable enthusiasm. The clear outcome was that students who had previously written and performed speeches were more proficient, adhering better to academic norms, structuring their discourse better, and delivering their speeches more naturally and appealingly.

Constraints

There are constraints to mentoring. Importantly, mentors and students must find the necessary time. While teachers are able to make informed professional choices as to how to manage their time in school, it is harder for students to perceive the value of a process they may not previously have engaged in. I have occasionally been perceived as "too keen" by some students and have learned to accept the fact that only students with the will to engage will be able to benefit from speaking in depth.

For committed instructors, mentoring requires specialized skills to enable a developmental relationship that provides information, support, and challenge as the conditions for facilitating reflective dialogue (Brockbank & McGill, 2000). Having studied and practiced mentoring techniques for some years, it remains a challenge for me to hold back and listen as objectively as possible. There is a delicate balance between patience and realizing the moment when students need to be nudged forwards with a question or a comment or granted time to think quietly. It is also a challenge to provide students with no more and no less than they need, regardless of my inclination to talk or teach.

Conclusion

My view is that not only does teaching for deep approaches facilitate students' academic development, it may affect the teacher positively too. The need exists for teachers to provide students with the opportunities to approach their learning in depth (Ramsden, 2003). At the same time, recognition of deep approaches dignifies the efforts of teachers who believe that their students can go further. One of our graduates confirmed that view, asserting, "The only time I ever said what I really wanted from a public platform was when I delivered my speech!"

Amanda Bradley has degrees from the University of Toulouse, in France, and the School for International Training, in the United States. She teaches English in Japan and has the good fortune to be able to invite students to say what they think on stage, through their English speeches.

CHAPTER 12

PowerPoint or Posters for EAP Students' Presentation Skills Development?

Caroline Brandt

INTRODUCTION

The research project that informs this chapter developed as a result of 23 years of teaching English for academic purposes (EAP) or English for specific purposes (ESP) in several different countries. Most recently, I have taught ESP at the University of Bahrain and the University of Brunei, and I am currently teaching academic communication skills to engineering undergraduates at the Petroleum Institute in Abu Dhabi, in the United Arab Emirates. Over the years, I have struggled to satisfy recipient lecturers by developing in my English as a second language (ESL) students the communication skills lecturers expect and need their students to have upon entry to their courses. My uncertainty about the match between my practice as an EAP and ESP tutor[1] over the years vis-à-vis subject lecturers' expectations eventually led to a qualitative research project in which lecturers' expectations of their ESL students were compared with the practice of tutors of EAP and ESP. I set out to answer the following questions: What skills do lecturers in various disciplines expect 1st-year university students to have, and why do they expect them to have these skills? What skills do EAP and ESP tutors teach, and why do they think these skills are important?

One set of outcomes related to the development of students' academic oral communication skills. In particular, I found that while EAP tutors tend to

---

[1] For convenience, those teaching EAP or ESP are referred to as *tutors*, and those teaching other subjects are referred to as *lecturers*. In practice, however, this distinction was not always maintained in the data. When referring to both groups, the term *faculty* is used.

prioritize the development of presentation skills over other academic speaking skills, many lecturers value the skills required to engage in academic discussion over those needed for public speaking, a finding supported by Kehe and Kehe (1996, p. 110) in their investigation into the expectations that university professors in the United States have of 1st-year students from overseas. Although other research, also conducted in the United States, has suggested that the requirement for undergraduates to give formal presentations as part of their major courses varies significantly from discipline to discipline and is not as common as is generally believed (Ferris & Tagg, 1996b, p. 301), I found that most students in international contexts can currently expect to give a formal presentation at some point in most undergraduate courses. This expectation is qualified by the fact that team-based presentations appear to be required far more often than individual presentations, however (Ferris & Tagg, 1996a, p. 49).

My study further suggested several issues specifically related to student use of presentation software programs such as Microsoft PowerPoint. For example, faculty observed that PowerPoint can have a negative, reductive effect on presentation content. They also noted that it can be difficult to discern students' levels of understanding of their material and their purposes, as students frequently deliver rehearsed and memorized monologues that may reflect a superficial grasp of the content of their presentation (see the Bradley chapter in this volume for more on this point).

Two difficulties emerge with the current situation. First, EAP tutors may be assigning undue emphasis to the development of formal presentation skills in their courses. Second, the situation is compounded by the expectation that students will employ an aid that makes it more difficult for them to participate in dialogue and the in-depth exploration of content through discussion. Therefore, an opportunity is missed to develop the very oral communication skills recipient lecturers value most highly.

This chapter explores and addresses such issues. By comparing students' use of PowerPoint with their use of posters as presentations aids, I will suggest that PowerPoint suits some presentation purposes better than others. These purposes relate in particular to a need to persuade or impress members of an audience. I contend that PowerPoint may not be ideally suited to an academic context where the aim is to develop students' ability to think critically and to participate confidently in spoken academic discourse. In this regard, I believe that poster presentations have greater potential because they lend themselves to discussing, sharing, and generating ideas. My overall recommendation is that EAP tutors should devote more time to developing the skills required to give effective poster presentations, rather than solely focusing instruction on the basics of making PowerPoint-based presentations.

Specifically, I will draw attention to key features of the two presentation aids, show how these features are affected by the choice of presentation aid, and discuss their implications for students. I will conclude by suggesting that ESL students need to be able to use *both* presentation aids effectively, and that awareness of these features in relation to each aid can enable them to do this.

CONTEXT

Research Base

To answer the research questions regarding the skills that lecturers expect 1st-year students to have and the skills that EAP/ESP tutors teach, I collected data over 4 years on 24 different courses at nine tertiary institutions in countries that included Indonesia, Australia, Bahrain, and the United Kingdom. Participants included 16 subject lecturers in the disciplines of law, humanities, social studies, and science, and 20 EAP tutors who were teaching on presessional or in-sessional EAP or ESP courses. Faculty were asked to complete a questionnaire of 24 open-ended questions (see Appendix A) plus questions aimed at gathering demographic data. The assumed proficiency level was students at or approaching a score of 5 or above in the International English Language Testing System (IELTS), run by the University of Cambridge ESOL Examinations in conjunction with the British Council. Respondents were asked to consider the needs of such students. The IELTS "measures ability to communicate in English across all four language skills—listening, reading, writing, and speaking—for people who intend to study or work where English is the language of communication" (IELTS, 2008).

Qualitative techniques, involving searching for themes within collated responses (Denzin & Lincoln, 1998; Miles & Huberman, 1994; Strauss & Corbin, 1990), helped me to identify consistencies or differences within the data. Having coded all data received to ensure anonymity, I adopted a five-stage approach to analysis that involved:

1. developing two data books, one for each set of data, that is, collating all responses to the same questions

2. collating responses to similar or related questions from the two sets of data

3. annotating all collated raw data in relation to the research questions

4. identifying recurring themes within annotations and grouping the annotations into those themes

5. identifying consistencies, differences, or issues within themes, labeled "issues" at this stage.

I subsequently sought written responses to these issues from faculty drawn from both groups who had not been involved in the first phase of the research. Analysis of these new data enabled me to substantiate and refine the preliminary issues. At this stage a small number were rejected, as they were poorly substantiated by the second phase, and others were modified or developed to take account of the new data. These two phases led to the identification of 25 outcomes, subsequently organized into seven themes for further discussion and investigation. I have selected seven key outcomes for discussion here, arranged into two broad topics: The role of student presentations in undergraduate courses (Table 1) and Students' use of presentation software programs (Table 2).

Issues in EAP Students' Presentation Skills Development

The seven outcomes were categorized into two broad areas: the role of student presentations in undergraduate courses, and students' use of a presentation software program. Four issues relating to the role of student presentations in undergraduate courses are provided in Table 1. The three outcomes in relation to students' use of presentation software are presented in Table 2.

Outcome 1.1 indicated that lecturers value highly students' abilities to engage in academic debate but tend to find that students' skills are less developed in this area. For example, a lecturer in Bahrain noted:

> While students need to be able to present, I think the skills required to argue a side, and support a view, give evidence and so forth, are more important but generally overlooked, both in writing and speaking. I find I have to spend quite a lot of time with them on this, to the extent even of sometimes having to explain what an academic argument is.

Outcomes 1.2 and 1.4, however, suggest that the emphasis on EAP and ESP courses tends to be on giving assessed presentations. Although all EAP and ESP courses aimed at developing students' oral communication skills required them to present and allocated time to develop associated skills, only two specifically mentioned a need to develop the skills required to engage in academic discussion or debate.

Outcome 1.3 indicates that students are rarely required in discipline-area courses to give individual presentations, and this approach creates a number of difficulties. For example, one tutor in Australia, writing about her Chinese students in an EAP course, observed that, ". . . they rush through a memorized speech, to get it over with. The relief is palpable when they hand over to a colleague . . . . I always have trouble making a judgement." The tendency to give a memorized speech appeared to be more common among students of educational backgrounds that emphasized the development of writing over speaking skills.

Outcome 2.1 suggests that students may use PowerPoint unreflectively. For example, a tutor in the United Kingdom noted that, "students mostly fail to consider alternatives to giving a PowerPoint presentation. . . . It's become the default [presentation aid]," and, according to a tutor in Bahrain, "PowerPoint looks the part. But students seem to think that because their slides look good, they will do well. They forget that there's far more to a good presentation than slides."

Outcomes 2.2 and 2.3 indicate that PowerPoint may be best suited to situ-

Table 1. The Role of Student Presentations in Undergraduate Courses

Outcome Number	Outcome Summary	Commentary
1.1	**Lecturers value the skills required to engage effectively in academic debate more than those required to present, and tutors tend to prioritize presentation skills.**	Lecturers value both presentation and academic debating skills, but, perhaps because students' presentation skills tend to be well developed, they emphasized that academic debating skills were more highly valued.
1.2	**Student presentations are standard pedagogical practice in higher education in many parts of the world.**	The requirement for 1st-year students to give oral presentations is standard practice in EAP and ESP courses and in many subject courses.
1.3	**Team-based presentations are required significantly more often than individual presentations but pose a number of difficulties.**	Problems include uneven student contribution and difficulty assessing individual performance, in particular when students' contributions are brief.
1.4	**Student presentations can carry high stakes in terms of summative assessment, but not all faculty find assessment of presentations straightforward.**	Assessment difficulty included: • brevity of presentation, leading to difficulty discerning students' levels of understanding of material • assessing fairly all required components (e.g., content, verbal and nonverbal communication, organization, visual aids, timing, pace, teamwork) in the limited time

ations in which communication is viewed as unidirectional and as a means of transferring or transmitting meaning. Tutors described finding that students cope poorly with interruptions and with questions, partly because they concentrate on performance and delivery rather than communication. This observation is in accord with an expert-led, *transfer* view of teaching and learning, and it suggests a monologic view of communication (also see the Hoa chapter in this volume). Monologue, of course, has its uses, but there are consequences:

> A person employing monologue seeks to command, coerce, manipulate, conquer, dazzle, deceive, or exploit. Other persons are viewed as "things" to be exploited solely for the communicator's self-serving purpose: they are not taken seriously as persons. Choices are narrowed and consequences are obscured. Focus is on the communicator's message, not on the audience's real needs. The core values, goals, and policies espoused by the communicator are impervious to influence exerted by receivers. Audience feedback is used only to further the communicator's purpose. An honest response from a receiver is not wanted or is precluded. (Johannesen, 1996, p. 69)

Table 2. Students' Use of Presentation Software Programs

Outcome Number	Outcome Summary	Commentary
2.1	**Students use a presentation software program as a matter of course, although they are rarely instructed to do so.**	• Alternative presentation aids tend not to be considered. • There appears to be an assumption that PowerPoint is best.
2.2	**PowerPoint can detrimentally affect the content and delivery of presentations.**	Concerns included: • the effect of students' use of PowerPoint on presentation content and delivery, which faculty described as "reductive" and "inflexible" • the tendency of students to give a polished, practiced performance, which may not reflect understanding of the material
2.3	**The use of PowerPoint may have a negative effect on student audiences.**	Student audiences may: • be passive and can show a tendency to disengage, particularly after finishing their own presentation • find it difficult to seek clarification when a point is not fully understood

How often do we expect our students to "command," "conquer," "deceive," or "exploit" in our academic contexts? How can the development of monologic skills help our students to learn essential skills for success in higher education? It is worth considering why EAP tutors aim to develop students' presentation skills and why the use of PowerPoint has become standard practice.

CURRICULUM, TASKS, MATERIALS

Why Do EAP Courses Address Presentation Skills?

In recent years, conceptions of learning have shifted from the *transfer* of knowledge approach referred to above, toward a more exploratory, or *transformational* approach. A transformational approach has a number of characteristics: It builds on existing knowledge, allows for different learning styles, provides opportunities for problem-solving, encourages autonomy, and is reflective (Tusting & Barton, 2003, pp. 34–36). Social interaction is believed to construct and transform processes because dialogue and discussion underpin collaborative enquiry. A collaborative, experiential approach to learning (through team-based research projects, for example) creates an educational environment in which transformational processes can thrive. An emphasis on collaboration makes particular demands upon students' oral communication skills, and presentations offer ideal opportunities for students to articulate their understanding of their work. This shift toward a more transformational approach to education has taken place within a context of rapid technological developments that have led to the widespread availability of slide-ware such as PowerPoint. Its availability, ease of use, and professional appearance have led to this software being viewed as a prerequisite to creating good presentations and to a consequent need for students to develop skills required to use it effectively.

It could be, however, that PowerPoint suits some purposes better than others. With this in mind, I decided to examine alternatives to PowerPoint for EAP and ESP students and began a classroom-based study of students using an alternative aid for academic presentations.

Changing Practice: Poster Presentations

In consultation with a group of students, I decided to conduct a study on the adoption of poster presentations into a course. After all of my research and classroom experience, I wanted to test my instinct that the visual aid of posters had the potential to address a significant number of the outcomes discussed in the previous section. For example, I suspected that a presentation supported by posters could provide an environment in which dialogue and discussion were more likely to take place, thereby allowing for more transformational learning processes.

> A poster presentation may be defined as the kind of presentation which: [C]ombines text and graphics to make a visually-pleasing presentation. Typically, a professional poster involves showing your work to numerous researchers at a conference or seminar . . . as viewers walk by, your poster should quickly and efficiently communicate your research. Unlike the fast pace of a slide show or verbal presentation, a Poster Session allows viewers to study and restudy your information and discuss it with you one-on-one. (Kiefer, Palmquist, Barnes, Levine, & Zimmerman, 2008)

I conducted this study at an English-medium national university in Southeast Asia during one semester in 2005–2006. The study involved 20 students enrolled in English for Business 3, the third of a four-level required course in English language. All students achieved an IELTS score of 5 or above during the semester following my study. The aims I set for the course emphasized the development of research skills and academic oral and literacy skills. Assessed coursework required students to summarize a journal article related to their area of study and to give an individual presentation of their summary. All students had prior experience doing class presentations with PowerPoint, both individually and as part of a team.

I asked the 20 students to give poster presentations of their article summaries, document their experience, and provide oral and written feedback. Written feedback included a reflective piece of writing in which they were asked to compare their experience of giving presentations using PowerPoint with those using posters. I also sought written feedback from faculty who visited the poster displays. These data were analyzed by the same qualitative processes employed in the primary questionnaire research.

Poster Presentations in Action

For various reasons connected with the availability of information technology resources at this university, the students in the study prepared their posters by hand, which is one option. To ensure a professional appearance, however, posters can be prepared with the aid of software packages such as Adobe Illustrator (http://www.adobe.com/products/illustrator/) or Photoshop (http://www .adobe.com/products/photoshop/index.html), among others. Posters can also be prepared in Microsoft PowerPoint by selecting a single blank slide layout and resizing the page as needed. An excellent example of a poster prepared using PowerPoint, on the relevant topic of "Poster Presentations: Theory and Application," is available on the Internet (Silva, 2006), as is a PowerPoint template that can be adapted for use (see Purrington, 2006).

Posters are ideally suited to the presentation of information that is best conveyed visually, such as tables, charts, or graphs. I learned that they are also suitable for conveying the content of a journal article, however, providing students adopt certain guidelines and standards. The guidelines in Table 3 were developed in conjunction with the students involved in the study.

The students' experience during the previous semester gave them some familiarity with several of these standards in relation to giving PowerPoint presentations (e.g., nos. 1, 7, 14, 16, and 18). Despite this background, however, I found that they did not transfer these standards automatically from one aid to another. This may owe to the dissimilarity between the two aids and the students' initial assumptions that poster preparation simply involved cutting up text, pasting the pieces onto a large sheet, and adding some decoration. I found that my students needed guidance and training to ensure that the standards were met. It is important not to underestimate the time required for this or the value of the process in the development of skills.

Poster Presentations: Responding to the Research Outcomes

Poster presentations addressed the concerns expressed in the initial research questionnaire outcomes (Tables 1 and 2) very successfully. The results were that posters:

- allowed students to convey the richness of their work by engaging with the topic through dialogue (responding to outcome 1.1)

- helped to ensure an even distribution of the work among team members, in part because faculty were able to ensure the adequate participation of all students in delivery (responding to outcome 1.3)

Table 3. Poster Presentation Guidelines

Preparation

1. Consider the audience and their needs before you begin.

2. Prepare a written article summary *before* beginning to design the poster.

3. Study examples of posters that meet the criteria described in guidelines 8–19 below. Many are available on the Internet (see Appendix B).

4. Plan in rough on A3 paper.

5. Proofread and edit. Print a scaled-down A4 version of the poster to do this. If you cannot read it, it will be too small for your poster, and you need to adjust the font size.

6. Ask others to evaluate the poster according to the criteria presented here, and revise it accordingly.

7. Rehearse with a willing friend several times before giving the presentation.

Layout

8. All posters need a title. This should be readable from 4–5 meters away. Include the name and affiliation of the author or authors here.

9. Use appropriate headings, such as "Introduction," "Research Question," "Literature Review," etc. Headings should provide a good overview of the content.

10. Use a hierarchy of size to reflect the relative importance of the content of poster sections.

11. Organize the poster into columns. Ensure the eye is guided to move from top to bottom and left to right.

12. Use devices such as color and arrows to guide the reader logically to key points.

13. Use color and font consistently throughout, including in tables and charts, and ensure that all visuals are readable at a distance of up to 1.5 meters. A minimum font size of 22 points with double spacing is recommended.

14. Use white space to relieve the eye, avoiding overly complex and dense information.

15. Avoid decoration for its own sake.

Content

16. Use bullet points and succinct language in phrases, not sentences.

17. Omit anything that is superfluous to your message.

18. Avoid too many details—these should be provided in discussion.

19. Avoid using too many citations, and remember to include references for any work you cite.

Delivery

20. Support a poster presentation with a handout that includes contact details.

21. Allow viewers to guide the discussion. Do not give a memorized speech, and do not read a poster.

22. Face the audience. Make eye contact, but look from time to time at your poster. This encourages viewers to do the same, and guides their vision.

- provided adequate assessment opportunities for faculty who could engage in discussion with a team member (responding to outcomes 1.3, 1.4, and 2.2)

- provided students with a wider range of possible aids for future presentations (responding to outcome 2.1)

- allowed for interactive, flexible delivery, responsive to audience needs (responding to outcome 2.2)

- placed peers into more active roles, allowing them to seek clarification as needed (responding to outcome 2.3) (also see the Carduner & Rilling chapter in this volume)

As well as considering posters as presentation aids in relation to the preliminary research outlined above, the second study allowed for a comparison between students' use of PowerPoint and their use of posters.

PowerPoint or Poster? A Comparison

Analysis of data gathered during the classroom-based study suggested nine features of presentation aids that faculty and students should consider. These are discussed below.

Feature 1: Purpose

PowerPoint may best be used when the presenter's purpose is to exert influence over the audience as suggested in the previous quotation from Johannesen (1996, p. 69). In an academic context, examples might include monologue-style presentations such as those for research proposals focused on persuasion. On the other hand, if the aim is to inform, as in the presentation of a research report, a poster presentation may be more effective because it allows greater opportunity for audience members to participate. This suggests that students will benefit from awareness of the need to match their choice of presentation aid more closely to its purpose.

Feature 2: Focus

PowerPoint presentations focus attention on the presenter and the slides, that is, on the technical means for formal academic communication. Poster presentations, which allow for audience control and participation, focus more on the message and the efficacy of communication, and may therefore be described as communication-centered. One student participant in the second study recognized this difference:

> I like how with a poster presentation that I am less the center of attention [than when giving a presentation using PowerPoint]. I can relax and concentrate on sharing my ideas.

Students, therefore, need to develop both the technical competence required to give effective presentations using different aids as well as the skills to participate in communicative relationships.

Feature 3: Content

Presenters who use posters are more able to respond to audience needs, adjusting content *in situ* according to feedback. This is a tailored approach and contrasts with a PowerPoint presentation, which allows for little response and represents a one-size-fits-all design because it is prepared in advance, as these students noted:

- I could be certain that the people I was talking to understood what I was saying. I knew they would ask me if anything wasn't clear to them.

- I was able to select what I felt it was important to say at the time in relation to the lecturer [I was addressing].

While oral skills are emphasized in PowerPoint presentations, students need to develop both listening and speaking skills equally to give effective poster presentations.

Feature 4: Understanding

Students observed that when attending a PowerPoint presentation, they had little or no influence over its delivery. If they failed to understand something as it was presented, they were usually expected to wait until the end before being able to seek clarification. Some noted that once understanding had broken down, it sometimes became difficult to follow the remainder of the presentation. This situation was less likely to arise while attending poster presentations because students felt able to seek clarification as the need arose. Students, as members of the audience of PowerPoint presentations, need to develop the ability to delay seeking clarification while continuing to engage with the presentation. With poster presentations, on the other hand, they need to learn how to seek clarification, or respond to a request for clarification that occurs during a presentation.

Feature 5: Audience Engagement

While PowerPoint presentations may be monologic, providing an opportunity for one person to speak at length, poster presentations provide opportunities for other voices to be heard through dialogue. Such dialogic communication offers possibilities that are altogether more dynamic, making listening skills more essential. Students observed that while attending PowerPoint presentations it was possible to stop listening.

> I can day dream in a PowerPoint presentation. It's impossible in a poster presentation. But if you did, you can ask for a repeat. You can't do that with [a] PowerPoint [presentation].

It may be that poster presentations are a more productive use of students' time because both presenter and audience can develop and practice speaking and listening skills during the event.

Feature 6: Preparation

The design of PowerPoint presentations is more likely to be linear and logical, and constrained by the software's templates. It may be that designing poster presentations encourages creativity, experimentation, and nonlinear thinking as students work toward what they know will be an entirely unique product. For example, this student observed,

> When I made a PowerPoint presentation, I took the main points of my work and organized them step by step using the template. But when I put my poster together, I added notes and points around the main points like a mind-map and I used pictures and cartoons. I could experiment more with ideas and it's easier to involve others and use their ideas too.

It might be the case that the two presentation aids suit different project types, with posters perhaps being more suitable for team presentations.

Feature 7: Display Time

The display time of a PowerPoint presentation is normally brief, and students in the audience need to adopt a range of strategies to maximize their engagement with content presented in this linear way, including repairing any breakdown in understanding. Poster presentations, on the other hand, have the dual benefits of visibility (i.e., the entire poster is visible at one time) and durability (i.e., posters can be displayed for a significant length of time, and may remain on display after the event). Viewers can revisit the presentation at will, both during the event and later. This feature provides opportunities to reinforce learning, and it also benefits assessor–tutors, who may find it easier to evaluate the work.

Feature 8: Formality

A PowerPoint-based presentation is essentially a formal event: Latecomers and early leavers are unwelcome, and audience silence is the norm. The audience is expected to be deferential, reflecting a view of the presenter as authoritative expert, in accord with a knowledge-transfer approach to learning. In such an approach, presenters may not appear open to alternative ideas and may resist challenges from the audience.

The presenter of a poster presentation engages in dialogue and, therefore, is more likely to participate in the exchange and development of ideas. This dialogue creates a more balanced and democratic learning environment. The opportunity for critical reflection is also more likely to arise, prompted by others' questions and observations.

Feature 9: Audience Control

Poster presentations offer greater flexibility in terms of audience attendance. While the audience of a PowerPoint presentation is established for the duration and dependent upon the presenter, the audience of a poster presentation is free to come and go at will, taking into account their level of interest in the topic and their available time. Fewer options are open to the audience of a PowerPoint presentation. Audience members are restricted to a passive role; students in the audience are expected to listen, take notes, and ask questions publicly, if desired, at the end. Poster presentation audiences, on the other hand, are likely to be more active and are able to discuss issues with a greater degree of privacy. Audience members are also able to take on different roles, such as that of questioner, devil's advocate, eavesdropper, or contributor. Role-play activities designed by tutors could enhance students' awareness of these different roles and help them develop related skills.

Students who are aware of these nine features and how they are affected by their selection of a presentation aid will be better equipped to identify the best aid for their particular topic and purpose, and to use it effectively.

REFLECTIONS

PowerPoint may be an effective aid when the presenter's purpose is to persuade or impress. It can facilitate the transmission of knowledge and the unquestioning acceptance of assumptions, and as such is consistent with a transfer view of learning. Also, students and professionals entering the workplace are expected to demonstrate proficiency with PowerPoint. As this expectation is likely to remain for the foreseeable future, students will need to develop the skills for effective PowerPoint use. Taking this reality into account, ESOL instructors may be able to develop a more interactive approach to presentation delivery using PowerPoint, suggesting opportunities for further research.

PowerPoint may not be ideally suited to an academic context where the aim is to develop students' ability to think critically and to participate confidently in spoken academic discourse, however. To meet such aims, poster presentations appear to have greater potential because they lend themselves to discussing, sharing, and generating ideas. They can facilitate collaborative knowledge generation by allowing for the recognition and testing of assumptions within supportive contexts. In addition, they can generate useful feedback on the success or failure of communication, as well as on the content of the exchange, and they allow participants to influence its direction. Based on these observations, I suggest that some of the time EAP tutors currently devote to training students in the use of PowerPoint needs to be redirected towards developing the skills required to give good poster presentations. For example, the preliminary data in my study indicated that in some general EAP courses, up to 20% of course time was devoted to training students in the use of PowerPoint. For such courses, my suggestion is to divide the time equally between PowerPoint and poster presentations. My feeling is that the skills required for the effective use of presentation software programs and posters complement one another. Appendix B provides an annotated list of useful links for teachers interested in learning more about using poster presentations in lessons.

Poster presentations demand active participation in a communicative relationship in the form of interaction between presenter and audience (see the Carduner & Rilling chapter in this volume for more on this point). The audience at a poster display is a willing one, able to take on a number of possible roles. That is to say that poster presentations support a transformational, democratic approach to learning in which both presenter and audience are viewed as equals who are able to learn from each other during the course of the event. The process can allow for and encourage critical reflection, the negotiation of meaning, the seeking and giving of clarification, and the development of understanding. These are all essential skills for students in higher education contexts to develop as they learn to articulate complex ideas that may not comfortably be reduced to a bullet point.

Caroline Brandt is currently an assistant professor at the Petroleum Institute, in Abu Dhabi, United Arab Emirates, where she teaches communication skills to engineering undergraduates through research projects. She is the author of Read, Research and Write: Academic Skills for ESL Students in Higher Education *(London: Sage Publications, 2008).*

APPENDIX A: RESEARCH INSTRUMENT SAMPLE

Section 2: Your Classroom Practice

In answering the questions below, please relate your responses to one group of EAP or ESP students in your current context. Please consider only those students with IELTS Level 5 or its equivalent, or whom you consider capable of achieving this level of proficiency during your course.

Your Students

2.1 EAP and ESP are characterized by an emphasis on students' needs and purposes. How are your students' needs identified at your institution, and who is involved in the process?

2.2 Generally speaking, at the start of your course, what do you consider to be your students' strengths and weaknesses in relation to the skills they need to study their chosen discipline?

Your Course

2.3 Which aspect of your course do you consider to be most successful in terms of addressing your students' needs, and why?

2.4 What do lecturers who receive your students say about your course? What is their attitude toward it?

Your Teaching

2.5 How would you characterize your philosophy–approach to teaching EAP and ESP?

2.6 How does teaching EAP and ESP differ from teaching general English? What areas do you address that would not be addressed in a general English course?

Your Materials

2.7 Who selects the teaching materials you use?

2.8 How satisfied are you with the materials you are currently using? Would you make any changes to them, and if so, in what way?

APPENDIX B: USEFUL LINKS FOR POSTER PRESENTATIONS

Hess, G. R. (2004). Effective scientific posters: Quick reference.

http://www.ncsu.edu/project/posters/NewSite/documents/QuickReferenceV2.pdf

A list of useful resources for poster presenters as well as brief tips for giving an effective poster presentation.

Hess, G. R. Tosney, K., & Liegel, L. (2006). Creating effective poster presentations.

http://www.ncsu.edu/project/posters

A detailed guide to creating effective poster presentations, with advice for preparation and delivery, examples of posters, and links to useful resources.

Kiefer, K., Palmquist, M., Barnes, L., Levine, M., & Zimmerman, D. (1993–2008). Writing guides: Poster sessions.

http://writing.colostate.edu/guides/speaking/poster/index.cfm

A comprehensive guide to all aspects of poster presentation preparation and delivery. Includes information on areas such as the different types of posters (pin up, table top, and floor), and offers suggestions for transporting and assembling posters, with examples and links to further resources.

Purrington, C. B. (2006). Advice on designing scientific posters.

http://www.swarthmore.edu/NatSci/cpurrin1/posteradvice.htm

An amusing, more personal overview of good poster presentation practice, including a long list of common mistakes to avoid and recommendations for further reading.

Silva, D. J. (2006). Poster presentations: Theory and application.

    http://ling.uta.edu/~lingua/utascil/2007/PosterPresentations.ppt

    A poster, prepared in PowerPoint that effectively illustrates good practice in poster preparation.

Tosney, K. (n.d.) How to create a poster that graphically communicates your message.

    http://www.bio.miami.edu/ktosney/file/PosterHome.html

    This site provides useful advice on a range of aspects of poster presentations, including examples of good and bad practice for purposes of comparison.

Focus on Feedback & Assessment

CHAPTER 13

The Speaking Log: A Tool for Posttask Feedback

Tony Lynch

INTRODUCTION

The speaking log is a learning and teaching tool that helps language learners to analyze their spoken English and get feedback from others. Its conception, design, and use draw on two principal strands of second-language (L2) acquisition theory. The first is the distinction, originally suggested by Corder (1967), between *slips*—mistakes that a learner is able to identify and correct—and *errors*, systematic mistakes reflecting the learner's current L2 competence, which will require another's help to correct. The second strand is part of the sociocultural theory of learning and draws in particular on research into collaborative work to encourage noticing (e.g., Swain, 1998).

CONTEXT

The teaching context in which the speaking log was conceived and developed is a presessional English for Academic Purpose (EAP) program at the Institute for Applied Language Studies at the University of Edinburgh, Scotland (for details, visit http://www.ials.ed.ac.uk/EL/English-Academic/GeneralEAP.htm). The majority of the 120 students attending the program are graduates preparing for entry into masters courses, others are about to begin doctoral research, and a few will be starting undergraduate degrees. Typically, about two-thirds will be native speakers of Chinese or Japanese. For virtually all of them, the presessional EAP program is their first experience of studying in a Western academic setting.

CURRICULUM, TASKS, MATERIALS

The presessional program consists of four study blocks of 3–5 weeks each. A student with a relatively low initial English proficiency score according to the International English Language Testing System (IELTS) or Test of English as a

Foreign Language Internet-based test (TOEFL iBT) would take all four blocks, totalling 15 weeks' tuition, aiming to reach the level of IELTS 6.5 or TOEFL iBT 92. Students with higher IELTS or TOEFL scores would attend between one and three blocks. The weekly schedule provides 20 contact hours in classes of up to 14 learners, who can also make 15 hours' further use of self-access facilities—a study room, a video room, and a computer lab—outside of class. The program has been running since 1979 and has undergone substantial curriculum revisions in response to the changes in the student demographic over those three decades (see Lynch, 1996a for details).

In the 1980s, the majority of our EAP students were Arabic speakers whose reading and writing skills tended to be less developed than their oral–aural proficiency skills, so the curriculum was designed to place greater emphasis on written-medium tasks. Rising incomes in Japan beginning in the 1980s, South Korea in the 1990s, and now China, have caused us to adjust the balance between program components to focus more on speaking and listening comprehension, which are often weaker skills among Asian learners of English. The speaking log is one of the tools we have developed in making these adjustments to the learning needs of the students attending our program today; the others include proof-listening (Lynch, 1996b) and self-transcribing (Lynch, 2007).

Over the 15 weeks of the program, the learners engage in a variety of speaking activities: scenarios simulating academic encounters, discussion of academic topics, short prepared talks on their specialty, and formal presentations to the rest of their class (for a detailed discussion of the construction and exploitation of the communication tasks involved, see Anderson, Maclean, & Lynch, 2004).

Technique

The log itself is a simple form and easy to use. It is a sheet of paper divided into three columns—"Slips," "Queries," and "Teacher's Comments"—and is accompanied by step-by-step instructions for use (see Appendix). As they listen to their recording, which could be of any of the speaking tasks mentioned above, the learners notice points they now realize are wrong, which they note and correct under "Slips." This noticing arises from the opportunity to revisit their original attempt at communication and to *reprocess* their output (Swain & Lapkin, 1995). Doing so free of the original pressure to communicate in real time allows the learners to devote more attention to what they said and therefore to monitor and note slips in their English. In addition, when they come across words or structures whose appropriateness or correctness they are unsure about on second hearing, they can write a note to their teacher in the "Queries "column and get a response, as shown in Figure 1.

The student passes the completed log to the teacher, who uses the "Comments" column to confirm (or not) the corrections of "Slips" and to respond to the "Queries." The teacher and student can then discuss the log prior to a follow-up performance.

Slips		Queries	Teacher's Comments
Original	**Correction**		
Temperatures are <u>hotter</u>	*are <u>higher</u>*		*OK*
		Can I say "required <u>many</u> time and labour"?	*A lot of (informal) A great deal of (formal)*

Figure 1. Sample Speaking Log

Students can use the log whenever recording their spoken English. Our audio-recording equipment is basic: 14 small cassette recorders with headphones, set out at seven pairs of tables in a large study room, far enough apart to prevent a pair's interaction interfering with their neighbors' recording. Student are given their own cassette tapes to keep and use at various points during the program, enabling them to record themselves in different spoken genres and then to listen to their spoken English in their own time.

Until now our video recording equipment has been limited to a VHS-C camera, which the teachers have used in some speaking classes (scenarios and presentations) to record paired and individual performances. After the teacher has replayed the video for initial feedback in class (see Lynch, 1996b), the recordings are made available in our self-access video room for review by the learners involved, using the speaking log.

Some examples of students' log entries follow:

Slips (→ speaker's own corrections)

the mechanism of brain → *the mechanism of the brain*

after entered to the university → *after entering the university*

there are three root causes who created that situation → *there are three root causes which created . . .*

even economical data includes in geography → *even economic data is included in geography*

Queries (and teacher's responses)

record the data by <u>human</u> hand?
   (T: record the data <u>manually</u>)

<u>disturbing situation</u>—can I describe water deficiency like that?
   (T: I'd say <u>a cause for concern</u>)

required <u>many</u> time and labour?
   (T: <u>a lot of</u> informal, or <u>a great deal of</u> formal)

> *I think I used <u>grew up</u> too many times!*
> (T: How about <u>rose</u>, <u>increased</u>, or <u>went up</u>?)

> *the temperature <u>arrives at or over</u> 35 degrees in summer*
> (T: <u>reaches at least</u> . . .)

REFLECTIONS

When the speaking log was used for the first time, it was introduced in the third of the four study blocks of our EAP program. To gauge the initial reactions to it, I added an item to the Block 3 evaluation questionnaire asking the students whether they would like to continue using the log in their final block; the response was a unanimous *yes* from the 34 students. Following are some of the comments from anonymous questionnaires completed by individual learners:

- By using speaking logs I could clear my doubts about my English and of course I could recognise my mistakes.

- This is almost the first time for me to review what I said by myself. In addition, the teacher's comments were most useful because it helped me not to repeat similar type of mistakes.

- It helps so much that the Queries space lets me describe what I really wanted to talk, because otherwise I choose the easier simple way and it is often different from what I really want to say.

- The log is improving my English speech by making me analyse my mistakes and trying to avoid them, on the next occasion.

On the other hand, the teachers expressed reservations about the time implications of providing log feedback (also see the Chernen chapter in this volume). In the original procedure, students completed the "Slips" and "Queries" columns and then passed both the log and their cassette to the teacher. For my colleagues, this meant that they had to listen to up to 14 recordings in real time. Here is a sampling of their comments:

- The log seems popular with the students, judging by the number of requests for feedback I've had (!!), but it's added to our marking load.

- Logistical problem: students who forget to leave the cassette in the right place. I spent ages trying to find the starts.

- A good idea, which my group really liked, but at times it was hard to turn round the cassettes fast enough.

The second of those comments, on locating the start of a student's recording, relates to a problem that should be reduced by digital technology, as students will be able to use personal MP3 players and mobile phones to make recordings and download them for the teacher to access (for more ideas and details, also see the Saitoh & Oh, Chartrand, and Yeh chapters in this volume).

Revising the Procedure

Given the very positive reception from learners, I decided to see what could be done to address the teachers' concerns. To reduce the additional load on teachers mentioned in the first comment and implied in the third comment, we changed the log procedure used in the EAP program so that the students now hand in only their completed log, without the cassette. Another modification made to the procedure is that at times when teachers are most heavily involved in grading assignments, the students pass their logs to the program director, who has fewer class contact hours and has more time to process the logs. These changes have been met with the approval of my colleagues who have taught with the program since, with no evident decrease in the level of satisfaction on the part of their students.

A recent further adjustment to the way we use the log—especially relevant to teachers working with classes of learners from different cultures and with different first languages—has been to add an optional second stage of *paired activity*, before the log is passed on to the teacher. Once the individual student has replayed his recording, monitored what he said, and completed the "Slips" and "Queries" columns, he gets another learner (preferably with a different first language) to listen to his recording, read the log, and provide a second opinion, noting additional mistakes and commenting on the queries. This second listener replays the recording and adds notes in the relevant column. Having looked through those comments, the first student decides whether he agrees with the corrections made by the listener before passing the log on to the teacher for further comment. This change has also worked well, perhaps because it involves learners in an extended version of the monitoring, output searching, and checking behavior that is thought likely to enhance proceduralization of L2 speaking skills (Bygate, 1998).

Benefits of Speaking Logs

In short, the log integrates three different perspectives into the provision of feedback on spoken English: self, peer, and teacher. As I have argued elsewhere (Lynch, 1996c), in the absence of firm evidence from L2 acquisition research that any one type of feedback is more effective than others, teachers should attempt to use as many sources as possible. The findings of research into the efficacy of teacher feedback (e.g., Lynch & Maclean, 2003) have shown that the majority of students who received feedback combining self-correction, oral feedback from peers, and written comments from a teacher improved the frequency of correct forms in their subsequent performances in the areas brought to their attention.

Similarly, a comparison of teacher-initiated and student-initiated feedback procedures, also conducted with students on our EAP program, found that the latter led to better retention and production of items highlighted in written feedback (Lynch, 2007).

The advantage of the speaking log is that it allows this synthesis of feedback from different sources and can do so with relatively basic technology. The log procedure also lends itself easily to adoption or adaptation by teachers working in other contexts, with access to more advanced facilities than I have described, such as a language laboratory or digital audio- or video-recording equipment. Clearly, students who are able to record themselves on a mobile phone or other MP3 device will have the added advantage that their recordings will be more portable than they would be on cassette, freeing them to listen and use the log at any convenient time. There is no obvious reason why the speaking log should not be used by learners at any level; beginners, too, can be encouraged to listen and identify mistakes in their L2 performances.

Conclusion

Learners' and teachers' experiences using the speaking log have been very positive. It creates an opportunity for learners to capture, analyze, and reflect on their own speech, which under normal circumstances is fleeting and hard to recall. Our EAP students have valued the chance to review their spoken output in the posttask phase and to self-correct before getting feedback in the form of peer- or teacher-correction. Whatever the recording medium used, the log provides an opportunity for language learners to reflect, to notice, and to learn. That they do so in their own time, at their own pace, and—most important of all—working with their own data, is arguably why the log has proved such a successful part of our EAP program.

Tony Lynch is senior lecturer at the Institute for Applied Language Studies at the University of Edinburgh, in Scotland, where he teaches EAP and master's courses, and supervises classroom-oriented research. He has written books for teachers and learners on spoken communication skills and is now working on Teaching Second Language Listening *(Oxford University Press).*

APPENDIX

How to use the Speaking Log

There are two columns for you to fill in as you listen to your cassette: "Slips" and "Queries."

Slips

Slips are mistakes that you realize are wrong, without anybody having to tell you. Sometimes you can hear something is wrong as soon as you have said it, or when you have the chance to listen to yourself on tape. Write in the "Slips" column both **what was wrong** and also **the correct version**.

Queries

When you're **not sure** that a word or expression is correct, or if you think there must be a **better way** of saying it, then ask the tutor a question about it in the "Queries" column.

Feedback from the Tutor

This final column is for the tutor to complete.

Using the Feedback

When you get the log back, study the tutor's notes and comments carefully. Ask about anything that is not clear. Later, try to use the language items and advice in the column next time you speak English.

CHAPTER 14

Demystifying Presentation Grading Through Student-Created Scoring Rubrics

Jeff Popko

INTRODUCTION

Public speaking is consistently listed as one of the most common phobias. Since first noted in *The Book of Lists* (Wallechinsky, Wallace, & Wallace, 1977), it has ranked among the top 10 anxieties or phobias (Horwitz, 2003; Rapee & Lim, 1992). Within the field of English for speakers of other languages (ESOL), even advanced students can feel intimidated by speaking in front of their peers, a requirement for most academic speaking classes. For example, Ferris (1998) found that 37% of student participants ($n=692$) reported having difficulty with formal speeches often or always. I teach credit-bearing English for academic purposes (EAP) courses at a university in the United States. My ESOL students consistently list classroom presentations as a common form of assessment in their major courses and one assignment they dread. While the assessment activity outlined in this chapter has been used in a variety of courses at various levels, the course I will describe to illustrate the technique, Graduate Seminar in Oral Communication, had an integrated approach that included reading, listening, and speaking.

In the year I conducted this study, six graduate students enrolled in the academic communication course. Graduate programs in other departments of the university had accepted all six students conditionally, pending completion of EAP courses. The method of assessment presented in this chapter addresses one key objective of the course: training students to give formal oral presentations in their content-area courses. This formative assessment allows for preparation, practice, and production of spoken language in a nonthreatening environment. Video recording performances enabled critical analysis, reflective learning, directed feedback, and student input on grading. Recognizing how common public speaking anxiety is and how detrimental it can be to student speaking performance, I created this assessment procedure to calm student fears about classroom presentations. My aim was to encourage ample practice and, more importantly, to demystify the grading process. This assessment process provides students with metacognitive awareness of the process of grading, introduces them to cultural expectations (e.g., eye contact), and helps them prepare and present a better speech or classroom presentation.

The course objective is to help students understand a range of attributes beyond content that makes a class presentation successful. I guide students through the process of picking a topic, narrowing it, outlining a presentation, presenting in front of the class (and the camera), and rating their own and their peers' presentations. Throughout each lesson, I model various aspects of successful presentations.

CONTEXT

International students at my university come from a variety of language backgrounds, primarily from the Middle East, and south and east Asia. The six students reported on in this chapter were enrolled in business administration, engineering quality management, studio art, and hotel and restaurant management programs. The course meets for 4 hours per week and includes the following: regular reading activities (students get a subscription to *Newsweek*), classroom discussions, listening activities based on minilectures in class, podcast assignments, cooperative group work, pair work, and prepared speaking activities. The focus of this chapter is the assessment of the formal speaking assignment, which uses a process approach to walk students through the various stages of creating a formal presentation. In fact, two formal presentations are created, performed in class, and assessed in parallel. The parallel system allows students to receive feedback on the first presentation that they can use to improve their second presentation.

CURRICULUM, TASKS, MATERIALS

The oral presentations were worth approximately one half of the grade in this graduate intensive English program (IEP) course. The two required presentations took roughly half of the 45 hours of instructional time. The process for these presentations was organized into six steps, each of which will be specifically addressed in this section. Students had to:

1. Choose presentation topics early in the semester.

2. Outline their topics.

3. Help the instructor create a rubric for grading their presentations.

4. Practice their presentations in pairs during lessons.

5. Make presentations while being assessed by the audience and video recorded.

6. View the recording and self-assess.

1. Choosing Topics for the Two Presentations

Preparation is crucial to a successful presentation and also to reducing public speaking stress. Therefore, I required the students to prepare early and revise often throughout the course. The general topics for the two presentations were chosen in the first week. Each student had chosen a specific topic for the first presentation by week two and for the second presentation by week three of the course.

One of the problems students reported on the needs analysis at the beginning of the course was that typically the choice of presentation topic is "too open." With little or no direction, they found it difficult to make good topic choices because they did not know how to go about it. One student reported feeling frustrated by information overload after going to the library to find a subject for his business class presentation. Using an online database, he typed in the word *business.* Overwhelmed by the number of references, he decided to use Business in My Country as his topic, but a business professor told him that this was not suitable because it was insufficiently academic in focus. Walking the students through the process of selecting a topic provided an opportunity for me to demonstrate how I organize my own presentations, by considering the audience and context first, picking a broad topic, and then narrowing it based on my own interests and on the research I do.

Topics can be chosen according to the specific course context. Because this course is preparation for graduate school, I required students to choose topics that demanded some sort of research, allowed them to use the target academic vocabulary, and had connections to their reading activity (*Newsweek*). Rather than allowing students to choose freely, I worked with them to help direct their choice of topics. For example, when one student suggested that the whole class present on food, we discussed how academics study food. We considered questions such as, "How could the business administration majors research food?" While there certainly are ways to make food a topic of academic discussion, the students decided that they were not really interested in doing so. The rules of thumb I gave them for a good topic were: (a) It should clearly fit the specific course (e.g., Economics 501 or Physiognomy 501), (b) it should be interesting to the audience, (c) there should be something about the topic that the presenter does not know (and thus needs to research), and (d) it should provide the audience with new information.

Working our way through the topics proposed by the students, we finally settled on a theme that was not really familiar to them, but one that was of interest to everyone. Because it was a political year in the United States, with both the Republican and Democratic national parties choosing presidential candidates, the theme the students chose for their first presentation was U.S. Presidential Candidates. Each student chose a different candidate based on personal interest. Then, they researched the candidate's career (drawing on official Web sites, debates, and news media coverage), examined one issue that was in some way related to their major (for example, our hotel and restaurant management student was interested in the immigration debate), and created a speech detailing the candidate's qualifications to be president of the United States. The theme they chose for the second presentation assignment was My Major in the News. Each student was required to research some aspect of their respective major subject area related to one of the *Newsweek* stories they had read. For example, the hotel and restaurant management student chose to examine the state of tourism in Thailand 1 year after the Indian Ocean tsunami of 2004.

2. Making a Presentation Outline

I asked the students to prepare and speak from an outline, rather than write out a complete speech. I limited the students to using an outline of no more than one page during both the pair practice and the graded presentation. I did this to encourage positive presentation behaviors such as maintaining eye contact with the audience, appearing spontaneous, and avoiding long and complicated quotations from their sources.

In class, students cooperated to create a generic outline for the first presentation by brainstorming what key information to include as subtopics in their speeches. Each student then focused on the subtopics as categories for conducting research on his or her chosen presidential candidate. Students peer-reviewed each other's outlines for the two presentations during class, with group members discussing gaps in the outlines.

During the outlining phase, I directed students to carefully consider the organization and flow of their presentations, timing, and relative significance of their ideas. For example, even though they decided that some background information on each candidate was important, they had to consider that the purpose of the presentation was not biographical. Therefore, many of the subtopics originally suggested during the brainstorming session were rejected from the final outline template. The outline was pared down to the following major headings:

I. Qualifications and Political Experience

II. Key Issues

III. Where the Candidate Stands on My Primary Issue

IV. Summary

3. Creating the Grading Rubric

I told students at the beginning of the course that they would be partially responsible for grading the presentations. Once they had chosen a topic and created an outline, I explained the purpose of classroom presentations, which led to a discussion of the main aspects of a good presentation. Rather than providing students with a list of possible categories to put on the rubric, I began by eliciting ideas about what makes a good presentation. The students came up with three main categories: content, language, and appearance. Because they had chosen the theme of U.S. Presidential Candidates, I asked them to watch one of the televised candidate debates for homework and to think about what the candidates did that fit into these three categories. The next day, they expanded their ideas into the 12 points listed in Table 1.

The students decided that they would prefer to be graded on the English as a second language (ESL) focus of the course rather than on the academic content of their presentations, and I accepted that decision. This had the effect of

Table 1. First Proposed Grading Rubric

Category	Guideline	Score
Appearance	Does the speaker dress professionally?	
Articulation	Is the speaker's voice clear?	
Comprehensibility	Are appropriate points made in a clear, understandable manner?	
Content	Is the speaker knowledgeable about the subject?	
Eye contact	How well does the speaker engage the audience by looking at all audience members?	
Fluency	Is the speaker's language rhythmic and fluid?	
Gestures	Does the speaker emphasize key points with appropriate hand gestures?	
Grammar	Is the speaker's grammar formal and correct?	
Multimedia	Does the speaker use visual media to support the presentation?	
Organization	Does the speaker cover all of the important points in a logical order?	
Persuasive argument	Does the speaker convince the audience?	
Time control	Does the presentation fit into the assigned time with a natural conclusion?	

allowing us to focus as a class on key aspects of presentations that would likely not be addressed in their major courses and provided me with a list of teachable points that were perceived by the students to be useful. The categories "Content" and "Persuasive argument" in Table 1 were voted off of the final grading rubric because the students argued that the course is not actually a content course. They stressed that their presentations were intended for a general audience rather than specialists, and the core purpose of the presentations was to inform rather than to persuade. Please note that the students made these decisions, and although I may have argued to include or exclude a given point, I did not veto any of their decisions.

The students organized the remaining 10 points into categories and created a grading scale. Initially, they decided that there were 10 categories, so if they assigned 10 points to each one, they would have a readymade 100-point scale. I encouraged them to rethink their position by asking if gestures were really as important to them as comprehensibility.

The students also discovered the difficulty of using a 10×10 scoring system; there would be little leeway to differentiate scores between *excellent* and *perfect*. If students had difficulty giving a perfect score for each category, they would mark 9, which in the grading system at our institution is an A−. Also, there would be less chance to monitor improvement. If a student received a 9 for eye contact on the first presentation and a 9 on the second, was there improvement? The class agreed that a rubric totaling 1,000 points would be more effective.

I divided the class to work on devising an adequate grading scale. The two groups each created a revised rubric aimed at weighting the scores more heavily for the most important features of the presentation. Then the groups debated the relative merits of the two rubrics. The students chose the rubric that focused on organization and language (see Appendix) over the one that focused more on personal style.

4. Conducting Pair Practice

I often use pair work to provide all of the students in a speaking course with equal practice time, so in this graduate course I elected to have students practice in rotating pairs. The students set up their desks face to face in two lines with as much space as possible between pairs (Figure 1). Line A began, and each student gave his or her presentation as the partners in Line B listened. After 7 minutes I signaled a change (the signal can be a key word, flicking the lights, or ringing a bell), and the A students knew it was time to wrap up. They then had 3 minutes to receive general feedback from the B students on the content and organization of their presentation. Students based their comments on the rubric. Next, Line B had 7 minutes for their presentation and 3 minutes for feedback. Subsequently, everyone in Line B moved one desk to the right, with the student sitting at the right end moving to the far left end, and they began again. In a 50-minute

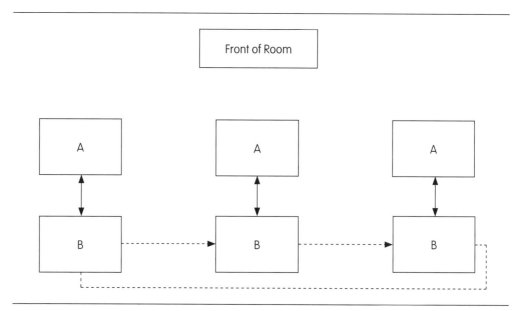

Figure 1. Rotating Pairs Seating Chart

period, each student presented twice and heard two different peers present, regardless of class size.

5. Recording Presentations

If anything makes people more nervous than speaking in front of a group, it is probably speaking on camera. Video recording the presentations provides two important contributions to the success of this activity, however: (a) It emphasizes the importance of the classroom presentation and (b) it provides students with a chance to be self-reflective. The fact that the presentations have been practiced in pairs with peers at least twice before the presentation day means that students are generally confident in the content and language they are using and can focus their attention on other important aspects of public speaking, such as gestures and eye contact. On the day of the presentations, I handed out copies of the rubric that the students had created so that they could complete one for each presenter. The students and I scored each presentation live. For this class I set up a DVD recorder. At the end of the session, I gave each presenter a DVD of his or her own presentation. Each student was asked to view the DVD, rate the presentation using the rubric, and then write an explanation of the rating. I instructed the students to observe their peers critically and to analytically assess their performance. These instructions encouraged them to compare their own performance with the performances of their peers (for more technical information, see the Chartrand and Yeh chapters in this volume).

6. Self-Assessing

After they submitted their presentation scores, each student received a score chart with peer and teacher ratings. I also wrote a narrative commentary on the presentation, highlighting what I felt went well and what needed improvement. This feedback provided students with the opportunity to see how well their self-assessment correlated to the assessments of their peers and of their teacher, increasing the accuracy of both their peer- and self-assessments (AlFally, 2004). Also, since they had a recording of their presentation, they could watch it a second time to better understand any discrepancies or to identify specific issues that my narrative assessment raised.

One aspect of this assessment activity that I consider essential to its success is repetition of each step in the process. Students repeat their presentations through practice, but they also have the opportunity to repeat the process of defining a topic, outlining a speech, giving and receiving feedback, and revising their presentation based on that feedback. Because the students asked to be allowed to prepare for several weeks, the two presentations were run in parallel (see Table 2). The outline for the first presentation was created, critiqued, and revised, and then the outline for the second presentation was created. The first presentation was practiced in pairs. In-class practice for the second presentation started before the first presentation was delivered for a grade. Since the schedule was offset, they practiced the first presentation in class twice (in weeks 5 and 6), while practicing the second presentation only once (in week 6). In week 7, I dedicated the entire class session to presenting the first speech, and in week 9 I dedicated the entire class session both days to final presentations of the second speech.

Table 2. Schedule of Activities

Week	Presentation 1	Presentation 2
1	Choose topic	
2	Narrow topic	Choose topic
3	Outline	Narrow topic
4	Critique outline	Outline
5	Practice	Critique outline
6	Practice	Practice
7	Present	
8	Score/Critique	
9		Present
10		Score/Critique

REFLECTIONS

This activity works when students are invested in learning how to improve oral presentations for a specific situation, such as in model teaching (Carrier, 2003). It might not be as useful in a setting where the students perceive it as being only an ESL activity, with no extrinsic motivation to improve (Pribyl, Keaton, & Sakamoto, 2001). In addition to using it at my university in the United States, I have used this assessment procedure in Spain in a business English course and in an English for medical purposes course with students who wanted to present at international conferences. In Indonesia, I used it with a group of high school students who wanted to improve oral skills to apply to international universities. The technology has improved from audio cassette, to VHS, and now to DVD recorders, but the central principles remain: to open up the grading system to students and allow them to prepare, practice, and produce spoken language in a nonthreatening environment. In addition, this oral presentation assessment procedure promotes critical analysis, reflective learning, and directed feedback.

I offer two measures of the effectiveness of the process: increased scores from the first presentation to the second presentation, and comments from student evaluations of presentations. Of the six students in the course, all but one improved the composite total score on the second presentation (see Table 3).

Adaptations

What makes this activity different from other oral presentations is the aspect of reflective learning provided by allowing students to create a rubric to grade their recorded performance. This self-reflection allows them to change their perceptions of their own performance (Foss & Reitzel, 1988). By watching themselves on video and having to look for and grade specific aspects of their own performance, students develop an observer, or external, perspective. This means that students do not have to rely on the memory of their performance under stressful conditions. Rather, they can view their own performance in a more detached manner by focusing on each category of the rubric they developed collectively.

Table 3. Presentation Scores

	Student 1	Student 2	Student 3	Student 4	Student 5	Student 6
Score 1	944	959.5	929	928	922	899
Score 2	955	969.5	972	938	953	895
Change	11	10	43	10	31	−4[a]

[a] Student 6 changed his presentation topic at the last minute from The Importance of Saudi Arabia in the U.S. Economy to Saudi Arabia, My Country and lost points in Organization and Fluency while gaining in other categories.

This procedure makes more accurate comparisons possible between their own abilities and those of their peers.

Keeping this assessment as the core of the activity, it is possible to adapt it to a variety of student populations. Constraints of class size, contact time, and program curricula need to be considered when deciding how best to apply this assessment procedure to a specific course. The primary limiting factor seems to me to be the ratio of students to the time available for presentations. With six students I was able to complete all presentations in 1 hour, but 40 students presenting 10 minutes each would take 7 hours of class time. A course I recently observed met twice a week. In that course, the 17 students were required to complete three presentations each. Unlike the course I describe in this chapter, there was no reading component, but it included listening and note-taking assignments. The instructor was able to have students negotiate a rubric and practice each presentation using rotating pairs but limited individual presentation times to 3–4 minutes. An alternative might be to divide a large class into groups that could present simultaneously in separate rooms, which would reduce the amount of class time required. This would increase scoring time, however, because the teacher would have to view presentations after class to score every student (for other ideas on assessing recordings of students, see the Chernen, Lynch, Saito-Stehberger & Oh, and Yeh chapters in this volume).

When I think about adapting activities for a variety of levels and age groups, I picture a mixing-board I call the ESL Task Equalizer (see Figure 2). Most tasks can be refined in a way that can lower the difficulty level for beginners or raise the challenge level for advanced learners. For example, a speaking task can be made easier by extending the time students have to prepare for it. An in-class writing assignment can be made easier by lowering the target accuracy required.

Figure 2. The ESL Task Equalizer

Using cooperative learning to provide peer support can make an assignment more manageable, while lowering teacher and peer input can make it more challenging.

I described oral presentation tasks in this chapter as I used them with adult graduate students in the United States. There are several ways to adjust the tasks for lower level students, however. The tasks can be made easier by using simpler topics, such as the student's hometown or family. For beginning students, the teacher might also lower expectations for grammar, and set age- and grade-appropriate vocabulary. The project can provide more scaffolding by increasing teacher support and lowering dependence on peer support. This is a productive activity, but a teacher can simplify it by allowing students to write and receive feedback on their reports first, and then allowing them to read their papers. Motivation can be made intrinsic rather than extrinsic by downplaying the need to prepare for oral presentations in other courses and to make a goal that is more meaningful for the students, such as meeting other students at a school party. While the tasks I describe in this chapter culminate in formal presentations, any oral activity would work: dialogues, recitations, or role-plays come to mind.

Student responses to the activity varied but were generally positive. As one student wrote in the final course evaluation, the process allowed "a chance to find problems and learn how to resolve them." Several students commented that they could see marked improvements in their eye contact, use of gestures, and vocal quality on the second video recording. One student remarked, "I even didn't realize that my voice was so quiet but when I see myself I could recognize it." After the second presentation, one particularly shy student stated that she felt more confident in her speaking skills: "I feel I am lucky . . . not only knowledge I got from you but also my attitude [towards public presentations] can be improved." Perhaps the most telling student response was the following, e-mailed to me after the course had concluded:

> In this class, it was my first time to give a presentation in English, so the feed back you did, It was very helpful. As a result, I got 100% in the presentation that I did in my MBA class. I am glad with all these achievements in short time.

These comments and other similar oral and written feedback from the students are a clear indication that the transparency of the assessment process in this activity had a lasting effect. The activity meets my basic objective to provide students with a set of strategies to help them overcome their fear of public speaking.

———————————————

Jeff Popko is an assistant professor of teaching ESOL and ESL at Eastern Michigan University. He has taught ESOL in Montana, Hawaii, Arizona, and Michigan, all in the United States, as well as in Japan, Spain, and Indonesia.

APPENDIX: STUDENT-CREATED PRESENTATION SCORING RUBRIC

	Category	Percentage/ Points	Score
Organization	Comprehensibility	200	
	Multimedia	100	
	Organization skills	150	
	Time control	100	
Language	Grammar	100	
	Articulation	100	
	Fluency	100	
Personal Style	Gesture	50	
	Eye contact	50	
	Appearance	50	
Total Score			

CHAPTER 15

Practical Strategies for Assessing Students' Oral Speeches Through Vlogs

Aiden Yeh

If I'm well-prepared, then there is nothing to fear.
—Student self-evaluation from speech training class

INTRODUCTION

At the college where I teach in southern Taiwan, Professional Public Speaking is a compulsory course for 1st-year English majors who enroll in a 2-year program. The purpose of this two-credit course is to teach students the fundamental skills and concepts needed to successfully deliver speeches. The course syllabus includes learning objectives such as: (a) students should be able to deliver different types of speeches in English, and (b) students need to make effective use of eye contact, gestures, and voice. Thus, the emphasis is placed on delivery or presentation. Despite constructive critiquing in the course objectives with peer–teacher feedback on speech presentations, however, pre- and post-performance self-evaluations are rarely carried out. Pedagogically, this has meant that support for students during the speech preparation process has been limited. Ultimately, the result has been poor-quality speeches presented in class.

To remove this flaw in the course design, I divided the speech task process into a five-stage learning cycle that I guide students through. This learning cycle integrates a number of feedback loops, such as preperformance feedback, peer–peer and student–teacher; postperformance peer–teacher; and self-evaluation feedback using a video portfolio or video blogs[1] (vlogs). The use of students' speech presentation video portfolios as an assessment tool is not commonly

---

[1]A *blog* is a short word for Web log, which is an interactive online journal (Doctorow, 2002, p. 96); blog entries can be a combination of texts, photos, voice (or music) recordings, and videos (see Yeh, 2007a).

practiced because of technical difficulties and the amount of tedious work involved in the preparation and distribution of videos. With Web 2.0, also known as second-generation online tools or emerging Web-based applications (Solomon & Schrum, 2007), however, creating and publishing a video portfolio using blogs and video servers makes it relatively fast and easy. These new interactive online technologies allow students to collaborate, enhance social networking, and manage and access Web content (i.e., their videos) in and outside the classroom (also see the Chartrand chapter in this volume).

In the following section, I discuss the concept and application of the learning cycle through a description of an actual speech task that I used in my Professional Public Speaking course to illustrate the process that students go through every time they make a speech presentation. Discussion of task materials and procedures is included to illustrate the use of Web 2.0 and the integration of materials in the learning cycle.

CONTEXT

There are typically 24 students in my Professional Public Speaking course; to accommodate students' learning needs, the class size is relatively small. Students entering the course are expected to have mastered basic academic skills necessary to deliver different types of speeches. The college is situated in an English as a foreign language (EFL) context, and English is used as the medium of instruction for the course, thus giving students more exposure to the target language. Lectures on the basic principles of public speaking and presentations on self-introductions and informative speeches are covered in the first semester, and persuasive speeches and speeches for special occasions are performed in the second semester. The learning objectives stated on the syllabus are based on *The Art of Public Speaking* (Lucas, 2007), the textbook chosen by the English Department for this course.

Even before the course starts, I plan and design class activities using a blended learning approach where multimedia and online technology are mixed into the traditional learning environment. Figure 1 shows how technology fits into the pedagogy and how it is integrated in the learning process that gives students the opportunities to improve their public speaking skills.

In addition, I create a class vlog using Yahoo! Groups and Blip.tv, a video server (or media host) that archives videos online (http://blip.tv); these Web 2.0 tools provide a virtual extension of the classroom that maximizes the learning opportunity. Our class Yahoo! Group serves as our online learning environment (OLE), where communications via the e-mail-based messaging system enhance class rapport. It also serves as an archive for syllabi and other learning materials. Blip.tv stores students' videos that are published on the class blog via blogger. com; this then becomes their online portfolio that showcases skills learned in the course.

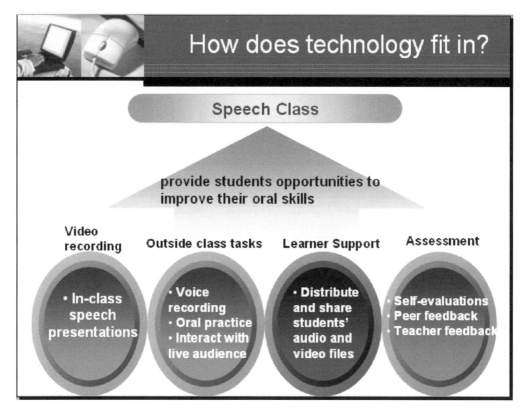

Figure 1. How Technology Supports Pedagogical Goals (Yeh, 2007a)

Learning Cycle

The learning cycle, shown in Figure 2, illustrates the various stages of a speech task. This cycle is based on the pedagogical framework of Kolb's learning cycle theory (1984) that emphasizes the importance of reflecting on what has been done, evaluating and making sense of it (experience), and doing it differently (see also Fry, Ketteridge, & Marshall, 2003.) In this cycle, students are engaged in active learning from the initial stages of their speech presentation to the very end. Thus, placing them at the center of the cycle diagram signifies the necessity of their involvement in the learning process.

In the following section, I illustrate each point in the cycle by using the speech task *speeches of introduction* from the course to show the relationships between the stages and illustrate how teachers can integrate Web 2.0 tools in the process.

CURRICULUM, TASKS, MATERIALS

Delivering an oral speech is difficult for many EFL learners. There are some speech activities (i.e., simulation), though, that could lessen the anxiety (also see the Popko chapter in this volume). Simulation is a fun activity, and according to

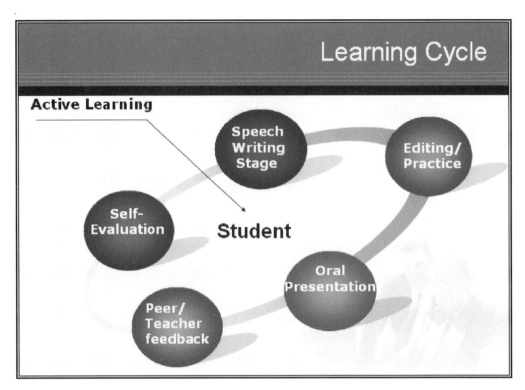

Figure 2. Learning Cycle (Yeh, 2007b)

Crookal and Saunders (1989), "it is more congruent to the learning process . . . than traditional classroom procedures" (p. 12). Simulation in an educational context models "real-world" activities and puts students in "true-to-life roles" (Millis & Hertel, 2002, p. 16). In addition, Taylor and Walford (1972, as cited in Cohen, Manion, & Morrison, 2000) posit that, "heightened interest and excitement in learning" is one of the motivational advantages of simulation, and that learning in "cognitive, social, and emotional" levels is inevitably provided (p. 377). Millis and Hertel argue, however, that no matter how closely an activity simulates a realistic situation, alterations will have to be made to fit learning goals.

A speech of introduction is one of the easier speech tasks in the course. The context of this task simulates a graduation ceremony where students are encouraged to think of themselves as ceremony hosts. Their principal responsibility is to introduce the main speaker. To effectively deliver a speech of introduction, Lucas (2007, pp. 470–473) suggests three goals that students need to meet:

- build enthusiasm for the upcoming speaker

- build enthusiasm for the speaker's topic

- establish a welcoming climate that will boost the speaker's credibility

In this speech task, I ask students to think of the event as their own graduation ceremony. To make it even more meaningful, the main speaker's topic should provide an inspiration that will motivate the graduates to embark upon a successful journey in their professional life.

As shown in the speech of introduction task guidelines and instructions (see Figure 3), the first thing that students need to do is to choose a guest speaker for their graduation ceremony. The main speaker must be a local figure, someone they think they look up to and would like to emulate. Thus, in selecting the main speaker, the students need to answer the following questions:

- If you were to invite someone inspirational, someone students could relate to, whom would that be?

- Aside from being inspirational, what other reasons do you have for inviting this person to be the main speaker?

- What is it about this speaker that makes him an expert on the subject?

They also choose a particular subject or theme (success, popularity, or influence) that is related to the speaker's background. For the performance, students prepare a PowerPoint slide that contains a picture of the invited guest speaker, thus creating an illusion that the guest speaker is present in the room. Students follow the guidelines below (adapted from Lucas, 2007) to successfully meet the task:

- Be brief (2–3 minutes).

- Provide accurate remarks about the invited guest speaker.

- Adapt remarks and statements to the occasion.

- Adapt remarks to the invited guest speaker.

- Adapt remarks to the audience.

- Create a sense of anticipation and drama.

Pretask Activity

As a pretask activity, I give lectures and workshops to help students develop ideas on how to prepare and deliver their own speech presentation. Workshops include exercises, discussions, and analyses of various speeches, as well as written compositions and video presentations. Speech samples are uploaded to the Files area of our Yahoo! Group and on the class blog where students can either download or view the files online. These compositions give them ideas about strategic organization of their main points and how they should go about writing their drafts. Video recordings of students' successful speeches presented in class model the desired outcomes of the speech task that help in refining their own presentation

Task: Speech of Introduction

1) Choose one important Taiwanese figure to be a keynote speaker for Wenzao Ursuline College's Graduation Ceremony for Batch 2006-2007.

2) Choose a particular subject or theme that you want to focus on in relation to the nature of your speaker's background (success/popularity/influence)

3) Follow the guidelines stated in your book (see Speeches of Introduction) and most importantly, make sure that you're able to answer the 4 questions posted below.

4) Prepare one powerpoint slide that contains a picture of your invited guest speaker.

5) Your speech should be at least 2-3 minutes (not less than 2 minutes, not exceeding 4 minutes)

6) Peer-feedback (assigned partner) and a comprehensive self-evaluation must be submitted a week after the presentation

Figure 3. Speech of Introduction Task Guidelines (Yeh, 2006a)

skills. During the workshop, I also distribute copies of the assessment rubric (see Appendix A). This way, students are made aware of the grading criteria and the requirements for meeting the task (Jackson & Larkin, 2002) (for more on assessment rubrics, see the Popko chapter in this volume).

Stage One: Speech Writing

Writing speech compositions is the first stage in which students take the plunge into the active process of producing a written product. This is usually a long and tedious process that many of them find daunting (also see the Bradley chapter in this volume). I give students 2–3 weeks to work on their drafts. In the 1st week, they brainstorm ideas for possible topics and choose their main speaker. To notify other students, they post the name of their chosen main speaker and theme on the class Yahoo! Group and Skrbl, a multiuser whiteboard where users can jot notes, scribble, and upload documents (http://www.skrbl.com/). An example of students' collaborative posting on Skrbl is shown in Figure 4. This communication limits the possibility of different students selecting the same main speaker. If students duplicate one another in their choice of main speaker or topic, the student who posted his choice first gets priority.

The first draft of their speech composition is turned in for editing at least 1 week prior to the performance. In their compositions for the speech of introduction, the same elements of a full speech—introduction, body, and conclusion—are used. They need to work on a good attention-getter and make the audience aware of the importance of having the main speaker present during the event.

a. Name	B. Topic
1. Annie Zhuang	Grace Jhan 詹慧君-- " Your dream could come true"
2. Stefanie	龍應台"Be the unique personalize on your career"
3. Emily	Kai-fu Lee (李開復) "true success"
4. Johnny	Roger Yang (培安)
5. Cassandra	Terry Kuo (郭台銘) - "The devil is in the details "
6. Selena	袁韻婕
7. Carly	Kevin Lin (義傑)
8. Zoe	Rocky yang (基寬)-"The way to success."
9. Frances Huang YE4A	B. Vincent Chang - Attitude Decides Your Future
10. Emma	Yundi Lee(李雲迪) - "The Incredible Pianist Genius Yundi Lee "
11. Claire	Yuan-Tseh Lee(李遠哲)-"Reaching for the stars"
12. Joyce Lin	Mr. Yu-Jan Lin 林裕展先生-- "Using What You've learned"
13. Vicky Wang	王齡嬌
14. Yvette	
15. Penny	YoYo Ma (馬友友)
16. Reiff	Chia- Tung Lee(李家) - "An Important Lesson to Everyone"
17. Vicky Li	Cing-Yuan Kao(高清愿)--" It is possible for your dreams to come true"

Figure 4. Postings of Main Speakers and Presentation Themes on Skrbl (Yeh, 2006b) (used with permission of Skrbl, http://www.skrbl.com)

Stage Two: Teacher–Student Conferences to Guide Editing and Practice

For many Taiwanese EFL college students, the inability to detect language errors makes speech compositions challenging. By conducting a teacher–student conference, I can provide feedback on three general areas of their speech compositions: grammar and lexical errors, organization of content (i.e., discussion of main points), and overall style and approach (see Figure 5). The Internet makes this possible even for students who are absent or fail to bring their drafts to class because they can easily upload their drafts (saved as Word documents) to the class Yahoo! Group for feedback. I do not give grades to students' drafts because they are still in the process of developing their speeches. As Ellis (1995) asserts, this kind of nonthreatening, open dialogue encourages students to revise their speech compositions. In addition, this allows me to verify whether the students have a clear understanding of the task requirements and how well the skills and knowledge taught in class are applied.

The peer feedback prior to the presentation is done in the classroom simultaneously as I engage learners in separate student–teacher conferences. The purpose of this activity is to foster collaborative interaction; students exchange drafts and provide feedback on each other's work using the speech task guidelines and rubric (see Appendix A) given to them during the pretask activity.

For oral practice prior to the performance, students practice, either individually or in small groups, after class or at home. I also suggest that they rehearse their speeches in front of a mirror, which according to some researchers (Bovée, 2003; Wood, 2005) can help students check distracting body language and notice

---

Introduction to Stanley Yen

Good Morning, everyone. Today we will have a very successful man come here
to share his personal experience and thoughts about how to success in our future
carrier. Being a high school graduate, he had distributed himself in many fields and
achieved enormous achievements. When he was 24 he was only a delivery in
American Express in 1971. Within four years, he became the first Asian general
manager in A.E. At the age of 32, he was invited to be a C.E.O. in a famous
international Hotel, and made this hotel being the top hotel that shares a very good
reputation. Besides, he also is a good writer. He wrote his story in "Lion Heart of
C.E.O." in 1997, and published his new book " Up with the Wind" in 2002. I think
many of you know who he is. Now, let's give the most welcome to Taiwan Tourism
Association president, Mr. Stanley Yen.

Figure 5. Speech Draft Sample (Yeh, 2006c)

inappropriate gap fillers (i.e., "um," "ah"). One student wrote this in her self-evaluation about the value of practice:

> I found that I still could not conquer the fear of presenting on the stage even though
> I had prepared and practiced at home in front of the mirror and my family. I believe
> that I will be able to improve my delivery, which needs more practice and a lot of
> work . . . .

Stage Three: Oral Presentation

Due to the number of students and limited class time available, I divide the class
into two groups; each group has about 12–13 presenters. The first group presents
for the first week, while the remaining half of the class presents during the second
week of presentations. The 2-week presentation schedule is decided in advance to
give students ample time to prepare. Time limitations often result in fast-paced
presentations where there is a quick rotation of presenters, however. During
presentations, students are asked to listen attentively, observe, take notes, and
comment on their classmates' performance by listing both positive and negative
points. I do the same by writing down my observations about the presentations.
Listening, watching, observing, and writing comments at the same time is difficult, however. Providing written feedback this way does not guarantee a comprehensive assessment of the students' performances. Even if a teacher is armed with
a scoring rubric (see Appendix A), written comments are still necessary to offer

students valuable feedback that they can comprehend. This is the reason why we record speech presentations on video: It provides instant playback for peer–teacher feedback and self-evaluations (see Figure 6).

The statement below, extracted from the postcourse survey, reveals one student's opinion about the integration of technology in this course:

> The technology is really useful and helpful in this course. The computer and Internet and digital camera make the learning process livelier and easier and I think these tools are necessary in public speaking class.

Vlogging

Video recording students' presentations requires the use of a digital video camera, secure digital (SD) cards, a tripod, and a computer. I record presentations using a Cannon IXY Digital 60 camera mounted on a small tripod. The video files are saved on a SD memory card, which is extracted and then converted to MP4 format to reduce file size. I then upload the converted files to Blip.tv for archiving and vlog distribution purposes (for a list of video server Web sites, see Appendix B).

Stage Four: Feedback

Peer Feedback

Peer review sessions are assigned as an outside-class activity. Students are required to work in pairs and to provide feedback to their partners. To enable better feedback, students watch the video playback of their peer's presentation to refresh

Figure 6. Screenshot of Students' Video Presentations (Yeh, 2006d)

their memories. Normally, classmates notice aspects of the presentation that they did not see during the actual speech performances. This activity allows students to refine their abilities to critically analyze all aspects of speech composition and delivery. Using the rubric as a checklist for evaluation (see Appendix A), they should be able to distinguish between weak and strong support, identify problems, and propose a workable solution.

Although peer feedback can also be done as an in-class oral discussion where students voice their opinions about their classmates' performances, I prefer written feedback that students upload on the Yahoo! Group or post on the comments area of the class blog. This way, students are not put on the spot and subjected to possible embarrassment (see Figure 7). In addition, written feedback gives students more time to prepare their constructive comments and present them in a nonjudgmental manner. Using the same assessment rubric for peer feedback can help elicit comments and suggestions from peers. The rubric template also provides language samples that address specific parts of the speech. Finally, written feedback gives students sufficient time to reflect. In my experience, it significantly contributes to their self-awareness and helps them come to terms with their speech performance.

---

annie said...

I think Vanessa did well at her speech of introduction. First of all, her voice was her biggest advantage of speech. It was very pleasing to the audience' s ear and controlled suitably.

Furthermore, I think her content of the speech was adapted to the occasion and the information was also related to the audience. Besides, she successfully established a welcoming climate that increase the speaker' s credibility and add the audience' s curiosity. However, there is one thing I think it can give to Vanessa to improve next time. Maybe it is because she was nervous when she made the speech, she did some unnecessary body language, and for instance she swung from the right hand side to the left hand side. I think she can avoid keeping this unnecessary body language. Otherwise, it was a good presentation.

luke said...

Alright, so how did Elliott do on this work? He clearly stated how the speech topic was related to the graduates and also introduced the speaker himself concisely. His gestures weren't many and his body remained still most of the time, but he kept the eye contact frequently which makes him look solemn and convincing. That's good. Although he forgot the line and stopped a little in the middle of the speech, it didn't matter much cause we all did. Generally, Elliott performed well on the is speech. And by the way, nice shirt.

Figure 7. Student Feedback Posted on the Class Blog (Yeh, 2006e)

Teacher Feedback

I like receiving comments from the teacher and other classmates so there is an interaction. Though I'm not really very good at speaking in public, I feel comfortable in this course because I can learn a lot.

—Feedback from a student

Postperformance evaluation is done using the following: the students' video presentations, the same scoring rubric given during the workshop (see Appendix A), notes taken during the actual performances, and a copy of the students' drafts and final speech compositions. I review the recorded presentations from beginning to end about 2–3 times, occasionally using the pause button to freeze-frame a scene. I then write a summative evaluation where I discuss my reactions to the performance. I begin by stating what the student presenter did best, followed by the weak points, and I conclude by giving my suggestions about how he could improve his performance. For mispronounced words and problems in articulation, I write down the words that are mispronounced and provide a link to an online dictionary (with audio) for reference (see Figure 8).

Stage Five: Self-Evaluations

Self-evaluation is a type of metacognitive thinking where students develop ways to assess their own learning (Blakey & Spence, 1990 as cited in Uden & Beaumont, 2006, p. 76). By evaluating their own speech performance (from composition to delivery), students notice their own learning problems. Knowing the criteria and guidelines for the speech of introduction task puts them in a better position to tackle their problems. Thus, being aware of what they know, what their abilities

---

"You may want to look into the following comments to help you in your next round of presentations:

- you have difficulty articulating long 'a' as in face and dedicate, see
  http://m-w.com/face
- http://m-w.com/dedicate

"When you address the main speaker, it would be better if you use appropriate titles such as "Mr.' as in "Mr. Hu will tell you…". During your presentation, you said, "Hu will tell you…" The 'Hu' here sounds like 'who', so the statement you uttered could be interpreted as a question, as in "Who will tell you…", thus resulting in confusion among audience members."

Figure 8. Sample Feedback on Delivery (Yeh, 2006f)

are, and what kind of knowledge they still need can help them to accomplish a task (Brown, 1980). In addition, the digital video recordings of their presentations also serve as evidence to help them judge their own work. Vocal variety, pronunciation, articulation, and visual cues such as posture, body language, and facial expression used to convey feelings are stored in the recordings, which simplifies assessing the quality of their own performance.

For short speeches such as the speech of introduction, I ask students to do an audio recording of their self-evaluation. The intent of this exercise is to give them another opportunity to work on their oral skills, get used to voice recording, and listen to their own voices. Using Chinswing (a free audio forum Web site), students can create a voice recording of their evaluation on the Internet (see Figure 9). They need to have a computer with access to the Internet, a microphone, and speakers to be able to complete this activity.

The following are transcribed snippets from the students' self-evaluations posted on Chinswing:

- After watching my video, I was relieved because it was not as bad as I thought . . . there are still things that I could have done better, such as speaking in a more natural tone, segmentation of the sentences, and try not to rely on notes. . . .

- I think I'm satisfied of (sic) my performance. . . . However, after watching the video on the blog, I realize that my arms were shaking during the

Figure 9. Speech of Introduction Reflection Forum at Chinswing (Yeh, 2007c)

presentation. . . . It was unnatural, and I will try to fix that up in the next speech.

- From the video . . . I think that at the beginning I successfully built the enthusiasm for the upcoming speaker. . .

REFLECTIONS

In this chapter, I discussed the stages of the learning cycle that students experience when doing a speech task. In the cycle I have described, feedback takes place throughout the speech development process, from the preparation of speech compositions to postperformance evaluation. The activities in each stage enhance students' involvement in their own learning process, thus giving them a sense of accountability for the outcome of their speech presentations. The integration and use of Web 2.0 technology as assessment tools helped my students to self-discover their own strengths and weaknesses. They reflected on and evaluated their own and their classmates performances in order to help one another become better speakers. As one student wrote in the end-of-course evaluation survey,

> In this course, I learned a lot of skills and methods that I haven't heard before to organize and deliver my speeches. After the training of these two semesters, I think I won't be afraid of giving speeches anymore. However, the most difficult part is how to write a good speech. I think it's the one I still have to improve.

From the teacher's perspective, perhaps the most troubling issue related to courses that introduce public speaking tasks is assessment. I have found that video recordings of speech presentations can go a long way toward addressing some assessment issues. The video recordings helped my students and me identify the strengths and weaknesses of speech presentations in a constructive manner that encouraged honest reflection and review and improved performance. The video content of our class vlog supports my claim that learning has actually taken place in the course.

Privacy is a primary concern when using vlogs. Videos posted on a blog can be seen by other people and, in a virtual sense, the whole world. One solution is to set the video preferences for private viewing; private videos are password protected and available only to people that you share them with. Another solution is to have students submit a signed consent form at the beginning of the course. Students should also have an option to have their videos removed from the blog or video server after all the evaluations are made.

Technology is improving at a rapid pace and many of the improvements have made basic Web applications more user-friendly. Integrating Web 2.0 in a speech class is relatively easy. By using the built-in buttons and support found in almost all Web-based applications, creating content on the Web, publishing, distributing, and sharing videos can all be done even by those who are less technologically savvy (also see the Chartrand chapter in this volume).

Each class is a learning community, and since Web 2.0 tools are about social networking, English for speakers of other languages (ESOL) teachers should have an understanding about how to cultivate and facilitate the use of these tools. The point is not to make use of Web 2.0 merely because the tools are there, but because they meet the learning needs of ESOL students enrolled in communicative courses in ways that are highly engaging, effective, readily accessible, and increasingly easy to manage.

Aiden Yeh is a doctoral student at the University of Birmingham in England and holds a master's degree in English language training management. She is a member of TESOL's Technology Advisory Committee and Computer-Assisted Language Learning Interest Section Electronic Village Online Coordinating Team, and TESOL's Nonnative English Speakers Caucus assistant listserv manager. She teaches at Wen Zao Ursuline College of Foreign Languages, in Taiwan.

APPENDIX A: SAMPLE SPEECH RUBRIC

Speeches of Introduction

Speaker: _____ Invited Keynote Speaker: _____ (PPT: _____)

Criteria	E	G	A	F	P	Comments	
Built enthusiasm for the upcoming speaker.	E	G	A	F	P		
Built enthusiasm for the speaker's topic	E	G	A	F	P		
Establish a welcoming climate that boosts speaker's credibility	E	G	A	F	P		
Accuracy of Remarks							
Remarks are completely accurate	E	G	A	F	P		
Got the speaker's name right	E	G	A	F	P		
Adapting Remarks to the Occasion	E	G	A	F	P		
Adapting Remarks to the Main Speaker							
(Avoided making the speaker uncomfortable, embarrassing facts that should have been avoided, unrealistic expectations from the speaker etc.)	E	G	A	F	P		
Adapting Remarks to the Audience							
Showed importance of the Main speaker's presence to the audience/occasion	E	G	A	F	P		
Made audience want to hear the Main Speaker on the specified topic	E	G	A	F	P		
Information presented related to the audience	E	G	A	F	P		
Information presented in an interesting manner	E	G	A	F	P		
Created a Sense of Anticipation and Drama	E	G	A	F	P		
Delivered extemporaneously	E	G	A	F	P		
Delivered with Sincerity and Enthusiasm	E	G	A	F	P		

Overall Evaluation:

Rubric Key: E = Excellent, G = Good, A = Average, F = Fair, P = Poor (Yeh, 2007a).

APPENDIX B: VIDEO SERVERS AND FILE SIZE LIMITS

- YouTube.com (http://youtube.com) 100 MB

- Blip.tv (http://blip.tv) There is no file size limit, but 100 MB or less is recommended

- Podomatic (http://podomatic.com) 250 MB

- Yahoo!video (http://video.search.yahoo.com/) 100 MB

- Google Video (http://video.google.com/) For 100 MB or less, use Web-based uploader; for more than 100 MB, use Google Video Uploader Client software

- Videoegg (http://videoegg.com) 5 minutes

- Web Server (e.g., http://geocities.yahoo.com, http://www.fileden.com) Less than 100 MB

- Springdoo Mail/Video (http://www.springdoo.com/) 20 MB

- Vimeo (http://www.vimeo.com) Weekly limit, 500 MB

CHAPTER 16

Promoting Oral Proficiency Through In-Class Speaking Tests

Stephen Soresi

INTRODUCTION

This chapter is for teachers who would like to implement in-class speaking tests. In many contexts, the default second-language (L2) testing method involves paper-based tests, usually covering target language phrases, grammar points, or vocabulary. Although much easier to implement, they neither directly nor effectively measure students' speech skills (Brown, 2000; Davies, Brown, Elder, Hill, Lumley, & McNamara, 1999; Spolsky, 1990). Recently, large testing institutions have begun offering more and more tests with speaking components such as the Test of English as a Foreign Language Internet-based test (often known as the TOEFL iBT) from Educational Testing Service. These institutional tests are impossible to use regularly, however, because of constraints such as cost, venue, and turnaround time for results (for ideas on using iBT-type items in speaking classes, see the Saito-Stehberger & Oh chapter in this volume).

If teachers implement a do-it-yourself, in-class speech test, pitfalls abound. Face-to-face interviews can exceed the allotted class time, meaning that all students are not tested equally. When teachers judge a very elusive entity such as spoken language, scoring can easily be influenced by who the speaker is, rather than actual speech performance. Even when a sophisticated scoring rubric is used, ratings might be done unevenly. The more complex the scoring system, the easier it is to lose track of. Additionally, fatigue can cause more sympathetic scoring and interviewing of the first interviewees compared with interviewees toward the end of oral exams.

A clear need exists for more useful in-class speaking test methodology. Teachers need an extremely practical testing tool with a straightforward scoring system. Learners need a test that directly rewards and informs their progress. The latter can rarely be done by simply assigning a numerical score for traits such as fluency, vocabulary use, and pronunciation, especially for lower-proficiency students. To answer this growing need, in this chapter I outline two in-class speech tests: the quick in-class speech test and the milestone in-class speech test. Table 1 provides an overview of both.

The quick test is designed for low-stakes regular testing, and the milestone test is used for higher-stakes testing that impacts course grades, streaming classes, or a threshold graduation requirement. Both in-class tests use a target speech rate range as the central scoring criterion. I determined these rate ranges through a good deal of trialing using various in-class speaking tasks. I found that when students knew the expected rate range, their participation greatly increased, especially in mixed-ability classes (Soresi, 2004). The two in-class tests have been used at five Japanese universities over the last 4 years in testing more than 500 students. Eleven teacher–raters used the tests during the same period. Repeated use underlines the tests' practicality. Each student's raw score can be tabulated immediately after the test session. Most importantly, regular testing with these instruments had positive effects on the speech quantity and quality of nearly all students.

CONTEXT

I work in Japan, where the in-class testing described in this chapter was carried out. Most Japanese university students may be considered *false beginners* (Grundy, 1994). Despite 6 years, or about 1,000 hours of English-language education,

Table 1. Two Types of In-Class Speech Tests

Quick In-class Speech Test
• Low stakes, used monthly or weekly
• Formative assessment aimed at developing basic fluency
• Classmates interview each other
• Test time is roughly 35 minutes for 12-question set (recommended)
• As many as 200 students can be tested at once
Milestone In-Class Speech Test
• Higher stakes, semiregular
• Summative assessment resulting in a score for grading purposes
• Teacher interviews students
• Test time is roughly 60 minutes for a 3-question set (recommended) given to a maximum of 25 students
• An extra interviewer (recommended for larger classes) is easily incorporated

most university students cannot sustain spontaneous speech. Table 2 shows a speech sample from an incoming 1st-year student who scored in the top 10% among her university peers on a standardized, computer-based achievement test of listening and vocabulary in April 2007. Shortly after completing the written exam, she did a face-to-face interview. Her response is to the prompt "Tell me about your hometown."

How should teachers engender spontaneous speech skills in this student? She produces only one sentence in 30 seconds. Her speech rate and amount are obviously problematic and yet representative of this context. In fact, administering the same interview to 56 of her peers resulted in a cumulative average of only about two sentences produced in 30 seconds. Thus, one of the most pressing issues for these students is an utterly insufficient speech rate and amount.

Some educators may wish to offer her a model answer for input or to focus on her very rudimentary syntax errors (i.e., preposition and article usage) in lines 2 and 6, which she makes despite having covered such points repeatedly in middle and high school. Instead of more drills or target language input, it may be more productive for these young adults to try to transfer their vast tacit or declarative knowledge to procedural knowledge (Canale & Swain, 1980; deBot, 1996). One way I have discovered to achieve this transfer of knowledge is through regular high- and low-stakes testing of spontaneous speech.

Table 3, a sample of spontaneous speech from the same student 3 months after the previous interview, illustrates my point. She had been tested four or five times previously with the developmental quick in-class speech test format and was aware she would take this milestone in-class test as a summative assessment. She did not know that the interview prompt would be to explain her hometown.

She produced seven sentences or clauses in 30 seconds, while overall her peers progressed from an average of about two to six. Admittedly, over 3 months of experience they became more familiar with the test format, extending

Table 2. April 2007 Speech Sample From Miss A

00:00 seconds
1. My . . . My hometown is . . .
2. *Ehto*[a] . . . in Gero, Gifu.
3. *Ehto* . . .
4. Gifu is
5. u . . . u . . .
6. u . . . a famous a . . . .
00:30 seconds

Note. The sample was taken in April 2007 from Miss A, an 18-year-old Japanese university student.
[a]*Ehto* is a Japanese language filler like *Um.*

Table 3. July 2007 Speech Sample From Miss A

00:00 seconds
1. My hometown in . . . is in Ge . . . Gero . . .
2. In a . . . (*recast*)
3. This is a . . . Ah . . . in Gifu prefecture.
4. And Ge, Gero is famous Ah . . .
5. because ah there are old houses
6. And I love, I love dagashi.
7. Ah . . . Maybe Dagashi is . . . (*recast*) Ah means cheap, cheap sweets in English maybe.
8. And Ah . . . Gero . . . (*recast*)
9. In Gero, many Ah dagashi's shop Ah, (*recast*)
10. There are many dagashi's shop.
00:30 seconds

Note. The sample was taken in July 2007 from Miss A, an 18-year-old Japanese university student.

spontaneous speech within a time limit. However, a control group composed of 15 similar students progressed from two to just three sentences on average in 30 seconds over the same period.

Importantly, the tests' criterion corresponds with the targeted ability and provides informational feedback, which can lead to more self-determined autonomous learning (Deci & Ryan, 2002). It is also interesting to note that recasts and even syntactic accuracy seem to proportionately increase as students become more comfortable with fluently delivering their message, a phenomenon that contradicts the accuracy–fluency dichotomy (Nation, 1991; Soresi, 2009).

CURRICULUM, TASKS, MATERIALS

In-Class Speaking Test Design and Mechanics

Following, I outline the four main design features for in-class speaking tests and discuss the mechanics for in-class testing.

Design Feature 1: Task Simplicity

The task objective is simple. Students reply to a prompt (e.g., Tell me about your hometown.) by generating as many sentences or clauses as they can within 30 seconds. A reasonable range that nearly all students can aim for is 5–12. As shown in the sample from Table 2, the major problem with Japanese students' spontaneous speech is that it is extremely limited in terms of amount and rate. This problem is very clearly demonstrated to a student when her speech amounts to fewer than five sentences or clauses in 30 seconds. On the other hand, a rate of more than 12 clauses or sentences usually results from trying to speak too fast, which I discourage. I have found that this target speech rate range provides a clear goal that assists my students to develop spontaneous and comprehensible speech skills in English.

One frustration for many ESOL professionals in this context is that students will rarely extend their speech voluntarily unless specifically instructed to do so. Therefore, instead of implicitly penalizing test-takers for failing to take such initiative, this test makes the demand for extended speech explicit.

Design Feature 2: Time Limit of 30 Seconds

A reasonable time limit pushes students to extend their speech, so teachers might ask why one would use a time limit of 30 seconds. During experimentation with the tests, I discovered that most students produced almost the same number of sentences in 30 seconds as they did in 1 minute when presented with similar prompts. In fact, many of my students seemed to run out of things to say after 20–30 seconds, creating an uncomfortable silence for them. Similarly, all participants reported that they "get stuck" (*tsumaru*) sometimes. This means the longer the time frame, the longer their silent discomfort. In other words, having just 30 seconds to answer actually made for a more pleasant overall test experience. However, a 1-minute time frame may suit different contexts and could be more appropriate for testing higher proficiency students.

Finally, I contend that the time limit encourages students to produce sentences, or more specifically clauses, the basic unit of output according to functional linguists. This productive push can be stressful at first but beneficial in several ways. In my experience teaching Japanese adults, I regularly see how the slightest doubt about syntax or usage prevents many students from even trying to express themselves. The following is one such example of a higher proficiency 1st-year university student based on her score from a standardized, computer-based achievement test taken 1 week before she was interviewed. She struggled to explain what she thought about the Japanese prime minister, saying: "Ah . . . He try to . . . to relation? . . . relationship? Ah . . . Ah (pause) Ah . . . with China . . . More good? . . . Better? . . . than before Koizumi . . . president? President."

This student is accustomed to seeking interlocutor support but does so almost to the point of paralysis. A target speech rate range demand may help her realize and overcome this so that she completes her thoughts. This demand can lead to improved comprehensibility in many cases but, admittedly, might cause a student to form shorter sentences or clauses, or encourage avoidance of certain language (Bachman, 1990).

Design Feature 3: Adjustability of Content and Difficulty

Since the target speech rate range remains constant, task difficulty is addressed through proper speech prompt selection. Before any testing, my students practice timed replies to very basic prompts. At first, most students struggle with basic questions such as "What did you do this morning?" Once we have practiced four or five times in class and held our first test, most of my students can regularly meet the target speech rate range in reply to very basic prompts. The speech themes can escalate in difficulty and become more relevant to the course or to students' majors. In content-based second-language learning courses, I suggest avoiding closed-answer questions, such as "When did the prime minister resign?" and adopting much more open-ended test questions. The one I use most is "Tell me about . . ." For example, I might use "Tell me about the prime minister's resignation." or ". . . your favorite chapter in our book," or ". . . one key concept you learned."

For students at lower speaking proficiency levels (nearly all students in my context), the initial test prompts should be as easy to understand and to answer as possible for several reasons. First, production of spontaneous speech needs to be an achievable goal, especially for less proficient students. Second, if there is difficulty understanding the prompt, the pacing of the test will slow. Third, easier prompts isolate speech measurement and allow for more specific feedback. Admittedly, one trend in second-language testing is toward integrated skills, but challenging prompts might muddy the speech score and lessen the test impact for students hoping to improve speech. Finally, when a student does not understand a prompt but is required to reply, it can significantly damage confidence and affect overall performance.

I have also found that some open-ended questions elicit more speech than others because they are more specific. For example, instead of "How was your day?" the teacher might ask, "What did you do this morning?" Or, instead of "Describe your family," a better prompt would be, "Tell me about your mother." Once students start meeting the target speech rate range, teachers can retest with more difficult or content-specific questions. In other words, a constant target speech rate range allows the test prompts to be contextualized at every stage of the course to reflect the students' overall level or course content demands. Finally, multilevel classes will be problematic with any task, but a target speech rate range gives a performance goal that is clear, meaningful, and achievable for heterogeneous proficiency groups.

Design Feature 4: Output Units—Spoken Sentences and Clauses

One novel and important feature of these in-class speaking tests is that students know a target speech rate range, the main criteria by which their speech will be judged. For an in-class speaking test to be practical, to positively impact learning and allow self-testing or peer-testing, a target speech rate range should be employed. Since these tests base scoring mostly on that output rate, I will briefly discuss the issue of output units.

The output unit used in studies of "articulation rate" is usually syllables (Derwing & Rossiter, 2004) or words per minute (Tauroza & Allison, 1990). While quite precise, smaller output units are completely impractical for in-class testing and self-training. Neither teachers nor students can count such small units while simultaneously listening to speech. Furthermore, the rate of production for small units such as words does not correlate with comprehensibility as well as the rate of production for consecutive sentences or clauses.

How should clauses be counted? Formal textual views of language define sentences as the most basic units (Greenbaum & Quirk, 1992), while a functional perspective of speech regards the clause as the basic unit (Halliday & Matthiessen, 2004). For speech testing in the Japanese university and adult education context, most clauses should be counted as one output unit. For example, "When I came to this university for the first time (=1 output unit) . . . I was afraid of the older students in my classes" (=1 output unit). Specific guidelines for counting spoken clauses in a more exact way are available (see Soresi & Suzuki, 2007). Ultimately, teachers may define output units differently according to educational prerogatives, but sentence and clause units are recommended.

Counting larger syntactic units such as sentences or clauses allows learners from junior high school students to adults to test themselves or each other. To do self-assessments, students choose a probable topic and then count how many sentences or clauses they can utter in 30 seconds or 1 minute. In practice, most of my Japanese students count with reasonable accuracy because of both prosody and the low oral proficiency. Furthermore, this output unit cognitively focuses students on smoothly producing spontaneous speech in consecutive subject–verb units, an important learning objective in this context.

Implementing the Two In-Class Speech Tests

Quick In-Class Speech Test

First I will explain the implementation of the low-stakes quick in-class speech test. It is designed as a formative assessment tool that is regularly implemented to promote oral proficiency. Students reply to 12 speech prompts, and classmates tally each others' comprehensible, spoken sentences or clauses. Test time is roughly 35 minutes for a 12-question set.

For the first round of the task, pair up students and align them in rows (Partner A and Partner B). The teacher announces the first three speaking prompts. Students write them down on a test score sheet. First, all the As speak about each prompt for 30 seconds while the Bs listen and tally the number of sentences or clauses spoken for each prompt. Then roles reverse, and the Bs speak on the same three prompts while the A partners tally. The teacher keeps time and fills in if the numbers are odd. Figure 1 shows the classroom configuration I use for this test.

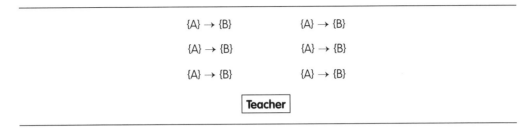

Figure 1. Classroom Seating Arrangement for Quick In-Class Speech Test

For the second round, rotate partners before the teacher announces the next three speech prompts. In this round, Bs talk first, and As count. Then, As speak and Bs count. Repeat the sequence four times to exhaust a set of 12 speaking prompts.

In my experience, using a set of three prompts for each round is the right amount. More than three prompts per round and more than 12 speeches required by each student may cause test-taker fatigue. After all 12 turns are completed, students calculate their totals and averages. I collect the score sheets and check them for calculation errors. I announce top, average, and most-improved scores in the next class meeting. Table 4 offers teachers a checklist to prepare for this assessment.

Milestone In-Class Speech Test

The milestone in-class speech test is the higher-stakes, teacher-mediated tool for summative assessment. This test consists of three total speech prompts. Students rotate one-by-one to the teacher's desk. The teacher says the prompt, keeps time, tallies each student's comprehensible sentences or clauses, and finally makes a qualitative assessment for each response.

With one interviewer in a 90-minute class, a maximum of 36 students can respond to three prompts each. That translates to about 23 students for a 60-minute period. To familiarize yourself and your students with the milestone in-class speech test, I suggest starting with the minimum two prompts per student for the first test, then increase to three per student in subsequent testing. Table 5 is a checklist that teachers can use to prepare for this test.

Table 4. Teacher Checklist for Quick In-Class Speech Test

1. Announce speech test in advance and confirm how to count sentences or clauses.
2. Give sample speech prompts, practice in class, and encourage at-home practice.
3. Carefully choose a set of 12 appropriate speech prompts for the test.
4. Prepare test score sheets for each student (a sample is provided in Appendix C).
5. Bring a timer to count down 30 seconds.

Table 5. Teacher Checklist for the Milestone In-Class Speech Test

1. Announce test and give sample questions for self-preparation.

2. On test day, all students line up in a set order to ensure smooth flow.

3. Students rotate to interview station(s).

4. Interviewer(s) conveys prompt (see sample prompts in Appendix A).

5. Teacher or time-keeper says "start," and student(s) begins response. (For multiple interview stations, students *simultaneously start & stop* answering.)

6. After 30 seconds, the teacher or timekeeper says "stop."

7. Interviewer(s) records number of comprehensible sentences and clauses spoken on test sheet (see sample in Appendix B). If the timekeeper cuts the student off in mid-sentence, assign a 0.5 score.

8. Interviewer makes a quantitative determination:

   • marks a star (*) for "excellent" speech, which may be defined as cohesive, well-developed with a high level of vocabulary and overall eloquence.

   • marks an "X" if the topic was not addressed at all or if the student merely "stacks" unconnected sentences

   • no mark for a "standard" answer composed of standard sentences that address the topic

9. Interviewer reads the next question.

10. Steps 3–8 are repeated until questions are exhausted.

11. Student(s) rotate after questions are exhausted.

12. Those who finish rotate to open desks where they:

    • tabulate their total spoken sentence/clause totals and average per question

    • write their test impressions in English on the back of their test sheets

13. Sheets are collected.

14. Top scores and most improved scores are reported at the next class.

I strongly suggest finding a second rater, which will double the interview stations and thus double the total speech prompts without significantly increasing the time needed for the test. In other words, instead of giving 36 students a total of three prompts in 90 minutes with a single interviewer, those students would be answering six prompts (i.e., three at each interview station) in the same time frame. Importantly, more prompts give students more chances to demonstrate ability, and less weight is placed on each prompt. A proficient student or school staff member can serve as the additional interviewer. The rotation for this format is shown in Figure 2.

There would be no cost to the students and teacher if teaching assistants, college staff members, or advanced students could volunteer as additional interviewers. Arranging for a second or third interviewer may incur a cost,

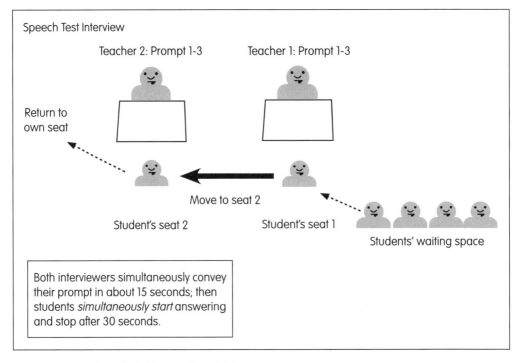

Speech Test Interview

Teacher 2: Prompt 1-3   Teacher 1: Prompt 1-3

Return to own seat

Move to seat 2

Student's seat 2   Student's seat 1

Students' waiting space

Both interviewers simultaneously convey their prompt in about 15 seconds; then students *simultaneously start* answering and stop after 30 seconds.

Figure 2. Test Flow for Milestone Speech Test

however. In a few cases, I did hire exchange students on our university campus to serve as interviewers and paid them for the test session and pretest training (see Figure 3).

If you use an additional interviewer, three things must be conveyed through pretest training. These points are outlined in Table 6.

I have found that simplifying raters' duties has several benefits. First, the interviewers' pretest rater training session can be completed in about 30 minutes. Second, the overall testing stays within the time limit. Finally, the simpler the raters' duties, the more reliable their scoring will be.

Pretest Preparation for Students

While a speech test will certainly motivate nearly any student to practice and improve his oral proficiency, preparing these students to be successful on the high-stakes tests will differ according to teaching context and educational demands. For example, I prefer my students to build upon the linguistic resources they have, but other teachers insist upon requiring students to reproduce target language as part of their answers.

Following are four teaching techniques that can be used in most contexts to prepare students for this high-stakes speaking test:

- Provide regular low-stakes in-class tests. I give one such practice test about every 3 weeks.

Figure 3. Teachers Serving as Interviewers at Toyo Eiwa University for a Large-Scale Milestone-Type Speech Test Involving 140 Students and 8 Teachers Over 90 Minutes

- Give cross-lingual advice. Teach students how to say phrases in their native language in English.

- Provide a large pool of possible topics to practice with.

- Integrate some writing tasks with course speaking tasks, and use similar topics for writing that you may use for the speech test.

Scoring Considerations for In-Class Speaking Tests

No test can ever perfectly judge the elusive entity of speech. Every language test has strengths and weaknesses. Critics of the tests I describe in this chapter may insist that quantitative factors should not be used to judge L2 speaking proficiency, or that scoring by rubric is superior. The caveats of scoring by rubric must be noted, however.

From a theoretical perspective, we can divide speech test scoring into two categories: holistic versus analytic approaches, or multiple and primary trait scoring. While the in-class tests presented here are based mostly on a primary score (i.e., speech rate), holistic rating scales almost always use rubrics with a different score for several different speech features (Fulcher, 2003).

Table 6. Pretest Training for Additional Raters or Interviewers

- **Master counting comprehensible sentences and clauses.**

  For training, I simulate students' speech samples while the interviewers practice counting sentences and clauses.

- **Practice qualitative checks:**

  ♦ **Detect stacking.** Students may be tempted to boost their sentence count by "stacking" sentences that are unrelated whatsoever to the prompt or by repeating the same sentence. If this occurs, raters mark an *X* next to the sentence count on the score sheet, and it is penalized later.

  ♦ **Reward eloquence and excellence.** Extra raters learn which speech samples would be considered "excellent" by listening to a teacher's example. An excellent speech is usually defined as coherent and well-developed with a high level of vocabulary and overall eloquence.

- **Practice being an interviewer who:**

  ♦ puts students at ease as they come to the interview station

  ♦ makes sure the prompt is conveyed

  ♦ never interrupts once a student's response time begins

Scoring by a rubric seriously risks what Alderson (1991) calls *cross-contamination*. He showed that one particular speech factor can strongly influence or cross-contaminate the scoring for other factors. For instance, a low score for pronunciation may trigger an overall low rating. Conversely, there may be a halo effect, causing higher scores for every category if a student greets interviewers enthusiastically, smiles, jokes, speaks loud, or exhibits other behaviors associated with confidence.

Risk of cross-contamination with a rubric is compounded with in-class testing because of prior knowledge of the student. In short, the students' classroom persona or histories can possibly prejudice the scoring either negatively or positively (also see the Popko, Saito-Stehberger & Oh, and Yeh chapters in this volume for other views on rubrics). Without some quantitative factor to judge speech, teacher-based assessment of their students' speech can easily be influenced by who the speaker is rather than how he speaks. By tallying test-takers' speech rate, teachers can gain a somewhat objective, quantitative baseline judgment of L2 speaking ability.

Furthermore, the students need to know what and how they will be judged. Speech rate based on spoken sentences or clauses allows for self-assessment, but I have found that the grade scale shown in Table 7 gives students a clearer and more meaningful goal for self-assessment. The grade scale also influences my final course grading.

Table 7. Grade Scale Sample for Speech Rates

A = 9–12 average sentences or clauses spoken in 30 seconds (more than 12 usually indicates hastened speech, which should be avoided).

B = 7–8 average sentences or clauses spoken in 30 seconds.

C = 5–6 average sentences or clauses spoken in 30 seconds.

D = 4 or fewer average sentences or clauses spoken in 30 seconds.

Note. This table matches letter grades with students' average speech rates. This assessment scale is then matched with the qualitative factors discussed previously. Grade scales may vary in different teaching contexts.

REFLECTIONS

I introduced two practical in-class speaking tests in this chapter. The tests focus on spontaneous speech, not on controlled output of prescribed target language forms. I illustrated how regular testing caused my students' spontaneous speech in monologue to improve dramatically in terms of volume and rate, a crucial aspect of extended speech. Speech usually needs to be annunciated within a reasonable timeframe, which simply describes the experience of speaking in a second or foreign language (Brazil, 1995; Halliday, 1985). Of course, some people may pause more or speak more slowly than others. This is accommodated in the test criterion and stated as the speech rate *range*.

I have seen my students progress in their overall speaking skills outside of these controlled testing situations during free-talk opportunities and classroom discussions. In addition to increases in their speech rate and amount, I have observed several paralinguistic changes. One is students' eye contact. In both video-recorded interviews and free-talk tasks, I noticed that many students increased the number of words spoken during eye contact. Many students initially uttered mostly just one word or term and then broke eye contact. As students become more comfortable speaking spontaneously, they tend to utter more phrases while maintaining eye contact. Other observed changes include a reduction in the proportion of errors to speech, more intersentence coherence, fewer sentence structure errors, increased voice volume, and an increase in recasts.

One thing that did not change was an unwillingness to speak out in front of the whole class, which may be rooted in sociocultural factors rather than linguistic development. Getting students to aggressively take the floor and speak out in front of the whole class may be valid for mainstreaming immigrants in a Western education system; however, the validity of universally insisting on such communication has been called into question (Canagarajah, 2005; Cook, 2002; Kumarava-divelu, 2003).

I consider the in-class tests to be part of a larger nonlinear, output-driven English-language teaching and testing approach (Soresi, 2009; Swain, 1995).

Input is not ignored because output-based tasks and regular testing create timely opportunities for learner-appropriate input. This approach focuses on cross-lingual issues and extending student speech. Supplementary explanation of proper nouns is one example (e.g., ". . . *Harajuku*. It's a major fashion district in Tokyo. ". . . *Gyudon*. It's a bowl of rice with stewed meat and onions on top.").

These types of cross-lingual issues are best revealed through output-driven tasks that encourage free talk or unguided output, where the content of the speech is determined by the student, not the textbook. That type of exercise helps students realize gaps in their first-language (L1) to L2 vocabulary. Admittedly, only bilingual teachers can answer L1 to L2 questions, and monolingual professionals would be disadvantaged. The opposite approach, controlled output, forces students to learn and use target language forms, which is easier for monolingual teachers.

Some may claim the in-class testing approach I am advocating increases fluency at the sacrifice of accuracy. A simple error analysis of recorded speech samples from 56 Japanese students in April and July 2007, however, shows the opposite may be true. This particular group of university students went from approximately 4 sentences per minute (SPM) to 12 SPM during a period of 15 weeks. I believe that the increase in speech rate is accompanied by an increase in automaticity and language control because my students' speech samples did not show an increase in the proportion of errors to speech amount. In other words, I believe that as their speech rate and automaticity increases, so does their language control. In short, they become more comfortable with spontaneous speech and can more accurately manipulate the spoken language.

Finally, I encourage teachers to consider implementing this testing methodology as both summative and formative assessment. The two tests presented in this chapter employ target speech rate ranges to offer learners a clear and meaningful path for developing spontaneous speech proficiency. They also provide ESOL professionals with a practical in-class assessment tool that directly tests speech. More precise speech measurements exist, but my experience shows that these two tests have very strong potential for positive learner impact. After all, the quality of learner outcomes from the testing experience is the heart of the matter (Breen, 2001).

Stephen Soresi teaches in Yokohama, Japan, in Toyo Eiwa University's Department of Social Sciences. He is completing his doctorate at the Aoyama Gakuin University's Graduate School for International Communication. He welcomes readers' comments and questions (ss@toyoeiwa.ac.jp).

APPENDIX A: SAMPLES OF MILESTONE IN-CLASS SPEECH TEST INTERVIEW SPEECH PROMPTS

Interviewer #1

- Tell me about your hometown. OK?

- Tell me about your university. OK?

- What do you think of _____, the prime minister?

Interviewer #2

- Tell me about your mother.

- After you graduate from university, what do you want to do?

- In your opinion, what is the best company in Japan?

APPENDIX B: SAMPLE OF MILESTONE IN-CLASS SPEECH TEST SCORE SHEET

Name:

1st Interviewer

(1) □ (# of comprehensible clauses or sentences spoken. To be written by 1st interviewer).

(2) □.

(3) □.

2nd Interviewer

(4) □.

(5) □.

(6) □.

Total Spoken Sentences = □.

Average Spoken Sentences per 30 seconds = □.

APPENDIX C: QUICK IN-CLASS SPEECH TEST SCORE SHEET

Name:

Round #1: Write the first three questions below. Write number of sentences spoken for each question in boxes.

(1) □.

(2) □.

(3) □.

Round #2: Write the next three questions below. Write number of sentences spoken for each question in boxes.

(4) □.

(5) □.

(6) □.

Round #3: Write the next three questions below. Write number of sentences spoken for each question in boxes.

(7) □.

(8) □.

(9) □.

Round #4: Write the next three questions below. Write number of sentences spoken for each question in boxes.

(10) □.

(11) □.

(12) □.

Total Spoken Sentences = □.

Average Spoken Sentences per 30 seconds = □.

CHAPTER 17

Taking Pronunciation Further With Oral Journals

Joann Chernen

INTRODUCTION

In the literature, oral journals are known variously as audio journals, taped journals, or oral dialogue journals. What they all have in common is a back-and-forth exchange of audio-recorded messages between instructor and student. The purpose of the exercise and the exact technique involved, of course, vary from context to context and from instructor to instructor. In a writing program, student writing, instructor feedback, and meaningful exchanges are recorded in print for future reference, reflection, and analysis. In a pronunciation or oral skills program, however, student speech, instructor feedback, and meaningful exchanges are often transitory words spoken in time that are difficult to capture and recall for future reference, reflection, and analysis. The oral journal is one way to capture and archive communication that is normally fleeting (also see the Lynch chapter in this volume for details on another speaking log).

I began using oral journals as a technique in my own teaching about 8 years ago within the context of a content-based program of instruction. When I first joined this program, I had never read about oral journals being used as a particular technique, nor did I know of anyone else using them. It just seemed like a natural thing to do as an occasional alternative to the writing journal, whereby I could build a rapport with my students through a conversational exchange on content. Additionally, I could provide individualized feedback on not only grammar and vocabulary, but also pronunciation.

As I began working with the journals, it became apparent that the oral journal process was popular with my students, particularly to help them with pronunciation, an area I had not set out to target. Since that time 8 years ago, I have refined the procedure and not only continue to use it as a teaching–learning tool but have instituted it as the cornerstone of a community college pronunciation course for which I have been project coordinator.

After consistently receiving positive student responses and results from oral journals, I decided to explore possible reasons for these reactions. This chapter provides a summary of my findings, together with a brief overview of oral journal use, particularly as practiced in the Pronunciation Course in the English Language Skills Department at Vancouver Community College (VCC) in Canada.

Oral Journal Use in General

A comprehensive look at published and Web-based literature turned up isolated and incidental mention of oral journal use as a supplementary instructional technique in a variety of settings, including classes for teacher education, oral skills, pronunciation, and writing. Oral journals are being used for:

- avoiding convergence on first-language (L1) pronunciation patterns and characteristics (Walker, 2005)

- critical reflection in content-based English courses (Dantas-Whitney, 2002)

- oral–aural expression and practice (Hughes, 2001)

- helping learners build confidence in their spoken English (Bradford, 1995)

- engendering teacher–student rapport (Henry, 1994)

- drawing attention to and correcting errors in all, one, or any combination of grammar, lexis, and pronunciation (Allan, 1991)

Without exception, all commentary about the potential benefits of oral journals for students is extremely positive. Furthermore, almost all of the methodological descriptions, regardless of specific objectives or target audience, identify the same three characteristics as being the most valuable features:

- the provision of a non-threatening environment for communication

- individualized feedback

- student–teacher rapport building

Oral journals are also described as time-consuming for the instructor, however. Ultimately in this chapter I address the perception that oral journals are burdensome, and I will make specific suggestions about how they can be made manageable for teachers.

CONTEXT

Background

Five years ago, I was asked to develop a new pronunciation course for intermediate- and advanced-level students. When I conducted my research, there were 545 full-time equivalent students in the English Language Skills department, the mandate of which is to address the English-language needs of adult

immigrants in the community. The development of a new course in this department was in response to pressure to raise the speaking standards for all English
language students.

Student Profile

In general, it would appear that there are four different types of students who
register in the pronunciation class:

- students with good proficiency who wish to make further improvements in
  the area of pronunciation and oral communication in general

- students who have significant articulation difficulties, especially at the
  segmental level

- students who tend to be highly communicative but may not be good at
  noticing and often have a rate of speech that is too fast

- students who lack confidence in their speaking and listening ability, whether
  it be real-time spontaneous encounters or situations where preparation is
  possible. As a result of their anxiety, speech is unclear. Many of our students
  fall into this last category.

Course Description

The pronunciation course is approximately 24 weeks in duration, and students
meet once or twice a week for 3 or 4 hours. There are typically six or seven different instructors teaching one section of 18 students at any one time. All instructors were trained by me. They all use oral journals as the core teaching–learning
tool. Other key components of the course include:

- instruction in selected features of the sound system of English

- learner training and the promotion of effective strategies for pronunciation
  and oral skills development

- fluency and delivery enhancement through recorded oral presentations and
  analysis

- authentic listening practice

A fundamental goal of the course, underpinning all components, is to increase
student confidence in the use and comprehension of spoken English.

CURRICULUM, TASKS, MATERIALS

General Procedure

The oral journal requires that students provide a recorded speech sample, 2 minutes in length, for the instructor to listen to and evaluate in terms of the level of

intelligibility, or speech clarity. A checklist for elements of clear speech appears in Table 1. Once every other week, one 40-minute visit to the audio laboratory is scheduled as part of class time for this express purpose.

Students are encouraged to prepare the oral journal ahead of time. If the students are not using their own words, they must be very familiar with whatever text they have chosen to use. That is, whether they are reading from a prepared text or speaking extemporaneously on a topic they have researched, students must "own" the language. I have seen in our course that even anxious students can own the language (for more on this point, see the Bradley chapter in this volume). The fluency of their delivery may suffer, but the extensive preparation that the course requires allows all students the opportunity to produce speech that they control as their own. The fact that they have 1 or 2 weeks to prepare works greatly in their favor, and over time the low-stress atmosphere helps them improve as a result of lowered anxiety.

My experience over the years has shown that if students process the oral journal ahead of time for grammar, vocabulary, and organization of ideas, the speech product is significantly better. Students themselves have consistently made the observation that they think their speech is better if they prepare, and while such preparation may not be authentic practice for the challenges involved in real-time processing, students appreciate the benefits that arise in the areas of delivery and fluency with rehearsed practice. Such rehearsed practice is heavily endorsed (Skehan, 1998, p. 119) not only for its ability to encourage automaticity, but also because it allows for noticing, a key requirement for improvement. Prior to collection of the audio recording by the instructor, students are advised to listen to their recording multiple times in an effort to hone their ear by noticing and reflecting upon areas for self-correction. They can then rerecord if necessary.

The audio laboratory at my college was recently upgraded from audio cassette recording to digitized recording, allowing journal entries to be exchanged virtually.

Topic Choice

Students are free to choose topics, although instructors may assign topics from time to time. In all cases students are exhorted to speak on something they care about. This is extremely important because if they do not care about what they are saying, delivery is often flat. Sometimes students need direction and motivation to help them decide on a topic for the oral journal. This is why we provide them with a handout entitled "101 Possible Topics for Oral Journals" at the beginning of the program. Suggested topics include My Background, My Job, My Childhood, A Good or Bad Vacation, How to Cook Something, Language Needed to Talk to a Hairdresser, and Lyrics to a Favorite Song.

Giving Feedback

After the students' recordings have been collected, the instructor listens to each and evaluates the language in terms of clear speech. Once the instructor has finished listening and taking notes, she makes an audio recording of her comments, tailoring feedback to individual student needs and goals. In general, the instructor will attend to the characteristics of clear speech listed in Table 1.

Positively Motivating Feedback

Because students are in need of more confidence regarding their spoken English, instructors make their commentary as positively motivating as possible. That is, teachers try to help students realize existing strengths with regard to intelligibility, thus serving to validate accents and the linguistic reality of English as an international language or a *lingua franca*. As Bradford (1995) notes, confidence is what all students need in order to progress in all facets of language learning, pronunciation included.

Negatively Motivating Feedback

The focus of the pronunciation course is clear speech, not native speaker mimicry. Therefore, instructors will choose for commentary those aspects of speech that have the greatest impact on comprehensibility. That is, they try to address only selected features of the sound system of English. Narrowing the spectrum of features for commentary also has the additional benefit of easing the workload involved in the feedback process.

Rapport Building

In addition to evaluative comments, the instructor may also want to respond briefly to the content in a conversational way, asking questions or simply commenting. This response reinforces the two-way communication feature of oral journals. It helps to develop a rapport between instructors and students and can have a positive effect on student confidence levels.

Table 1. Checklist for Evaluating Speech Clarity

- A strong, confident voice
- A moderate rate of speech
- Pausing after tone units
- Correct placement of word stress
- Correct placement of nuclear stress, the most prominent stress within a tone unit
- Careful articulation of consonants and consonant clusters (especially those consonants that fall within the realm of the *lingua franca* core (LFC)
- Careful articulation of vowels (vowel quantity more than vowel quality)
- Attention to word endings and linking

Encouraging Self-Correction

Instructors find it very rewarding when they listen to the recordings and hear students self-correct, incorporate corrections, and show evidence of increased awareness and progress (see Table 2). They will comment on such things to the students in order to build confidence and help feed the students' motivation to continue to self-monitor.

Processing Feedback

At my institution, instructors normally return their recorded evaluations to students within 1 week via e-mail or by posting to a Web site. Students are encouraged to listen repeatedly to the feedback in an effort to further analyze instructor comments and practice in accordance with suggestions. In the case of the virtual exchange of recordings, students will usually transfer recordings to such personal listening devices as iPods and other MP3 players.

The process begins again the following week and continues until the end of the course. The hope is that over time students will internalize instructor commentary and effect permanent positive change in their speech. Ultimately, the goal is for students to develop increased awareness of their own speech and their ability to self-monitor and self-correct, thus becoming more autonomous in their learning. The appendix contains an illustrative example of one student's oral journal experience along with the transcript from the student's first and last oral journal entries and one of my corresponding responses. The transcript illustrates the role the oral journal process can play in building confidence and the positive impact this can have on speech.

The following description is representative of many students' experience.

> A young man from Hong Kong spoke in such a flat, unexpressive monotone that it made me, as a listener, less inclined to want to listen to what he was

Table 2. Examples of Improvements

Sometimes improvements noted in student speech are small:
• student begins to consistently articulate the /d/ in *I'd like*
• student pays obvious attention to articulation of /v/ and /w/
Other times the improvements noted are greater:
• student begins to curb the overuse of upward-rising intonation contours
• student begins to show instances of self-correction on the /l/ and r/ confusion, for example, saying *loom* initially and then self-correcting to *room*
Other examples of improvements in pronunciation that have become apparent through oral journal sessions include:
• making an obvious effort to pause after thought groups
• beginning to inject more feeling into speaking as evidenced by a greater intonation range and more effective use of accentual stress

saying because he sounded so very bored and uninterested. I communicated my feelings to him through the oral journal and using the language he had uttered in the oral journal, I gave him imitative models to analyze and compare. I also mentioned to him that his speech would likely sound more engaging if he relaxed and smiled a bit when he spoke. After four oral journal exchanges for which accentual stress and a greater pitch range were the focus areas, the student showed marked improvement. The challenge then became one of having the student carry his improvements over into face-to-face communication.

REFLECTIONS

Investigating the Effectiveness of Oral Journals

Research that I conducted on journal use by others in the field confirmed my own experience and anecdotal evidence that oral journals are an extremely useful technique for pronunciation and oral skills development. There is a consensus among practitioners, myself included, that two of the main reasons for the success of oral journals are their ability to provide students with a nonthreatening environment for communication and the enabling of individualized correction and feedback (Allan 1991; Bradford, 1995; Henry, 1994; Walker, 2005). To further investigate the perceived effectiveness of oral journals, I gathered data from 61 students studying in the 2006 winter term of the pronunciation course in the English Language Skills Department at VCC through focus groups and a detailed questionnaire.

The Questionnaire

The questionnaire consisted of 57 questions that required answers based on a sliding scale, where "1" represented disagree, "2" represented neither agree nor disagree, and "3" represented agree. There were also two open-ended questions for freer commentary. The questionnaires were administered to students by their instructors in class, and instructors were available to answer questions about interpreting the questionnaire. For the most part, students answered the questionnaire easily, with little clarification needed.

Profile of Students

Sixty-one adult students completed the questionnaire. Of the 61 respondents, 57% were native speakers of Chinese and 47% were speakers of other languages. Other native languages included Spanish, Russian, Korean, Farsi, French, Bulgarian, Kurdish, Arabic, Azerbaijani, Thai, Vietnamese, Romanian, Bengali, and Serbo-Croatian. With regard to education, 56% were university educated, 29% were college educated, and the rest had high school education. The students were equally divided between advanced- and intermediate-level speakers of English.

The average length of English study was 1.3 years in Canada and 5.3 years in the home country of the student. Prior to taking the pronunciation course at the college, 92% of the students had never used oral journals, 69% had not owned a tape recorder or personal recording device, and 46% had never used a tape recorder or personal recording device before for English study or practice.

Results of the Questionnaire

For the purpose of presenting the questionnaire results, I adopted the following terms to refer to differing levels of consensus and agreement among students: *overwhelming* (80–100%); *significant* (69–79%); *slightly more than half* (50–60%); and *just under half* (41–49%).

The Sliding Scale Questions

There was overwhelming consensus (80–100%) among students on 19 sliding scale questions. It was revealed, among other things, that most students:

- believe that their pronunciation and speaking are better when they are more confident

- like to listen to their teacher's voice

- look forward to hearing their teacher's feedback

- want and value individualized feedback and correction

There was significant consensus (60–79%) on another 19 questions. A partial summary of the answers to these questions showed that a majority of students:

- believe that oral journals lead to clearer speech

- consider oral journals to be a personally motivating way to practice pronunciation and oral skills

- are motivated to try their best because they know their speech will be evaluated

- can remember correction offered through oral journals because they allow for unlimited repetition

Slightly more than half of the students (50–60%) agreed on 9 of the 57 questions. Answers to some of these questions showed that a slight majority of students:

- find the oral journal offered an opportunity to ask the teacher questions about things that they would not have asked

- find that the oral journal has improved their ability to analyze speech—both their own and that of others

Finally, just under half of all students surveyed (41–49%) showed agreement on six questions. The answers to some of these questions indicated that just under half of all students:

- feel that oral journals provide them with one of the few opportunities they have for a social or personal connection with a fluent speaker of English

- feel that oral journals enhance fluency

The Open Questions

One open-ended question asked students to comment on what they thought was the best thing about oral journals. The most significant finding was that 61% of the respondents indicated the best thing was getting individualized feedback and correction.

When asked to comment on what they thought was the worst thing about oral journals, the most significant finding was that 25% of the students surveyed indicated there was nothing negative about oral journals. The next most significant finding was that 23% of respondents found the 2-minute time limit for an oral journal entry to be too short.

Discussion of the Survey Results

The oral journal attribute most valued by students was receiving individualized feedback and correction, which confirms findings showing that adult learners have a strong desire for error correction (Allan, 1991; Chenoweth, Day, Chun, & Luppescu, 1983). Given the intensity of affective concerns over one's voice and pronunciation, the instructional challenge lies in finding a safe, nonthreatening way to offer personalized feedback. It would appear, given the overwhelming endorsement shown for correction and feedback in the questionnaire results, that oral journals satisfy this challenge.

An Integrated Approach Paradigm

The students' perception that oral journals are an effective teaching–learning tool and lead to clearer speech is significant. To determine why it is that they find the technique effective necessitates a closer look at the "most significant" findings that showed a consensus opinion of 60% or greater. My examination reveals that highly prized attributes of the oral journal fall into different categories— categories which, interestingly, mirror the three pillars of Morley's (1995) integrated approach paradigm: affective involvement, cognitive involvement, and physical involvement. I believe Morley's pronunciation paradigm is comprehensive, embodying much of what is considered valid and current today, including significant attention to strategies. Although Morley's description of her approach is more than a decade old, I feel she has captured the essence of effective pronunciation teaching and learning. Next, I employ Morley's framework to analyze the pedagogic merits of oral journal methodology as described in this chapter.

Affective Involvement

Regarding affective involvement and the psychological component of learning, it would appear that the oral journal technique as described in this chapter provides students with the all-important safe zone needed for more confident self-expression and processing of error correction. The value of this attribute cannot be overestimated, as increased confidence often has the happy consequence of increased speaker comprehensibility generated by a stronger voice and slower, more relaxed speech. Having a human connection, not a disembodied voice as exists on a commercial tape or computer program, is also important for the student on the affective level.

Cognitive Involvement

At the level of intellectual and cognitive involvement, the oral journal succeeds first by satisfying the student's desire for correction, that is, providing instructor commentary that the students can repeatedly listen to. Furthermore, students can train their ear and hone their ability to self-correct by repeatedly listening to the voice of their instructor as compared to their own voice, with a view to noticing both strengths and weaknesses. The fact that the oral journals are archived is also helpful from a cognitive point of view by allowing students to self-monitor and track their own progress through comparisons with earlier recordings.

Physical Involvement

With oral journals, the student can replay instructor models again and again. In this way, the oral journal allows for intensive imitative practice opportunities and engagement of the student at the physical level.

Oral Journals in Use: Concerns and Suggestions

Instructors at my college have found oral journals to be highly effective for helping students develop clear speech. There is a perception, however, that using oral journals in English for speakers of other languages (ESOL) classes is extremely time-consuming and labor intensive for the instructor. I would like to address this perception and offer specific suggestions for making the technique manageable. To inform this aspect of my investigation, I interviewed eight different instructors about their experiences with oral journals over the course of a 3-month term.

Time Consuming

The average number of students in each instructor's class was 18. Initially, all of the instructors reported that they felt overwhelmed by the prospect of the work involved in listening and recording feedback to 18 different students. All of the instructors, however, commented that over time and with practice, the time they needed to listen and offer feedback decreased significantly. They discovered that 8 minutes per student entry was sufficient. For a 2-minute student recording,

8 minutes was the length of time that I had determined through my own experience. It is also the amount of time suggested by other oral journal practitioners in the field as a realistic expectation. The technological switch from cassette tapes to audio files has allowed me to shave a further 2 minutes off the time necessary to listen and respond to each journal entry. For the instructors to be able to listen and respond within 6–8 minutes, they had to overcome a number of hurdles. These obstacles included:

- not knowing what to say to the student

- not being able to pinpoint the pronunciation issue

- not being happy with their response and needing to record again

- scripting feedback before recording because of uncertainty

All instructors reported that with practice they became more efficient as their ability to analyze sound features of student speech and offer constructive feedback improved. It simply became easier to identify and comment on sound features as their ear for such listening sharpened.

The number-one hurdle for instructors to overcome, however, was their inclination to correct every mistake, grammar and vocabulary included. Once the instructor narrowed her focus to select features of pronunciation and aspects of delivery, there was an immediate reduction in the amount of time spent on the oral journal process. One instructor reported that the most helpful hint was to listen to the student recording only once. In general, repeated listenings should be avoided to save time and avoid overly critical responses.

Recently, as another time-saving measure, I have begun asking students for oral journal entries that are 1½ minutes in duration as opposed to 2 minutes, and have found the length to be more than adequate for the exercise. Additionally, I am experimenting with peer feedback by having students exchange recordings and offer feedback to each other.

Finally, I think it is helpful if instructors remind themselves that the type of feedback they are giving is rare for the student to receive, and thus is highly valued and appreciated. Not often are students given commentary on their individual strengths and weaknesses in pronunciation and oral skills. Therefore, instructors need to remember that a little can go a long way.

Labor Intensive

While it is true that time expenditure can be effectively dealt with, there is no escaping the fact that listening to oral journals to analyze and offer constructive feedback is focused work that requires concentrated attention from the instructor. One instructor reported that she could not even drink a cup of tea while working on oral journals and commented that, by comparison, marking essays can be relaxing. Even so, the instructors at my institution reported a high level of satisfaction with oral journals due to the exceedingly positive student response and the results that they see their students achieve.

Technological Concerns

Sometimes instructors worry about students being able to secure the use of a computer or tape recorder for listening and recording purposes. In reply to this concern, I tell teachers to encourage their students to purchase some form of technology that will allow them to listen to and record language. In the rare circumstance that the environment or the economic circumstances make this impossible, I recommend that students set aside a regular time to visit a school library or learning center.

In circumstances where there is no audio laboratory, the instructor could, with one tape recorder, set up a recording station outside of the classroom that students could take turns visiting to record an oral journal entry. One instructor who was using oral journals with her students in a work-site training program compensated for the fact that there was no audio laboratory by bringing in her digital recorder for students to use. She would then upload the oral journal entries onto her computer at home or in her office to listen and respond, ultimately converting the entries into sound files that she could send to her students.

Conclusion

Oral journals have been avoided for too long by ESOL instructors teaching speaking, largely because of the claim that they are too time consuming. In this chapter, I attempted to show teachers that this claim is not valid. Adjustments can be made to ensure the manageability of oral journals. ESOL educators should reconsider oral journals because they are versatile and able to effectively address the three different levels deemed so important for adult learners in the advancement of pronunciation and oral skills: the affective level, the cognitive level, and the physical level. Additionally, oral journals are effective for teaching speaking because they simultaneously anchor pronunciation instruction and learning within meaningful and authentic contexts, the hallmarks of current best practice in language teaching, no matter the domain.

Joann Chernen is an instructor and teacher trainer at Vancouver Community College in Canada with more than 27 years experience in the delivery of many types of English as a second language (ESL) programs. She is also involved in curriculum and materials design. Her areas of expertise include pronunciation and content-based language instruction. She is the department head of ESL at Vancouver Community College.

APPENDIX: ILLUSTRATIVE EXAMPLE OF ONE STUDENT'S ORAL JOURNAL EXPERIENCE

Case Summary

A young mother, an immigrant of 2 years from Korea, described in her first oral journal entry a recent experience at a Burger King restaurant that upset her and caused her to believe that her "pronunciation [was] not good enough to communicate with people in Canada." She had ordered a cup of coffee, and instead of pronouncing [f] she pronounced [p]. This is a typical Korean–English mistake, yet one the student was seemingly unaware of.

What follows is this student's first and last oral journal entries. Also included is my response to the student's first entry.

Oral Journal Entry #1

After some experience I found that my pronunciation is not good enough to communicate with people in here. That's why I'm taking this course. For example, I was at Burger King for a cup of *copy* not so long ago. I spoke to the staff three times, *copy*, but they couldn't understand me. I tried to make exact pronunciation in a *diperent* way, *copy, copy, copy*, but it didn't work. I was so upset. I don't think it's a very difficult word to pronounce. I'm not sure what my problem exactly is. Maybe accent or maybe my voice is not loud enough. I never imagine my pronunciation is as bad as that level. I'm sure part of my problem is related to confidence. I want to find my problem and make progress, that's my goal.

Instructor Response #1 [shortened]

Hi (Student's Name), I agree with you. Your problem is more related to confidence. What happens when you lose your confidence? Well, usually people do speak more quietly, so a combination of unfamiliar pronunciation and quiet voice equals difficult to understand. So, for example, your Burger King example . . . a very good example and thank you for telling me about it. If you had said *copy* louder, mmm no, maybe that alone wouldn't have helped, but you have to think, what would help your listener? If you said "a cup of coffee," even if you didn't pronounce *coffee* correctly, and said "I'd like a cup of *copy*," "a cup of *copy* please." Just the *cup*, the *cup of* together . . . that would have helped your listener. That's a really good strategy to think of, okay, add another key word or two, and make sure your voice is strong and loud enough. Now, your problem, I'm surprised you're not aware of it. Maybe you are. A typical Korean problem is the /p/ and the /f/, right? So, not *copy*. *Copy* is what you do, what you do with a photocopy machine, right? You make *copies, copies*, but here you want *coffee, coffee*. Top teeth, bottom lip, [f], like the number *five*, 1, 2, 3, 4, 5, like the number *four*, 1, 2, 3, 4. /f/, /f/, *coffee, coffee, coffee*. So, now that you know that that is a problem word, do not lose confidence. Go back to Burger King and say it again,

"Yes, I'd like a cup of coffee please." Now if you practice before you go, and say it with a loud voice, and with confidence, I bet you'll be successful, and I really think you should do it again and again a few times just to build your confidence because it is a very common word.

Oral Journal Entry #6

I think I made improvements about English since the beginning of this course. I think I learned how to enjoy speaking English. I realized that many people have their pronunciation problems like me and it gives me courage to speak. Before I think pronunciation is difficult to overcome and boring. Now I focus more on pronunciation. I think English is more interesting, so now I'm kind of more practicing. I always want to speak in order to practice, practice. Last week you gave me a question about how I will get conversation with native English speakers. I am planning to join a swimming class or cooking class, something like that. If I register in a swimming class or cooking class I can learn how to cook, how to swim, and also I can have conversation with many people.

References

ABC News (2006). Blood pressure boost for workaholics, ABC News Medical Minute. Retrieved August 29, 2006, from http://abcnews.go.com/Technology/Podcasting/

Akabari, R. (2008). Transforming lives: Introducing critical pedagogy into ELT classrooms. *ELT Journal, 62*(3), 276–283.

Alcón Soler, E. (2005). Does instruction work for learning pragmatics in the EFL context? *System, 33*, 417–435.

Alderson, C. J., & Bachman, L. F. (2004). Series editors' preface to *Assessing Speaking*. In S. Luoma, *Assessing speaking* (pp. ix–xi.). Cambridge: Cambridge University Press.

Alderson, J. C. (1991). Bands and scores. In J. C. Alderson & B. North (Eds.), *Language testing in the 1990s* (pp. 71–86). London: British Council/Macmillan.

AlFally, I. (2004). The role of some selected psychological and personality traits of the rater in the accuracy of self- and peer-assessment. *System, 32*(3), 407–426.

Allan, D. (1991). Tape journals: Bridging the gap between communication and correction. *ELT Journal, 45*(1), 61–66.

Allwright, D. (2005). From teaching points to learning opportunities and beyond. *TESOL Quarterly, 39*(1), 9–31.

Anderson, K., Maclean, J., & Lynch, T. (2004). *Study speaking* (2nd ed.). Cambridge: Cambridge University Press.

Arnold, J. (1999). *Affect in language learning*. Cambridge: Cambridge University Press.

Asami, E. (2007, November 27). More medical institutions seen adopting English-language use, *The Japan Times Online*. Retrieved November 27, 2007, from http://www.japantimes.co.jp

Atkinson, D. (1997). A critical approach to critical thinking in TESOL. *TESOL Quarterly, 31*, 71–94.

Auerbach, E. R., & Burgess, D. (1985). The hidden curriculum of survival ESL. *TESOL Quarterly, 19*, 475–495.

Bachman, L. F. (1990). *Fundamental considerations in language testing*. Oxford: Oxford University Press.

Bailey, K. M., & Nunan, D. (Eds.) (1996). *Voices from the language classroom*. New York: Cambridge University Press.

Bailey, K., Curtis, A., & Nunan, D. (1998). Undeniable insights: The collaborative use of three professional development practices. *TESOL Quarterly, 32*, 546–556.

Baugh, L. S. (1997). *How to write term papers and reports* (2nd ed.). New York: McGraw-Hill.

Bebermeier, H., Frederichs, M., Hartmann-Kleinschmidt, E., & Stoll, U. (2004). *Making the grade with Ginger 1*. Berlin: Cornelsen.

Becker, C., Gerngross, G., Puchta, H., & Zebisch, G. (2004). *Playway to English 3—Show what you know*. Leipzig, Germany: Klett.

Blakey, E., & Spence, S. (1990). *Developing metacognition*. (ERIC Document Reproduction Service No. 32 7 218.) Retrieved August 5, 2007, from ERIC database.

Bleutge, C., & Obermann, J. (2004). Sprachförderung mit Musik und Bewegung: Silly little song [Supporting language growth through music and movement: Silly little song]. *Grundschulmagazin Englisch, 4*, 9–11.

Bonwell, C. C., & Eison, J. A. (1991). *Active learning: Creating excitement in the classroom*. Washington, DC: ERIC Clearinghouse on Higher Education.

Böttger, H. (2005). *Englischlernen in der Grundschule* [Learning English in the primary school]. Bad Heilbrunn, Germany: Klinkhardt.

Boutell, T. (2008). WWW FAQs: How do I make a video podcast? Retrieved January 20, 2008, from http://www.boutell.com/newfaq/creating/makevideopodcast.html/

Bovée, C. (2003). Contemporary public speaking (2nd ed.). San Diego, CA: Rowman and Littlefield.

Bradford, B. (1995). The pronunciation clinic. *Speak Out!, Newsletter of the IATEFL Pronunciation Special Interest Group, 16*, 20–25.

Brazil, D. (1995). *A grammar of speech*. Oxford: Oxford University Press.

Breen, M. (2001). Overt participation and covert acquisition in the language classroom. In M. Breen (Ed.), *Learner contributions to language learning* (pp. 112–140). Harlow, England: Pearson Education.

Brinton, D., Snow, M. A., & Wesche, M. B. (1989). *Content-based second language instruction*. Boston: Heinle & Heinle.

Brockbank, A., & McGill, I. (2000). *Facilitating reflective learning in higher education*. Buckingham, England: Open University Press.

Brown, A. L. (1980). Metacognitive development and reading. In R.J. Spiro, B. Bruce, & W. F. Brewer (Eds.), *Theoretical issues in reading comprehension* (pp. 453–479). Hillsdale, NJ: Lawrence Erlbaum.

Brown, G., & Yule, G. (1983). *Teaching the spoken language*. Cambridge: Cambridge University Press.

Brown, H. D. (1987). *Principles of language learning and teaching*. Englewood Cliffs, NJ: Prentice-Hall.

Brown, H. D. (2001). *Teaching by principles* (2nd ed.). White Plains, NY: Addison-Wesley Longman.

Brown, H. D. (2004). *Language assessment: Principles and classroom practices*. New York: Longman.

Brown, H. D. (2007). *Principles of language learning and teaching* (5th ed.). New York: Addison Wesley Longman.

Brown, J. D. (2000). University entrance examinations: Strategies for creating positive washback on English language teaching in Japan. *Shiken: JALT Testing & Evaluation SIG Newsletter*, 3(2), 4–8.

Bygate, M. (1996). Effects of task repetition: Appraising the development of second language learners. In J. Willis & D. Willis (Eds.), *Challenge and change in language teaching* (pp. 136–146). Oxford, England: Heineman.

Bygate, M. (1998). Theoretical perspectives on speaking. *Annual Review of Applied Linguistics, 18*, 20–42.

Cameron, L. (2001). *Teaching languages to young learners*. Cambridge: Cambridge University Press.

Campton, D. (1977). *Us and them*. London: Samuel French Ltd.

Canagarajah, A. S. (2005). Critical pedagogy in L2 learning and teaching. In E. Hinkel (Ed.), *Handbook of research in second language teaching and learning* (pp. 931–949). Mahwah, NJ: Laurence Erlbaum.

Canagarajah, A. S. (2006). TESOL at forty: What are the issues? *TESOL Quarterly, 40*, 9–34.

Canale, M., & Swain, M. (1980). Theoretical bases of communicative approaches to second language teaching and testing. *Applied Linguistics, 1*(1), 1–47.

Carrier, K. A. (2003). NNS teacher trainees in Western-based TESOL programs. *ELT Journal, 57*(3), 242–250.

Celce-Murcia, M., Dörnyei, Z., & Thurrell, S. (1995). Communicative competence: A pedagogically motivated model with content specifications. *Issues in Applied Linguistics, 6*(2), 5–35.

Chartrand, R. (2006). Asynchronous language learning through podcasting. *International Association of Teachers of English as a Foreign Language (IATEFL) CALL Review,* Winter 2006, 18–22.

Chenoweth, N. A., Day, R. R., Chun, A. E., & Luppescu, S. (1983). Attitudes and preferences of non-native speakers to corrective feedback. *Studies in Second Language Acquisition, 6*(1), 79–87.

Cohen, L., Manion, L., & Morrison, K. (2000). *Research methods in education.* London: Routledge.

Connor, U. (2006). Fear and loathing on the convention stage. *Essential Teacher, 3*(4), 22–24.

Cook, V. (2002). *Portraits of the L2 user.* Cleveland, OH: Multilingual Matters.

Corder, S. P. (1967). The significance of learners' errors. *International Review of Applied Linguistics, 5,* 161–170.

Cotton, K. (2001). Classroom questioning. *School Improvement Research Series.* Retrieved November 10, 2007, from http://www.nwrel.org/scpd/sirs/3/cu5.html

Crookall, D., & Saunders, D. (1989). Towards an integration of communication and simulation. In D. Crookall & D. Saunders (Eds.), *Communication and simulation: From two fields to one theme* (pp. 3–32). Clevedon, England: Multilingual Matters.

Crookes, G., & Lehner, A. (1998). Aspects of process in an ESL critical pedagogy teacher education course. *TESOL Quarterly, 32,* 319–328.

Cummins, J. (1996). *Negotiating identity: Education for empowerment in a diverse society.* Los Angeles: California Association for Bilingual Education.

Curran, C. A. (1977). *Counseling–learning, a whole person model for education.* Apple River, IL: Apple River Press.

Dantas-Whitney, M. (2002). Critical reflection in the second language classroom through audiotaped journals. *System, 30*(4), 543–555.

Davies, A., Brown, A., Elder, C., Hill, K., Lumley, T., & McNamara, T. (1999). *Dictionary of language testing.* Cambridge: Cambridge University Press.

deBot, K., (1996). The psycholinguistics of the output hypothesis. *Language Learning, 46*(3), 528–555.

Deci, E. L., & Ryan, R. M. (2002). *Handbook of self-determination research.* Rochester, NY: Rochester University Press.

Denzin, N. K., & Lincoln, Y. S. (Eds.). (1998). *The landscape of qualitative research: Theories and issues.* Thousand Oaks, CA: Sage Publications.

Derwing, T. M., & Rossiter, M. J. (2004). Second language fluency: Judgments on different tasks. *Language Learning, 54*(4), 655–679.

Diaz-Rico, L. T. (2008). *A course for teaching English learners*. Boston: Pearson Education.

Dickson, S. V., Chard, D. J., & Simmons, D. C. (1993). An integrated reading/ writing curriculum: A focus on scaffolding. *LD Forum, 18*(4), 12–16.

Diehr, B. (2006). Reden und reden lassen [Talk and let talk]. *Grundschule, 9,* 36–40.

Diehr, B., & Frisch, S. (2008). *Mark their words. Sprechleistungen im Englischunterricht der Grundschule fördern und beurteilen [Mark their words. Supporting and assessing speaking in the primary school EFL class]*. Braunschweig, Germany: Westermann.

Dieu, D., & Stevens, V. (2007). Pedagogical affordances of syndication, aggregation, and mash-up of content on the Web. *TESL-EJ, 11*(1), 1–15.

Doctorow, C. (2002). *Essential blogging*. Sebastopol, CA: O'Reilly.

Doughty, C., & Varela, E. (1998). Communicative focus on form. In C. Doughty & J. Williams (Eds.), *Focus on form in classroom second language acquisition* (pp. 114–138). Cambridge: Cambridge University Press.

Doyé, P., & Lüttge, D. (1977). *Untersuchungen zum Englischunterricht in der Grundschule. Bericht über das Forschungsprojekt FEU* [Investigating the teaching of English in primary school. Report on the FEU research project]. Braunschweig, Germany: Westermann.

Dudley-Evans, T., & St. John, M. (1998). *Developments in English for specific purposes: A multidisciplinary approach*. Cambridge: Cambridge University Press.

Edge, J. (2001). *Action research*. Alexandria, VA: TESOL.

Edge, J. (Ed.). (2006). *(re)locating TESOL in an age of empire*. Hampshire, UK: Palgrave Macmillan.

Educational Testing Service. (2005). *Helping your students communicate with confidence*. Princeton, NJ: Author.

Ellis, K. (1995). Apprehension, self-perceived competency and teacher immediacy in the laboratory-supported public speaking course: Trends and relationships. *Communication Education, 44*(1), 64–77.

Ellis, R. (1985). *Understanding second language acquisition*. Oxford: Oxford University Press.

Ellis, R. (1997a). *Second language acquisition*. Oxford: Oxford University Press.

Ellis, R. (1997b). *SLA research and language teaching*. Oxford: Oxford University Press.

Ellis, R. (2000). *Second language acquisition*. Oxford: Oxford University Press.

Ellis, R. (2001). *SLA research and language teaching*. Oxford: Oxford University Press.

Ellis, R. (2003). *Task-based language learning and teaching*. Oxford: Oxford University Press.

Ellis, R., & Brakhuizen, G. (2005). *Analysing learner language*. Oxford: Oxford University Press.

Entwistle, N. J. (1984). Contrasting perspectives on learning. In F. Marton, D. Hounsell, & N. Entwistle (Eds.), *The experience of learning* (pp. 3–22). Edinburgh, Scotland: Scottish Academic Press.

Fairclough, N. (Ed.). (1992). *Critical language awareness*. London: Longman.

Farrell, T. S. C. (2007). A place for teachers in research. *Essential Teacher*, 4(1), 14–16.

Ferris, D. (1998). Students' views of academic aural/oral skills: A comparative needs analysis. *TESOL Quarterly*, 32, 289–318.

Ferris, D., & Tagg, T. (1996a). Academic oral communication needs of EAP learners: What subject-matter instructors actually require. *TESOL Quarterly*, 30, 31–58.

Ferris, D., & Tagg, T. (1996b). Academic listening/speaking tasks for ESL students: Problems, suggestions, and implications. *TESOL Quarterly*, 30, 297–320.

Flavell, J. (1976). Metacognitive aspects of problem solving. In L. Resnick (Ed.), *The nature of intelligence* (pp. 231–236). Hillsdale, NJ: Erlbaum.

Folse, K. S. (2006). *The art of teaching speaking*. Ann Arbor: The University of Michigan Press.

Forbes, S. (2003). *Holistic education: An analysis of its ideas and nature*. Brandon, VT: Solomon Press.

Foss, K. A., & Reitzel, A. C. (1988). A relational model for managing second language anxiety. *TESOL Quarterly*, 22, 437–454.

Fotos, S. (1996). Integrating grammar instruction and communicative language use through grammar and consciousness-raising tasks. *TESOL Quarterly*, 28, 323–351.

Fotos, S. (2002). Structure-based interactive tasks for the EFL grammar learner. In E. Hinkel & S. Fotos (Eds.), *New perspectives on grammar teaching in second language classrooms* (pp. 135–154). Mahwah, NJ: Lawrence Erlbaum.

Freire, P. (1972). *Pedagogy of the oppressed*. New York: Seabury Press.

Freire, P. (1973). *Education for critical consciousness*. New York: Seabury Press.

Freire, P. (1993). *Pedagogy of the oppressed*. New York: Continuum.

Fry, H., Ketteridge, S., & Marshall, S. (2003). *Handbook for teaching & learning in higher education: Enhancing academic practice* (2nd ed.). London: Routledge, Taylor & Francis.

Fulcher, G. (2003). *Testing second language speaking.* Edinburgh: Pearson.

Galbraith, R. E., & Jones, T. M. (1976). *Moral reasoning: A teaching handbook for adapting Kohlberg to the classroom.* Minneapolis, MN: Greenhaven Press.

Gass, S. M., & Selinker, L. (2001). *Second language acquisition.* Mahwah, NJ: Lawrence Erlbaum.

Geoghegan, M. W., & Klass, D. (2007). *Podcast solutions: The complete guide to podcasting* (2nd ed.). Berkeley, CA: Friends of Ed.

Graman, T. (1988). Education for humanization: Applying Paulo Freire's pedagogy to learning a second language. *Harvard Educational Review, 58*(4), 433–450.

Greenbaum, S., & Quirk, R. (1992). *A student's grammar of the English language.* Harlow, England: Pearson Education.

Grundy, P. (1994). *Beginners: Resource books for teachers.* Oxford: Oxford University Press.

Halder, T. (2005). Eine geglückte Einführung. Fremdsprachenlernen an baden-württembergischen Grundschulen [A successful initiative. Foreign language learning in Baden-Wurttemberg primary schools]. *Primary English, 2,* 17–19.

Halliday, M. A. K. (1985). *Spoken and written language.* Victoria, Australia: Deakin University Press.

Halliday, M. A. K., & Matthiessen, C. M. I. M. (2004). *An introduction to functional grammar* (3rd ed.). London: Arnold.

Henry, L. M. (1994). *Oral dialogue journals: A learner-centered approach.* (Doctoral dissertation, School for International Training, Brattleboro, VT.) East Lansing, MI: National Center for Research on Teacher Learning (ERIC Document Reproduction Service No. ED 375 671).

Hinkel, E. (2006). Current perspectives on teaching the four skills. *TESOL Quarterly, 40,* 109–131.

Holliday, A. (2004). Issues of validity in progressive paradigms of qualitative research. *TESOL Quarterly, 38,* 731–734.

Holliday, A. (2005). *The struggle to teach English as an international language.* Oxford: Oxford University Press.

Holmes, H., & Guild, S. (1979). The parable. In D. Hoopes & P. Ventura (Eds.), *Intercultural source book: CC training methodology* (pp. 155–157). Chicago: Intercultural Press.

Hones, F. D. (1999). U.S. justice? Critical pedagogy and the case of Mumia Abu-Jamal. *TESOL Quarterly, 33,* 27–32.

Horwitz, E. (2003). Language anxiety and achievement. *Annual Review of Applied Linguistics, 21,* 112–126.

Hughes, A. (2001). The idea corner: Speaking on the Web. *Clear News.* Retrieved March 14, 2006, from http://clear.msu.edu/clear/newsletter/files/fall2001.pdf

International English Language Testing System. (2008). Retrieved June 4, 2008, from http://www.ielts.org/default.aspx

Jackson, C. W., & Larkin, M. J. (2002). Rubric: Teaching students to use grading rubrics. *Teaching Exceptional Children, 35*(1), 40–44.

Jenkins, J. (2000). *The phonology of English as an international language: New models, new norms, new goals.* Oxford: Oxford University Press.

Johannesen, R. L. (1996). *Ethics in human communication* (4th ed.). Prospect Heights, IL: Waveland Press.

Johnson, D. W., Johnson, R. T., & Smith, K. A. (1991). *Active learning: Cooperation in the college classroom.* Edina, MN: Interaction Book Company.

Johnson, K. E. (2006). The sociocultural turn and its challenges for second language teacher education. *TESOL Quarterly, 40,* 235–257.

Johnson, K. E., & Golombek, P. R. (Eds.). (2002). *Teachers' narrative inquiry as professional development.* Cambridge: Cambridge University Press.

Johnston, B. (2003). *Values in English language teaching.* Mahwah, NJ: Lawrence Erlbaum.

Kahl, P. W., & Knebler, U. (1996). *Englisch in der Grundschule—und dann? Evaluation des Hamburger Schulversuchs ab Klasse 3* [English in primary school—what next? Evaluating the Hamburg school survey in grade 3 and beyond]. Berlin: Cornelsen.

Karbe, U. (2004). *Colourland. Let's check 4.* Leipzig, Germany: Klett.

Kasper, G. (2001). Four perspectives on pragmatic development. *Applied Linguistics, 22,* 502–530.

Kasper, L. F. (2000a). The short story as a bridge to content in the lower level ESL course. In L. F. Kasper (Ed.), *Content-based college ESL instruction* (pp. 107–121). Mahwah, NJ: Lawrence Erlbaum.

Kasper, L. F. (2000b). Film imagery: A visual resource for clarifying content and developing academic writing skill. In L. F. Kasper (Ed.), *Content-based college ESL instruction* (pp. 122–134). Mahwah, NJ: Lawrence Erlbaum.

Kehe, D., & Kehe, P. (1996). Professors' expectations of foreign students in freshman-level courses. *JALT Journal, 18*(1), 108–115.

Kern, R. (2006). Perspectives on technology in learning and teaching languages. *TESOL Quarterly, 40,* 183–210.

Kiefer, K., Palmquist, M., Barnes, L., Levine, M., & Zimmerman, D. (1993–2008). Writing guides: Poster sessions. Retrieved January 16, 2007, from http://writing.colostate.edu/guides/speaking/poster/pop2a.cfm

Kirkpatrick, A. (2007). *World Englishes: Implications for international communication and ELT*. Cambridge: Cambridge University Press.

KMK (2003). *Bildungsstandards für die erste Fremdsprache (Englisch/Französisch) für den Mittleren Schulabschluss. Beschluss vom 4.12.2003* [Standards governing the first foreign language (English/French) at the end of secondary school. Resolution taken on 2003/12/04]. Retrieved February 2, 2008, from http://www.kmk.org/schul/Bildungsstandards/1.Fremdsprache_MSA_BS_04-12-2003.pdf

Kohlberg, L. (1963). The development of children's orientations toward a moral order. *Vita Humana, 6*, 11–33.

Kolb, D. A. (1984). *Experiential learning: Experience as the source of learning and development*. Englewood-Cliffs, NJ: Prentice-Hall.

Krashen, S. (1981). *Second language acquisition and second language learning*. Oxford: Pergamon.

Krashen, S. (1982). *Principles and practice in second language learning and acquisition*. Oxford: Pergamon.

Krashen, S. (1988). *Second language acquisition and second language learning*. Hemel Hempstead, England: Prentice-Hall.

Kubota, R. (2002). The author responds: (Un)Raveling racism in a nice field like TESOL. *TESOL Quarterly, 36*, 84–92.

Kumaravadivelu, B. (2006a). TESOL methods: Changing tracks, challenging trends. *TESOL Quarterly, 40*, 59–81.

Kumaravadivelu, B. (2006b). *Understanding language teaching: From method to postmethod*. Mahwah, NJ: Lawrence Erlbaum.

Kumaravadivelu, R. (2003). A postmethod perspective on English language teaching. *World Englishes, 22*(4), 539–550.

Le Beau, C., & Harrington, D. (1998). *Speaking of speech*. Tokyo: Macmillan Languagehouse.

Le, V. C. (2007). A historical review of English language education in Vietnam. In Y. H. Choi & B. Spolsky (Eds.), *English education in Asia: History and policies* (pp. 167–179). Seoul: Asia TEFL.

Levelt, W. J. M. (1989). *Speaking: From intention to articulation*. Cambridge, MA: MIT Press.

Levine, D. R., & Adelman, M. B. (1992). *Beyond language: Cross cultural communication*. Englewood Cliffs, NJ: Prentice Hall.

Littlewood, W. (1992). *Communicative language teaching*. Cambridge: Cambridge University Press.

LoCastro, V. (2003). *An introduction to pragmatics: Social action for language teachers*. Ann Arbor: University of Michigan Press.

Long, M. (1983). Native speaker/non-native speaker conversation and the negotiation of comprehensible input. *Applied Linguistics, 4*, 126–141.

Long, M. H. (1991). Focus on form: A design feature in language teaching methodology. In K. de Bot, R. Ginsberg, & C. Kramsch (Eds.), *Foreign language research in cross-cultural perspective* (pp. 39–52). Amsterdam: John Benjamins.

Lucas, S. (2007). *The art of public speaking* (9th ed.). New York: McGraw-Hill.

Lynch, T. (1996a). Influences on course revision: An EAP case study. In T. Dudley-Evans & M. Hewings (Eds.), *Evaluation and course design in EAP* (pp. 26–35). London: Prentice Hall Macmillan.

Lynch, T. (1996b). "Proof-listening": A feedback technique in speaking classes. *Modern English Teacher, 5*(4), 41–45.

Lynch, T. (1996c). *Communication in the language classroom.* Oxford: Oxford University Press.

Lynch, T. (2007). Learning from the transcripts of an oral communication task. *ELT Journal, 61*(4), 311–320.

Lynch, T., & Maclean, J. (2001). "A case of exercising": Effects of immediate task repetition on learners' performance. In M. Bygate, P. Skehan, & M. Swain (Eds.), *Researching pedagogic tasks: Second language learning, teaching and testing* (pp. 141–162). New York: Longman.

Lynch, T., & Maclean, J. (2003). Effects of feedback on performance: A study of advanced learners on an ESP speaking course. *Edinburgh Working Papers in Applied Linguistics, 12*, 19–44.

Maley, A. (1992). An open letter to "the profession." *ELT Journal, 46*(1), 96–99.

Maley, A., & Duff, A. (1982). *Drama techniques in language learning* (2nd ed.). Cambridge: Cambridge University Press.

Marton, F., & Saljo, R. (1976). On qualitative differences in learning, outcome and process I. *British Journal of Educational Psychology, 46*, 4–11.

McCarthy, M. J., & Carter, R. A. (1995). Spoken grammar: What is it and how can we teach it? *ELT Journal, 49*(3), 207–218.

Miles, M. B., & Huberman, A. M. (1994). *Qualitative data analysis: A sourcebook of new methods.* Beverly Hills, CA: Sage Publications.

Millis, B., & Hertel, J. P. (2002). *Using simulations to promote learning in higher education: An introduction.* Sterling, VA: Stylus Publishing.

Ministerium für Kultus, Jugend und Sport Baden-Württemberg (2001). *Bildungsplan für die Grundschule. Ergänzung Fremdsprachen Englisch/Französisch* [Primary school syllabus. Supplement for foreign languages English/French]. Villingen-Schwenningen: Neckar Verlag.

Ministerium für Kultus, Jugend und Sport Baden-Württemberg (2004). *Bildungsplan für die Grundschule* [*Primary school syllabus*]. Villingen-Schwenningen: Neckar Verlag.

Ministry of Justice. (2005). Estimated number of registered foreign nationals. Retrieved October 1, 2007, from http://www.moj.go.jp/PRESS/060530-1/060530-1.html

Mohan, B. A. (1986). *Language and content*. Reading, MA: Addison-Wesley.

Morita, N. (2000). Discourse socialization through oral classroom activities in a TESL graduate program. *TESOL Quarterly, 32*, 279–310.

Morita, N. (2004). Negotiating participation and identity in second language academic communities. *TESOL Quarterly, 38*, 573–603.

Morley, J. (1995). Maximizing pronunciation learning: Multi-faceted instructional programming. *Speak Out!, Newsletter of the IATEFL Pronunciation Special Interest Group, 11*, 4–6.

Moskowitz, G. (1978). *Caring and sharing in the foreign language class*. Rowley, MA: Newbury House.

Nation, I. S. P. (1991). Fluency and learning. *The English Teacher, 20*, 1–8.

Nguyen, T. M. H., & Nguyen, Q. T. (2007). Teaching English in primary schools in Vietnam: An overview. *Current Issues in Language Planning, 8*(1), 162–173.

Nguyen, X. V. (2003). English language teaching in Vietnam today: Policy, practice and constraints. In H. W. Kam & R. Y. L. Wong (Eds.), *English language teaching in East Asia today* (pp. 455–474). Singapore: Times Media Private Limited.

Norman, D., Levihn, U., & Hedenquist, J. A. (1986). *Communicative ideas*. Hove, England: Language Teaching Publications.

Nunan, D. (2004). *Task-based language teaching*. Cambridge: Cambridge University Press.

O'Keefe, A., McCarthy, M., & Carter, R. (2007). *From corpus to classroom: Language use and language teaching*. Cambridge: Cambridge University Press.

O'Malley, J. M., & Pierce, L. V. (1996). *Authentic assessment for English language learners*. New York: Addison Wesley.

Orr, T. (Ed.). (2002). *English for specific purposes*. Alexandria, VA: TESOL.

Ovando, C., Collier, V., & Combs, M. (2003). *Bilingual and ESL classrooms: Teaching in multicultural contexts*. Boston: McGraw-Hill.

Pennycook, A. (1999). Introduction: Critical approaches to TESOL. *TESOL Quarterly, 33*, 329–348.

Pennycook, A. (2000). *Critical applied linguistics: A critical introduction*. Mahwah, NJ: Lawrence Erlbaum.

Perry, B., & Stewart, T. (2005). Insights into effective partnership in interdisciplinary team teaching. *System, 33*(4), 563–573.

Phillips, D. (2005). *Preparation course for the iBT.* New York: Longman.

Pica, T., Holliday, L., Lewis, N., & Morgenthaler, L. (1989). Comprehensible output as an outcome of linguistic demands on the learner. *Studies in Second Language Acquisition, 11,* 63–90.

Pinter, A. (2006). *Teaching young language learners.* Oxford: Oxford University Press.

Pribyl, C. B., Keaton, J., & Sakamoto, M. (2001). The effectiveness of a skills-based program in reducing public speaking anxiety. *Japanese Psychological Research, 43*(3), 148–155.

Purrington, C. B. (2006). Advice on designing scientific posters: "PowerPoint poster template." Retrieved January 21, 2008, from http://www.swarthmore.edu/NatSci/cpurrin1/postertemplate.ppt

Ramsden, P. (2003). *Learning to teach in higher education.* New York: Routledge.

Rapee, R. M., & Lim, L. (1992). Discrepancy between self-and observer ratings of performance in social phobics. *Journal of Abnormal Psychology, 101*(4), 728–731.

Reid, J. (1994). *The process of paragraph writing.* New York: Prentice Hall.

Reid, J. (1999). Affect in the classroom: Problems, politics and pragmatics. In J. Arnold (Ed.), *Affect in language learning* (pp. 297–306). Cambridge: Cambridge University Press.

Richards, J. C. (1998). *Beyond training.* New York: Cambridge University Press.

Richards, J. C. (2001). *Curriculum development in language teaching.* New York: Cambridge University Press.

Richards, J. C., & Lockhart, C. (1996). *Reflective teaching in second language classrooms.* Cambridge: Cambridge University Press.

Richards, J. C., & Rodgers, T. S. (2001). *Approaches and methods in language teaching* (2nd ed.). Cambridge: Cambridge University Press.

Rogers, B. (2007). *The complete guide to the TOEFL test.* Boston: Thomson.

Rosenshine, B., & Meister, C. (1992). The use of scaffolds for teaching higher-level cognitive strategies. *Educational Leadership, 49*(7), 26–33.

Rost, M. (1991). *Listening in action.* New York: Prentice Hall.

Rowe, M. B. (1986). Wait-time: Slowing down may be a way of speeding up. Retrieved February 5, 2008, from http://sce4361-01.sp01.fsu.edu/waittime.html

Sagliano, M., Stewart, T., & Sagliano, J. (1998). Professional training to develop content-based instruction in higher education. *TESL Canada Journal, 16*(1), 36–53.

Santos, T. (2001). The place of politics in second language writing. In T. Silva & P. K. Matsuda (Eds.), *On second language writing.* Mahwah, NJ: Lawrence Erlbaum.

Savignon, S. J. (1983). *Communicative competence: Theory and classroom practice.* Reading, MA: Addison-Wesley.

Schmidt, R. (1992). Psychological mechanisms underlying second language fluency. *Studies in Second Language Acquisition, 14*(4), 357–385.

Schmidt, R. W. (1990). The role of consciousness in second language learning. *Applied Linguistics, 11,* 129–158.

Schmidt, R. W., & Froda, S. (1986). Developing basic conversational ability in a second language: A case-study of an adult learner of Portuguese. In R. Day (Ed.), *Talking to learn: Conversation in second language acquisition* (pp. 237–326). Rowley, MA: Newbury House.

Shinzaki, R., & Takahashi, Y. (2004). *Dynamic listening and speaking.* Tokyo: Hamano.

Shohamy, E. (2004). Reflections on research guidelines, categories, and responsibilities. *TESOL Quarterly, 38,* 728–731.

Shor, I. (1992). *Empowering education: Critical teaching for social change.* Chicago: University of Chicago Press.

Silva, D. J. (2006). Poster presentations: Theory and application. Retrieved January 21, 2008, from http://ling.uta.edu/~lingua/utascil/2007/PosterPresentations.ppt

Simon, S. B., Howe, L. W., & Kirschenbaum, H. (1972). *Values clarification.* New York: Hart Publishing.

Skehan, P. (1998). *A cognitive approach to language learning.* Oxford: Oxford University Press.

Slavin, R. E. (1989). *Cooperative learning: Theory, research, and practice.* Englewood Cliffs, NJ: Prentice-Hall.

Solomon, G., & Schrum, L. (2007). *Web 2.0: New tools, new schools.* Eugene, OR: International Society for Technology in Education.

Soresi, S. (2004). A progressive approach to fluency with SPM. *ESL Magazine, 42*(2), 7–9.

Soresi, S. (2009). *Output-driven English language teaching and testing: Using target speech rates to develop oral proficiency.* Unpublished doctoral dissertation, Aoyama Gakuin University, Tokyo.

Soresi, S., & Suzuki, T. (2007). The SPM-based speaking test at Toyo Eiwa: A look into the contextualized scoring system. *Toyo Eiwa Journal of the Humanities and Social Sciences, 25,* 13–32.

Spada, N., & Lightbrown, P. M. (2008). Form-focused instruction: Isolated or integrated? *TESOL Quarterly, 42,* 181–207.

Spolsky, B. (1990). *Measured words.* Oxford: Oxford University Press.

Stengel, I. (Ed.) (2000). *Voice and self: A handbook of personal voice development therapy.* London: Free Association Books.

Stevick, E. (1990). *Humanism in language teaching—A critical perspective.* Oxford: Oxford University Press.

Stewart, T. (1997). Wanting to talk: Discussion building in a Japanese college classroom. *Comparative Culture, 3,* 8–11.

Stewart, T. (2001). The value of action research in exploring methodology: A case of instruction on questioning in debate. *Pan-Asia Consortium Journal, 1,* 79–92.

Stewart, T. (2003). Debate for ESOL students. *TESOL Journal, 12,* 9–15.

Stewart, T. (2006). Teacher-researcher collaboration or teachers' research? *TESOL Quarterly, 40,* 421–430.

Stewart, T., & Pleisch, G. (1998). Developing academic language skills and fluency through debate. *The Language Teacher, 22*(10), 27–32.

Stewart, T., Sagliano, M., & Sagliano, J. (2002a). An alternative team teaching model for content-based instruction. In Y. Cheng, K. Tsui, K. Chow, & M. Mok (Eds.), *Subject teaching and teacher education in the new century: Research and innovation* (pp. 457– 488). Hong Kong: Kluwer Academic Publishers.

Stewart, T., Sagliano, M., & Sagliano, J. (2002b). Merging expertise: Promoting partnerships between language and content specialists. In J. Crandall & D. Kaufman (Eds.), *Content-based language instruction* (pp. 29–44). Alexandria, VA: TESOL.

Strauss, A., & Corbin, J. (1990). *Basics of qualitative research.* London: Sage Publications.

Sukegawa, N., & Harrington, T. (2006). *How are you feeling today?: English for nurses* (11th ed.). Tokyo: Seibido.

Sullivan, P. N. (2000). Playfulness as mediation in communicative language teaching in a Vietnamese classroom. In J. P. Lantolf (Ed.), *Sociocultural theory and second language learning* (pp. 115–132). New York: Oxford University Press.

Swain, M. (1985). Communicative competence: Some roles of comprehensible input and comprehensible output in development. In S. Gass & C. Madden (Eds.), *Input in second language acquisition* (pp. 235–256). Rowley, MA: Newbury House.

Swain, M. (1995). Three functions of output in second language learning. In G. Cook & B. Seidlhofer (Eds.), *Principle and practice in applied linguistics: Studies in honour of H. G. Widdowson* (pp. 125–144). Oxford: Oxford University Press.

Swain, M. (1998). Focus on form through conscious reflection. In C. Doughty & J. Williams (Eds.), *Focus on form in classroom SLA* (pp. 64–81). Cambridge: Cambridge University Press.

Swain, M. (2000). The output hypothesis and beyond: Mediating acquisition through collaborative dialogue. In J. P. Lantolf (Ed.), *Sociocultural theory and second language learning* (pp. 97–114). Oxford: Oxford University Press.

Swain, M. (2007) The output hypothesis: Its history and its future. Retrieved November 14, 2007, from http://www.celea.org.cn/2007/keynote/ppt/Merrill%20Swain.pdf

Swain, M., & Lapkin, S. (1995). Problems in output and the cognitive processes they generate: A step towards second language learning. *Applied Linguistics, 16*(4), 371–391.

Swan, M. (2005). Legislation by hypothesis: The case of task-based instruction. *Applied Linguistics, 26*(3), 376–401.

Tauroza, S., & Allison, D. (1990). Speech rates in British English. *Applied Linguistics, 11*(1), 90–105.

Taylor, J. L., & Walford, R. (1972). *Simulation in the classroom.* Harmondsworth, England: Penguin Books.

TESOL (n.d.-a). *Convention tips for presenters.* Retrieved October 6, 2008, from http://www.tesol.org/s_tesol/seccss.asp?CID=1518&DID=8281

TESOL (n.d.-b). *Preparation guidelines for poster sessions.* Retrieved October 6, 2008, from http://www.tesol.org/s_tesol/seccss.asp?CID=1518&DID=8281

Tusting, K., & Barton, D. (2003). *Models of adult learning: A literature review.* National Research and Development Centre for Adult Literacy and Numeracy. London: Institute of Education.

Uden, L., & Beaumont, C. (2006). *Technology and problem-based learning.* Hershey, PA: Information Science Publishing.

Ur, P. (1987). *Grammar practice activities.* Cambridge: Cambridge University Press.

Ur, P. (2002). The English teacher as professional. In J. C. Richards & W. A. Renandya (Eds.), *Methodology in language teaching: An anthology of current practice* (pp. 388–392). Cambridge: Cambridge University Press.

van Lier, L. (1996). *Interaction in the language curriculum: Awareness, autonomy & authenticity.* Harlow, England: Addison-Wesley Longman.

Via, R. (1972). English through drama. *English Teaching Forum,* July–August.

Vu, V. T. (1995). Some cultural features of Vietnamese life and teacher education. In B. Alex (Ed.), *Intercultural interaction and development: Converging perspectives.* Sydney: University of Technology.

Vygotsky, L. (1980). *Mind in society.* Cambridge, MA: Harvard University Press.

Walker, R. (2005). Using student-produced recordings with monolingual groups to provide effective, individualized pronunciation practice. *TESOL Quarterly, 39*, 550–557.

Wallechinsky, D., Wallace, I., & Wallace, A. (1977). *The book of lists.* New York: Bantam.

Wallerstein, N. (1983). *Language and culture in conflict: Problem-posing in the ESL classroom.* Reading, MA: Addison-Wesley.

Walsh, C. E. (1991). *Literacy as praxis: Culture, language, and pedagogy.* Norwood, NJ: Ablex.

Waters, R., & Wright, R. (1973). Us and Them [Recorded by Pink Floyd]. On *Dark side of the moon* [CD]. London: Capital Records.

Weir, C. (1990). *Communicative language testing.* Hemel Hemstead, England: Prentice Hall.

Wennerstrom, A. (2003). *Discourse analysis in the language classroom: Vol. 2. Genres of writing.* Ann Arbor: University of Michigan Press.

Wessels, C. (1987). *Drama.* Oxford: Oxford University Press.

Widdowson, H. G. (1996). Comment: authenticity and autonomy in ELT. *ELT Journal, 50*(1), 67–68.

Widdowson, H. G. (2003). *Defining issues in English language teaching.* Oxford: Oxford University Press.

Wilderdom. (2006, April 2). Survival scenario exercise. Retrieved October 8, 2007, from http://wilderdom.com/games/descriptions/SurvivalScenarios.html

Wingate, J. (1993). *Getting beginners to talk.* Hemel Hempstead, England: Prentice Hall.

Woo, Y., Herrington, J., Agostinho, S., & Reeves, T. C. (2007). Implementing authentic tasks in Web-based learning environments. *Educause Quarterly, 30*(3), 36–43.

Wood, J. (2005). *Communication in our lives.* Belmont, CA: Wadsworth.

Woods, D. (1996). *Teacher cognition in language teaching: Beliefs, decision-making, and classroom practice.* New York: Cambridge University Press.

Wylde, A. (2005). Improved goals, action plans, planning ahead and reflection: Students' self-assessment of coaching. *Investigations in University Teaching & Learning, 2*(2), 54–58.

Yeh, A. (2006a). *Speech of introduction task guidelines.* Retrieved July 30, 2007, from http://speech2006.blogspot.com/2007/02/task-speech-of-introduction.html

Yeh, A. (2006b). *Postings of main speakers and presentation themes on Skrbl.* Retrieved July 30, 2007, from http://www.skrbl.com/aidenyeh

Yeh, A. (2006c). *Speech draft sample.* Retrieved July 30, 2007, from http://groups .yahoo.com/group/speechye3b/

Yeh, A. (2006d). *Screenshot of students' video presentations.* Retrieved July 30, 2007, from http://groups.yahoo.com/group/speechye3b/

Yeh, A. (2006e). *Student feedback posted on the class blog.* Retrieved July 30, 2007, from http://speech2006.blogspot.com/2007_03_11_archive.htm

Yeh, A. (2006f). *Sample feedback on delivery.* Retrieved August 1, 2007, from http:// groups.yahoo.com/group/speechye3b/

Yeh, A. (2007a, March). *Vlogging students' oral speeches for assessment purposes.* Workshop presented at the 41st TESOL Annual Convention & Exhibit, Seattle, WA.

Yeh, A. (2007b). Critical issues: Blended learning. In J. Egbert, E. Hanson-Smith, & K. Huh (Eds.), *CALL environments: Research, practice, and critical issues* (2nd ed.) (pp. 404–420). Alexandria, VA: TESOL.

Yeh, A. (2007c). *Speech of introduction reflection forum at Chinswing.* Retrieved August 1, 2007, from http://tinyurl.com/3b6ql2

Yu, M.-C. (2005). Sociolinguistic competence in the complimenting act of native Chinese and American English speakers: A mirror of cultural value. *Language and Speech, 48*(1), 91–119.

Zeichner, K., & Liston, D. (1996). *Reflective teaching: An introduction.* Mahwah, NJ: Lawrence Erlbaum.

Zemach, D. (2006). Burnout from teaching. *Essential Teacher, 3*(3), 16–17.

Index

Page numbers followed by an *f* or *t* indicate figures or tables.

A

A4esl.org, podcasts and, 101
Abcnews.go.com/health, podcasts and, 101
Academic achievement, curricula and, 29
Accountability, disempowerment and, 1–2
Accuracy
    DLS method and, 73
    vs. fluency, 2–3
Acquisition, defined, 31
Action research, productive speech and, 57
Actional competence, 125, 134
Activities
    high-volume speaking activities and, 45–51
    presentation skills and, 158*t*
    public speaking skills and, 129*f*
    values exploration and, 14–15
Adjustability. *See* Flexibility
Affective involvement, oral journals and, 232
Affective response, problem-posing approach and, 83, 86*t*
"Alligator River," 13–27, 17*f*, 18*f*, 19*f*, 20*f*, 21*f*, 22*t*
Announcement/Discussion Task, 33*t*
Appearance, assessment of, 183*t*
Apple, Inc., 94, 96
Application, problem-posing approach and, 84, 86*t*
Art of Public Speaking, The (Lucas), 192
Articulation, assessment of, 183*t*
Articulator stage, 54*f*

B

Assessment
    in-class testing and, 207–222
    Internet-based, 29–43
    oral journals and, 223–236
    presentation skills and, 157*t*, 162
    productive speech and, 63
    public speaking skills and, 133
    self-, 134, 186, 201–203
    speaking logs and, 171–177
    student-created rubrics and, 179–190
    as topic, 8*t*
    vlogs and, 191–205
Audacity, 32–34, 95
Audience
    control of, 165
    evaluation of, 135
    presentation skills and, 163–164
Audio files, Internet 2.0 and, 95–96
Autonomous learning, as topic, 8*t*

B

Beyond Language (Levine & Adelman), 15
Blogs, video, 191–205
Book of Lists, The (Wallechinsky, Wallace, & Wallace), 179
Brainstorming, iBT and, 39
Breakingnewsenglish.com, podcasts and, 101
Burnout, teacher, 117

C

CALL. *See* Computer-assisted language learning

Also Available from TESOL

TESOL Classroom Practice Series
M. Dantas-Whitney, S. Rilling, and L. Savova, Series Editors

Classroom Management
Thomas S. C. Farrell, Editor

Language Games: Innovative Activities for Teaching English
Maureen Snow Adrade, Editor

❈ ❈ ❈ ❈ ❈

Language Teacher Research Series
Thomas S. C. Farrell, Series Editor

Language Teacher Research in Africa
Leketi Makalela, Editor

Language Teacher Research in Asia
Thomas S. C. Farrell, Editor

Language Teacher Research in Europe
Simon Borg, Editor

Language Teacher Research in the Americas
Hedy McGarrell, Editor

Language Teacher Research in the Middle East
Christine Coombe and Lisa Barlow, Editors

Language Teacher Research in Australia and New Zealand
Jill Burton and Anne Burns, Editors

❈ ❈ ❈ ❈ ❈

Perspectives on Community College ESL Series
Craig Machado, Series Editor

Volume 1: Pedagogy, Programs, Curricula, and Assessment
Marilynn Spaventa, Editor

Volume 2: Students, Mission, and Advocacy
Amy Blumenthal, Editor

Volume 3: Faculty, Administration, and the Working Environment
Jose A. Carmona, Editor

* * * * *

Collaborative Partnerships Between ESL and Classroom Teachers Series
Debra Suarez, Series Editor

Helping English Language Learners Succeed in Pre-K–12 Elementary Schools
Jan Lacina, Linda New Levine, and Patience Sowa

Helping English Language Learners Succeed in Middle and High Schools
F. Pawan and G. Sietman, Editors

* * * * *

TESOL Language Curriculum Development Series
Kathleen Graves, Series Editor

Developing a New Curriculum for Adult Learners
Michael Carroll, Editor

*Planning and Teaching Creatively
within a Required Curriculum for School-Age Learners*
Penny McKay, Editor

* * * * *

CALL Environments: Research, Practice, and Critical Issues, 2nd ed.
Joy Egbert and E. Hanson-Smith, Editors

Learning Languages through Technology
Elizabeth Hanson-Smith and Sara Rilling, Editors

Global English Teaching and Teacher Education: Praxis and Possibility
Seran Dogancay-Aktuna and Joel Hardman, Editors

Content-Based Instruction in Primary and Secondary School Settings
Dorit Kaufman and JoAnn Crandall, Editors

Teaching English as a Foreign Language in Primary School
Mary Lou McCloskey, Janet Orr, and Marlene Dolitsky, Editors

ESOL Tests and Testing
Stephen Stoynoff and Carol A. Chapelle

PreK–12 English Language Proficiency Standards
Teachers of English to Speakers of Other Languages, Inc.

*Paper to Practice:
Using the TESOL English Language Proficiency Standards in PreK-12 Classrooms*
M. Gottlieb, A. Katz, and G. Ernst-Slavit

Local phone: (240)646-7037
Fax: (301)206-9789
E-Mail: tesolpubs@brightkey.net
Toll-free: 1-888-891-0041
Mail Orders to TESOL, P.O. Box 79283, Baltimore, MD 21279-0283

ORDER ONLINE at www.tesol.org and click on "Bookstore"